THE MAN ADAM

Edited by Joseph Fielding McConkie
and Robert L. Millet

BOOKCRAFT
Salt Lake City, Utah

Library of Congress Catalog Card Number: 89-81705

ISBN 0-88494-724-6

First Printing, 1990

Printed in the United States of America

Contents

Preface   vii

1   Adam in the Premortal Life
    Larry E. Dahl   1

2   Adam in Eden: The Creation
    Robert L. Millet   11

3   The Mystery of Eden
    Joseph Fielding McConkie   25

4   The Fall of Man
    Robert J. Matthews   37

5   The Revelation of the Gospel to Adam: The
    Meaning of the Atonement
    Robert J. Matthews   65

6   "Our Glorious Mother Eve"
    Vivian M. Adams   87

7   Adam's Role from the Fall to the End—and Beyond
    Larry E. Dahl 113

8   The Book of Adam in Judaism and Early Christianity
    Stephen E. Robinson 131

9   Adam: As Understood by Four Men Who Shaped
    Western Christianity
    Roger R. Keller 151

10 Adam: A Latter-day Saint Perspective
    Robert L. Millet............................. 189

    Subject Index 195

    Scripture Index 207

Preface

Perhaps no person in all eternity, save Jesus only, has been more directly involved in the plan of salvation—the creation, fall, and ultimate redemption of mankind—than the man Adam. His ministry among the sons and daughters of earth stretches from the distant past of premortality to the distant future of resurrection and judgment and beyond. As Michael, the archangel, he led the forces of God against the armies of Lucifer in the War in Heaven. Under the direction of Elohim and Jehovah, he assisted in the creation of the earth. After taking a physical body, Adam (with Eve) brought mortality into being through partaking of the fruit of the tree of the knowledge of good and evil; with the fall of our first parents came blood and posterity and probation and death, as well as the need for redemption through a Savior, a "second Adam" (see 1 Corinthians 15:45). To Adam the gospel was first preached. Upon Adam the priesthood was first bestowed. From Adam and Eve the message of the gospel of salvation went forth to all the world. Even following his death, which occurred almost a millennium after he entered mortality, Adam's watch care over his posterity continued. Revelations have come and angels have ministered under his direction. Priesthoods have been conferred and keys delivered at his behest.

All too often Adam's place and role in the plan of the Father have been misunderstood. To many in the religious world he is an enigma, to others a myth. Some despise him for his actions in Eden. The praise he receives from some others takes the strange form of adoration and worship. Though there is yet much to be revealed in regard to the Creation, the Fall, the Atonement, and the final redemption of earth and its inhabitants, the fundamental doctrines of the gospel — including a proper understanding of Adam and Eve and our relationship to them — have been made known through modern seers and revelators. Latter-day Saints need not be confused and certainly need not be led astray by the views of the hopelessly ignorant, the sophistries of learned men, or the vagaries of the willfully perverse. We have the scriptures, the standard works, to guide our study. And, perhaps more important, we have the prophetic utterances of those called to lead the destiny of the restored Church in this final dispensation of grace.

The chapters of this book have been prepared by individuals committed to the practices and beliefs of the Church. Each of the individual contributors is responsible for his or her own conclusions, and the volume is a private endeavor and not a production of either Brigham Young University or The Church of Jesus Christ of Latter-day Saints. Although the writers have sought to be in harmony with the teachings of the standard works and the leaders of the Church, the reader should not regard this work as a primary source but should turn instead to the scriptures and the words of the living oracles for authoritative doctrinal statements.

Larry E. Dahl

Adam in the Premortal Life

The scriptures, especially latter-day scriptures, and prophetic commentary by Joseph Smith cast a flood of light upon the subject of Adam's role in bringing to pass the immortality and eternal life of all those who have dwelt or will yet dwell upon this earth. Adam is identified as "Michael, the prince, the archangel" (D&C 107:54). "[The Lord] hath . . . given unto him [Michael] the keys of salvation under the counsel and direction of the Holy One, who is without beginning of days or end of life" (D&C 78:16).

ADAM'S PLACE IN THE PLAN OF SALVATION — AN OVERVIEW

Joseph Smith explained the central role Adam plays in the Father's great plan:

Adam . . . was the first man, who is spoken of in Daniel as being the "Ancient of Days," or in other words, the first and oldest of all, the great, grand progenitor . . . the first and father of all, not

Larry E. Dahl is Professor and Chairman of the Department of Church History and Doctrine at Brigham Young University.

only by progeny, but the first to hold the spiritual blessings, to whom was made known the plan of ordinances for the salvation of his posterity unto the end, and to whom Christ was first revealed, and through whom Christ has been revealed from heaven, and will continue to be revealed from henceforth. Adam holds the keys of the dispensation of the fullness of times; i.e., the dispensation of all the times have been and will be revealed through him from the beginning to Christ, and from Christ to the end of the dispensations that are to be revealed. . . .

Now the purpose in [God] Himself in the winding up scene of the last dispensation is that all things pertaining to that dispensation should be conducted precisely in accordance with the preceding dispensations.

And again, God purposed in Himself that there should not be an eternal fullness until every dispensation should be fulfilled and gathered together in one, and that all things whatsoever, that should be gathered together in one in those dispensations unto the same fullness and eternal glory, should be in Christ Jesus; therefore He set the ordinances to be the same forever and ever, and set Adam to watch over them, to reveal them from heaven to man, or to send angels to reveal them. . . .

These angels are under the direction of Michael or Adam, who acts under the direction of the Lord.[1]

Regarding Adam's priesthood position and authority, the Prophet further explained:

The Priesthood was first given to Adam; he obtained the First Presidency, and held the keys of it from generation to generation. He obtained it in the Creation, before the world was formed, as in Genesis 1:26, 27, 28. He had dominion given him over every living creature. He is Michael the Archangel, spoken of in the Scriptures. Then to Noah, who is Gabriel: he stands next in authority to Adam in the Priesthood; he was called of God to this office, and was the father of all living in this day, and to him was given the dominion. These men held keys first on earth, and then in heaven.

The Priesthood is an everlasting principle, and existed with God from eternity, and will to eternity, without beginning of days or end of years. The keys have to be brought from heaven whenever the Gospel is sent. When they are revealed from heaven, it is by Adam's authority. . . .

. . . He (Adam) is the head, and was told to multiply. The keys were first given to him, and by him to others. He will have to give an account of his stewardship, and they to him. . . .

. . . Christ is the Great High Priest; Adam next.[2]

This, then, is the nature of the Priesthood; every man holding the Presidency of his dispensation, and one man holding the Presidency of them all, even Adam; and Adam receiving his Presidency and authority from the Lord, but cannot receive a fullness until Christ shall present the Kingdom to the Father, which shall be at the end of the last dispensation.[3]

It is abundantly clear from the foregoing quotations that Adam's role in the plan of salvation as it pertains to this earth did not begin with his being placed in the Garden of Eden, nor did it end with his death. This brief chapter deals with Adam's role in the premortal life. A later chapter will discuss his earthly ministry and continuing watch care over his posterity throughout the history of the earth — through all dispensations — including his involvement in the last dispensation, the judgment, the resurrection, and in the eternities to come. Let us now turn our attention to Adam's premortal role.

A Spirit Child of God

In an official statement issued in 1909 by the First Presidency (Joseph F. Smith, John R. Winder, and Anthon H. Lund), we read:

Adam, our progenitor, "the first man," was, like Christ, a pre-existent spirit, and like Christ he took upon him an appropriate body, the body of a man, and so became a "living soul." The doctrine of the pre-existence, — revealed so plainly, particularly in latter days, pours a wonderful flood of light upon the otherwise mysterious problem of man's origin. It shows that man, as a spirit, was begotten and born of heavenly parents, and reared to maturity in the eternal mansions of the Father, prior to coming upon the earth in a temporal body to undergo an experience in mortality. It teaches that all men existed in the spirit before any man existed in the flesh, and that all who have inhabited the earth since Adam have taken bodies and become souls in like manner.[4]

Adam's spirit was "begotten and born of heavenly parents, and reared to maturity in the eternal mansions of the Father," as were the spirits of all mankind. And all the spirits that were to inhabit this earth were thus created before the creation of the earth itself (see Moses 3:5). While being shown a vision of these premortal spirits, Abraham learned that many of them were "noble and great" and chosen even there to be God's rulers upon the earth (Abraham 3:22–23). Adam stood preeminent (under Christ) among all these spirit children of our Heavenly Father. He was not just *an* archangel but *the* archangel, or chief angel.[5]

ADAM LED THE RIGHTEOUS FORCES
IN THE WAR IN HEAVEN

"And there was war in heaven: Michael and his angels fought against the dragon; and the dragon fought and his angels, and pre-vailed not; neither was their place found any more in heaven. And the great dragon was cast out, that old serpent, called the Devil, and Satan, which deceiveth the whole world: he was cast out into the earth, and his angels were cast out with him." (Revelation 12:7–9.)

There was a war because the devil and "a third part of the hosts of heaven" who chose to follow him rebelled against God and the plan of salvation (D&C 29:36). John tells us the devil was "the ac-cuser of our brethren" and that he "accused them before our God day and night" (Revelation 12:10). Obviously the War in Heaven was not a brief afternoon skirmish—it went on "day and night." Who were the "brethren" that were being so persistently accused? Undoubtedly, Adam, as the leader of the righteous spirits, would have been a prime target of the devil's scorn. And who were the "angels" who fought either with Adam or the devil? No doubt all the sons and daughters of God were aware of the underlying issues being discussed over which the War in Heaven was fought. As is the case in our present existence, we would assume that there was much variance in the commitment and valiance of individual spirits; surely some championed their respective causes more vig-orously than others.

What were the issues, and what weapons were employed? The issues centered around who was to be the savior, how his mission was to be carried out, and who was to receive honor. Both the devil and Jesus offered to be the savior. The devil claimed he would save everyone, "that one soul shall not be lost," demanding God's place or honor for his efforts (Moses 4:1). Jesus simply wanted to honor his Father by doing his Father's will. Commenting on this circumstance, the Prophet Joseph Smith explained: "The contention in heaven was — Jesus said there would be certain souls that would not be saved; and the devil said he could save them all, and laid his plans before the grand council, who gave their vote in favor of Jesus Christ. So the devil rose up in rebellion against God, and was cast down, with all who put up their heads for him."[6]

Satan's "guarantee" of salvation for all had deep implications. Anyone who guarantees something must have complete control. Hence the subjects must forfeit their agency. The Lord affirmed to Moses that Satan "sought to destroy the agency of man, which I, the Lord God, had given him" (Moses 4:3). How did Satan persuade a third part of the hosts of heaven to follow him in a course that would bring such consequences? Did he tell them that if they followed him he would take away their agency? Surely not! He is more clever than that. Agency is too prized a possession for such an approach. How then were they persuaded? The promise of salvation without price — without risk and pain and sorrow — is on the surface an attractive and persuasive proposition. That this was one of Satan's arguments seems probable given John's statement concerning those who did not succumb to the devil's ploy. John says those who chose Christ in that premortal war "loved not their lives unto the death" (Revelation 12:11). The devil and his angels evidently did love their lives unto death; or, in other words, they held tenaciously to a program promising ease and comfort — rather than the prospects of a world of risk and pain — to such an extent that it brought death to them, a spiritual death. What sad irony — demanding your own way to the point of spiritual death, wherein the devil "doth seal you his; therefore the Spirit of the Lord hath withdrawn from you, and hath no place in you, and the devil hath all power over you; and this is the final state of the wicked" (Alma 34:35).

What the devil promised, he could not deliver. Godhood cannot be attained without our proving ourselves. And proving ourselves requires agency, with risks, trials, and pain counterbalancing the pleasures and comforts of life.

> For it must needs be, that there is an opposition in all things. If not so . . . righteousness could not be brought to pass, neither wickedness, neither holiness nor misery, neither good nor bad. Wherefore, all things must needs be a compound in one; wherefore, if it should be one body it must needs remain as dead, having no life neither death, nor corruption nor incorruption, happiness nor misery, neither sense nor insensibility.
> Wherefore, it must needs have been created for a thing of naught; wherefore there would have been no purpose in the end of its creation. Wherefore, this thing must needs destroy the wisdom of God and his eternal purposes, and also the power, and the mercy, and the justice of God. (2 Nephi 2:11–12; see also D&C 29:39; Moses 6:55.)

Adam and his angels understood the futility of the devil's proposal and "overcame him by the blood of the Lamb, and by the word of their testimony; and they loved not their lives unto the death" (Revelation 12:11). We have already discussed the last of these three weapons or means by which the devil and his angels were overcome. What of the other two? What is meant by the "blood of the Lamb"? I propose that it means the *true* doctrine of the Atonement as opposed to Satan's counterfeit notions — the necessity of an "infinite and eternal sacrifice" (Alma 34:10) "to appease the demands of justice" (Alma 42:15). Some, as seemed to be the case with Corianton, are offended at God's justice (see Alma 41:1–3; 42:1). They wonder why God cannot simply forgive without requiring payment in the form of suffering for broken law. Alma explained to his son Corianton that if God offered mercy without satisfying justice He "would cease to be God" (Alma 42:13, 22, 25), that satisfying the demands of justice through the Atonement is the very thing that allows God to be "a perfect, just God, and a merciful God also" (Alma 42:15). But if justice were not satisfied, how would God cease to be God? Who would see to it? He would cease to be God because he would be without one of the necessary attributes that make him God—justice. And if he did not possess the attribute of justice, and if we did not know that he did possess it, we could not have faith in him unto salvation. Therefore, he would cease to be a God—to us. The *Lectures on Faith*, prepared by or under the direction of Joseph Smith, affirm this relationship of God's justice and our faith:

> It is also necessary, in order to the exercise of faith in God unto life and salvation, that men should have the idea of the existence of the attribute justice in him; for without the idea of the existence of the attribute justice in the Deity, men could not have confidence sufficient to place themselves under his guidance and direction; for they would be filled with fear and doubt lest the judge of all the earth would not do right, and thus fear or doubt, existing in the mind, would preclude the possibility of the exercise of faith in him for life and salvation. But when the idea of the existence of the attribute justice in the Deity is fairly planted in the mind, it leaves no room for doubt to get into the heart, and the mind is enabled to cast itself upon the Almighty without fear and without doubt, and with the most unshaken confidence, believing that the Judge of all the earth will do right.[7]

The scriptures are clear concerning what was required to balance justice and mercy. Jesus Christ "wrought out this perfect atonement through the shedding of his own blood" (D&C 76:69), suffering "even more than man can suffer, except it be unto death" (Mosiah 3:7), which suffering caused him, "even God, the greatest of all, to tremble because of pain," to "bleed at every pore," to "suffer both body and spirit," and to yearn to endure the ordeal without shrinking from it. He did it all so that justice could be satisfied and mercy offered. "For behold, I, God, have suffered these things for all, that they might not suffer if they would repent; but if they would not repent they must suffer even as I." (D&C 19:16–18.) Suffering, his and/or ours, is not an arbitrary inconvenience; it is a necessary part of the plan of salvation. Understanding of and commitment to the true doctrine of the Atonement, as suggested by John's phrase "the blood of the Lamb," was one means that enabled Michael and his angels to prevail against the devil and his angels in the War in Heaven.

The third weapon or means identified by John as employed by Michael and his angels in that pre-earth war is "the word of their testimony" (Revelation 12:11). This suggests a few pertinent questions: How are issues of eternal consequence decided? When people disagree over eternal verities, how can things be resolved? Suppose two-thirds rather than one-third of the hosts of heaven had sided with the devil — would the plan of salvation have been different? The only difference, it seems to me, would have been that two-thirds rather than one-third of the hosts of heaven would have denied themselves the opportunity to continue on toward the goal of eternal life.

There is only one path to happiness, which, as the Prophet Joseph Smith declared, is "the object and design of our existence."[8] That path consists of eternal principles made operative through the power of the Gods, principles which cannot be changed by argument or by vote. One of these principles is agency, whereby each individual may choose among given alternatives with given consequences. The alternatives and consequences cannot be juggled and mixed to our liking. "There is a law, irrevocably decreed in heaven before the foundations of this world, upon which all blessings are predicated — and when we obtain any blessing from God, it is by obedience to that law upon which it is predicated" (D&C 130:20–21). When one-third of the hosts of heaven knowingly and completely rejected the path, incorrigibly intent on reconstructing it, the consequence was sure and would have been the same regardless of the number of the rebellious; for "that which breaketh law, and abideth not by law, but seeketh to become a law unto itself, and willeth to abide in sin, and altogether abideth in sin, cannot be sanctified by law, neither by mercy, justice, nor judgment. Therefore, they must remain filthy still." (D&C 88:35.) For Michael and his angels, arguing at that point about the merits of *the* path compared to *their* path (the counterfeit path espoused by Satan and his followers) must have seemed fruitless. What was left was to bear testimony, testimony borne of the Spirit, with the power "to seal both on earth and in heaven, the unbelieving and rebellious" (D&C 1:8). Perhaps it should be noted here that that testimony was surely not borne with a taunting sense of victory or in haughty self-righteousness. Undoubtedly it was borne in solemnity and humility, and probably in sadness; truly, "the heavens wept" at the result of the War in Heaven (D&C 76:26).

ADAM HELPED CREATE THE EARTH

Abraham was privileged to see a vision of the pre-earth life. Concerning the creation of the earth, he wrote: "And there stood one among them that was like unto God, and he said unto those who were with him: We will go down, for there is space there, and we will take of these materials, and we will make an earth whereon these may dwell" (Abraham 3:24). The one "like unto God" was clearly Jesus Christ, as "by him, and through him, and of him, the worlds are and were created" (D&C 76:24; see also John 1:3; Hebrews 1:2; Mosiah 4:2). But who were "those who were with him"? Surely Adam, as the chief angel or archangel — the one designated to be the "first man" (Moses 3:7) on the earth and to preside over his posterity throughout earth's history — had a prominent role in that enterprise. Though the scriptures currently available to us do not identify by name those who were with Christ in the Creation, we know, as Elder Bruce R. McConkie wrote, "from other sacred sources . . . that Jehovah-Christ, assisted by 'many of the noble and great ones' (Abraham 3:22), of whom Michael is but the illustration, did in fact create the earth and all forms of plant and animal life on the face thereof."[9] In addition, Joseph Smith taught that Adam received the priesthood "in the Creation, before the world was formed."[10] Also, in 1863 President Heber C. Kimball made the following observation: "We have been taught that our Father and God, from whom we sprang, called and appointed his servants to go and organize an earth, and, among the rest, he said to Adam, 'You go along also and help all you can; you are going to inhabit it when it is organized, therefore go and assist in the good work.' It reads in the Scriptures that the Lord did it, but the true rendering is, that the Almighty sent Jehovah and Michael to do the work."[11] Similar statements about Adam's role in the Creation can be found in the writings of many of the presiding authorities of the Church from the beginning of this dispensation to the present.

CONCLUSION

Adam, who is also known as Michael, the archangel, holds the keys of salvation, under Christ, for all the inhabitants of this earth. He was one of the noblest and greatest of the spirit children of God in the premortal life. There he was given authority over all other spirits (except Christ) designated to experience mortality upon this earth. He led the forces of the righteous against the devil and his angels in the War in Heaven, following the Grand Council called to consider the Father's plan of salvation. Michael and his angels overcame the devil and his angels in that war "by the blood of the Lamb, and by the word of their testimony; and they loved not their lives unto the death" (Revelation 12:11). He also played a key role, under the direction of Christ, in the creation of the earth.

NOTES

1. *Teachings of the Prophet Joseph Smith,* comp. Joseph Fielding Smith (Salt Lake City: Deseret Book Co., 1976), pp. 167–68.

2. *Teachings of the Prophet Joseph Smith,* pp. 157–58.

3. *Teachings of the Prophet Joseph Smith,* p. 169.

4. *Messages of the First Presidency,* comp. James R. Clark, 6 vols. (Salt Lake City: Bookcraft, 1965–75), 4:205.

5. See D&C 107:54; 128:21; Jude 1:9. Adam is the only one designated in the scriptures as the archangel.

6. *Teachings of the Prophet Joseph Smith,* p. 357.

7. *Lectures on Faith* 4:13.

8. See *Teachings of the Prophet Joseph Smith,* pp. 255–56.

9. Bruce R. McConkie, *The Promised Messiah* (Salt Lake City: Deseret Book Co., 1978), p. 62.

10. *Teachings of the Prophet Joseph Smith,* p. 157.

11. In *Journal of Discourses,* 10:235.

2

Robert L. Millet

Adam in Eden:
The Creation

In order to understand fully the nature of the Creation, we must first grasp the reality that there were in fact three creations. The first creation is called the *spirit* creation and pertains to the birth of our spirits in premortality. The second creation, the *spiritual* creation, pertains to the nature of life on earth before our first parents were dismissed from Eden. The third creation or organization of things came as a result of the Fall; this, the *natural* creation, opened the door to mortality and corruption and death. We shall now speak briefly of the spirit creation, after which we shall discuss at some length the nature of the spiritual state of life in Eden. Life after the Fall will be treated in a subsequent chapter.

THE SPIRIT CREATION

The first creation of man of which the prophets speak — the spirit creation — entailed the creation of our spirits as organized intelligences (Abraham 3:22). That is to say, in a pristine past, in

Robert L. Millet is Associate Professor and Chairman of the Department of Ancient Scripture at Brigham Young University.

premortality, men and women were begotten as individual spirit entities and thereby became the children of a Father and Mother in heaven. The doctrine of the Latter-day Saints is clear: man is a child of God in the purest and most literal sense, and we inherit from our exalted Sire the powers and attributes and capacities to become, in process of time, even as he is. "We believe," Elder Lorenzo Snow explained,

> that we are the offspring of our Father in heaven, and that we possess in our spiritual organizations the same capabilities, powers and faculties that our Father possesses, although in an infantile state, requiring to pass through a certain course or ordeal by which they will be developed and improved according to the heed we give to the principles we have received. . . .
>
> We are born in the image of God our Father; he begot us like unto himself. There is the nature of deity in the composition of our spiritual organization; in our spiritual birth our Father transmitted to us the capabilities, powers and faculties which he himself possessed, as much so as the child on its mother's bosom possesses, although in an undeveloped state, the faculties, powers and susceptibilities of its parent.[1]

We need to observe at this point in our discussion that, as President Joseph Fielding Smith explained, "there is no account of the creation of man or other forms of life when they were created as spirits. There is just the simple statement that they were so created before the physical creation. The statements in Moses 3:5 and Genesis 2:5 are interpolations thrown into the account of the physical creation, explaining that all things were first created in the spirit existence in heaven before they were placed upon this earth. We were created untold ages before we were placed on this earth."[2]

PERSONALITIES IN THE CREATION

The Prophet Joseph Smith learned, as a result of his studies of the Egyptian papyri, that "everlasting covenant was made between three personages before the organization of this earth, and relates to their dispensation of things to men on the earth; these personages, according to Abraham's record, are called God the first, the Creator; God the second, the Redeemer; and God the third, the witness or Testator."³ God the Father, the Almighty Elohim, is designated as the Creator. Indeed, in the ultimate sense, all creation is accomplished in and through his power and under his divine direction. We therefore know "that there is a God in heaven, who is infinite and eternal, from everlasting to everlasting the same unchangeable God, the framer of heaven and earth, and all things which are in them" (D&C 20:17).

The scriptures also attest that Jehovah was and is the creator of worlds without number (Moses 1:32–33); that the Lord Omnipotent, acting under the direction of his Eternal Father, brought worlds into existence out of chaotic matter and thereafter formed and prepared those orbs for habitation by intelligent and sentient life. That is to say, God the Father "created all things by Jesus Christ" (Ephesians 3:9). "In the beginning," the Apostle John wrote, "was the gospel preached through the Son. And the gospel was the word, and the word was with the Son, and the Son was with God, and the Son was of God. The same was in the beginning with God. *All things were made by him;* and without him was not anything made which was made." (JST, John 1:1–3; italics added.) Paul likewise testified to the Hebrew Saints that the Father had "spoken unto us by his Son, whom he hath appointed heir of all things, by whom also he made the worlds" (Hebrews 1:2; compare D&C 76:24). "Behold, I am Jesus Christ the Son of God," the Master declared to the Nephites. "I created the heavens and the earth, and all things that in them are." (3 Nephi 9:15.)

In addition, "Adam helped to form this earth," President Joseph Fielding Smith taught. "He labored with our Savior Jesus Christ. I have a strong view or conviction that there were others also who assisted them. Perhaps Noah and Enoch; and why not Joseph Smith, and those who were appointed to be rulers before the earth was formed?"⁴ In expanding our view even more regarding those who may have been involved in the work of creation — including perhaps some of that group of men and women designated as the "noble and great ones" — Elder Bruce R. McConkie observed:

Christ and Adam were companions and partners in preexistence. Christ, beloved and chosen of the Father, was foreordained to be the Savior of the world; Adam, as the great Michael, led the armies of heaven when Lucifer and one-third of the spirit hosts rebelled. The Lord Jesus, then reigning as the Lord Jehovah, was the number one Spirit Son; described as being "like unto God" (Abraham 3:24), he then ascended the throne of eternal power; and with him, by his side and serving under his direction, was Michael, who is Adam, and who was then foreordained to be the first man and the head of the human race.

And we cannot doubt that the greatest of all female spirits was the one then chosen and foreordained to be "the mother of the Son of God, after the manner of the flesh." (1 Nephi 11:18.) Nor can we do other than suppose that Eve was by her side, rejoicing in her own foreordination to be the first woman, the mother of men, the consort, companion, and friend of mighty Michael.

Christ and Mary, Adam and Eve, Abraham and Sarah, and a host of mighty men and equally glorious women comprised that group of "the noble and great ones," to whom the Lord Jesus said: "*We* will go down, for there is space there, and *we* will take of these materials, and *we* will make an earth whereon these may dwell." (Abraham 3:22–24. Italics added.) This we know: Christ, under the Father, is the Creator; Michael, his companion and associate, presided over much of the creative work; and with them, as Abraham saw, were many of the noble and great ones. Can we do other than conclude that Mary and Eve and Sarah and myriads of our faithful sisters were numbered among them? Certainly these sisters labored as diligently then, and fought as valiantly in the war in heaven, as did the brethren, even as they in like manner stand firm today, in mortality, in the cause of truth and righteousness.[5]

After describing Abraham's vision of the noble and great ones; after a significant discussion of their foreordination and the purpose of mortality (to "prove them herewith, to see if they will do all things whatsoever the Lord their God shall command them"); and after a brief recitation of Lucifer's rebellion (Abraham 3:22–28), the scriptural record continues: "And then the Lord said: Let us go down. And they went down at the beginning, *and they, that is the Gods*, organized and formed the heavens and the earth." (Abraham 4:1; italics added.) It is possible that those here called "the Gods" — those involved in the preparation of the earth to receive plants, animals, and, most important, man himself — are those previously referred to as "noble and great ones." If so, they are gods not in the sense that they are resurrected beings and have received the fulness of the glory and power of the Father (see D&C 132:19–20) but in the sense that they are involved in the accomplishment of the creative work of the Father; they are members of the family of God, sons and daughters of God; and they are those to whom the word of God came and by whom it was carried out (John 10:34–35).

NEAR THE THRONE OF GOD

This earth was created in a different environment, a very different atmosphere from the one we know now. It was created near Kolob, near to where God himself dwells. In speaking of the ultimate renewal and regeneration of the planet on which we reside, Joseph Smith simply stated, "This earth will be rolled back into the presence of God, and crowned with celestial glory."[6] President Brigham Young explained: "When the earth was framed and brought into existence and man was placed upon it, it was near the throne of our Father in heaven. And when man fell—though that was designed in the economy, there was nothing about it mysterious or unknown to the Gods, they understood it all, it was all planned—but when man fell, the earth fell into space, and took up its abode in this planetary system, and the sun became our light. . . . This is the glory the earth came from, and when it is glorified it will return again unto the presence of the Father, and it will dwell there."[7] On an earlier occasion President Young had taught that "this earthly ball, this little opake [sic] substance thrown off into space, is only a speck in the great universe; and when it is celestialized it will go back into the presence of God, where it was first framed."[8]

In instructing one of the sisters of the Church, John Taylor spoke of her divine origins:

Knowest thou not that eternities ago thy spirit, pure and holy, dwelt in thy Heavenly Father's bosom, and in His presence, and with thy mother, one of the queens of heaven, surrounded by thy brother and sister spirits in the spirit world, among the Gods? That as thy spirit beheld the scenes transpiring there, and thou

grewest in intelligence, thou sawest worlds upon worlds organized
and peopled with thy kindred spirits who took upon themselves
tabernacles, died, were resurrected, and received their exaltation
on the redeemed worlds they once dwelt upon. Thou being willing
and anxious to imitate them, waiting and desirous to obtain a
body, a resurrection and exaltation also, . . . thou longed, thou
sighed and thou prayed to thy Father in heaven for the time to arrive when thou couldest come to this earth, *which had fled and
fallen from where it was first organized, near the planet Kolob.*
Leaving thy father and mother's bosom and all thy kindred spirits
thou camest to earth, took a tabernacle, and imitated the deeds of
those who had been exalted before you.[9]

Furthermore, because the Fall was yet to occur, because the
earth was created in the proximity of God's dwelling, the earth
was on a different system of time in the morn of creation. In the
Abrahamic account of the creation, the Gods instructed Adam and
Eve: "Of every tree of the garden thou mayest freely eat, but of the
tree of knowledge of good and evil, thou shalt not eat of it; for in
the *time* that thou eatest thereof, thou shalt surely die. Now I,
Abraham, saw that *it was after the Lord's time, which was after
the time of Kolob; for as yet the Gods had not appointed unto
Adam his reckoning."* (Abraham 5:12–13; italics added.)

THE PARADISIACAL CREATION

We state as an article of our faith that in the Millennium "the
earth will be renewed and receive its paradisiacal glory" (Articles
of Faith 1:10). Reasoning in reverse, and knowing that during the
thousand years of peace the earth will exist in a terrestrial glory,
we can conclude that life on the Edenic earth was of a terrestrial
order. This state was indeed paradisiacal. Man knew his God and
walked and talked with him. Adam was, as Joseph Smith taught,
"lord or governor of all things on earth, . . . at the same time
enjoying communication and intercourse with his Maker, without
a vail to separate between."[10] The Prophet also observed: "The
designs of God, . . . have been to promote the universal good of
the universal world; to establish peace and good will among men;
to promote the principles of eternal truth . . . , and to bring about
the millennial glory, when 'the earth shall yield its increase, resume
its paradisean glory, and become as the garden of the Lord.' "[11]

As we have already observed, the accounts of the Creation from the records of Moses and Abraham depict the placement of Adam, Eve, and all forms of life in a physical state. They had substance. They were tangible. And yet they were what the scriptures describe as being *spiritual.* That is, they were immortal, not subject to death. In speaking of the body in the resurrection, Paul wrote that "it is sown in corruption; it is raised in incorruption: . . . it is sown a natural body; it is raised a spiritual body" (1 Corinthians 15:42, 44). Amulek likewise testified that "this mortal body is raised to an immortal body, that is from death, even from the first death unto life, that they can die no more; their spirits uniting with their bodies, never to be divided; thus the whole becoming spiritual and immortal, that they can no more see corruption" (Alma 11:45). Finally, a modern revelation attests that notwithstanding the righteous die, "they also shall rise again, a spiritual body" (D&C 88:27). The nature of things in Eden before the Fall can therefore be described as physical-spiritual: physical and tangible in its makeup but not subject to the decaying and deteriorating effects of death. Joseph Fielding Smith summarized as follows:

> The account of creation in Genesis was not a spirit creation, but it was in a particular sense, a spiritual creation. This, of course, needs some explanation. The account in Genesis, chapters one and two, is the account of the creation of the physical earth. The account of the placing of all life upon the earth, up and until the fall of Adam, is an account, in a sense, of the spiritual creation of all of these, but it was also a physical creation. When the Lord said he would create Adam, he had no reference to the creation of his spirit for that had taken place ages and ages before when he was in the world of spirits and known as Michael.
>
> Adam's body was created from the dust of the earth, but at that time it was a spiritual earth. Adam had a spiritual body until mortality came upon him through the violation of the law under which he was living, but he also had a physical body of flesh and bones.[12]

"Man, when he was first placed upon this earth," Elder Orson Pratt explained, "was an immortal being, capable of eternal endurance; his flesh and bones, as well as his spirit, were immortal and eternal in their nature; and it was just so with all the inferior creation . . . ; all were immortal and eternal in their nature; and the earth itself, as a living being, was immortal and eternal in its nature."[13] More specifically, Joseph Fielding Smith wrote: "Adam [and, by extension, all of the animal creation] had no blood in his veins before the fall. Blood is the life of the mortal body." After Adam partook of the forbidden fruit, blood became "the life-giving fluid in Adam's body, and was inherited by his posterity. Blood was not only the life of the mortal body, but also contained in it the seeds of death which bring the mortal body to its end. Previously the life force in Adam's body, which is likewise the sustaining power in every immortal body, was the spirit."[14]

Inasmuch as blood did not become a part of the physical organization of animal life until after the Fall, death was held in abeyance. The revelations attest that by reason of transgression came the Fall, and through the Fall came death (Moses 6:59; compare 2 Nephi 9:6). In addition, because blood is the medium of mortality and thus the means by which mortal life is propagated, before the Fall there was no procreation. That is to say, the command to our first parents and to all forms of life to multiply and replenish the earth (see Moses 2:22, 28) could not be obeyed until man had fallen and until blood had entered the human and animal systems.

Thus Lehi explained to Jacob that "if Adam had not transgressed he would not have fallen, but he would have remained in the garden of Eden." He and Eve and all plant and animal life would have persisted in their spiritual state, and they would still be in the garden today, after some six thousand years! "And all things which were created" —man and woman, plant and animal —"must have remained in the same [immortal, spiritual, paradisiacal] state in which they were after they were created; and they must have remained forever, and had no end. And they would have had no children; wherefore they would have remained in a state of innocence, having no joy, for they knew no misery; doing no good, for they knew no sin." (2 Nephi 2:22–23; compare Moses 3:9.) After the Fall, and with a more elevated perspective of the events in Eden, Eve, in what is certainly one of the most profound declarations in scripture, exulted: "Were it not for our transgression we never should have had seed, and never should have known good and evil, and the joy of our redemption, and the eternal life which God giveth unto all the obedient" (Moses 5:11).

Having come thus far, we are in a better position to understand the otherwise enigmatic words of God to Moses regarding man's creation. Having written of the six days (periods or times) of creation and the particular events of those days — including the placement of man on earth — Moses recorded the Lord's words as follows: "These are the generations of the heaven and of the earth, when they were created, in the day that I, the Lord God, made the heaven and the earth, and every plant of the field before it was in the earth, and every herb of the field before it grew. For *I, the Lord God, created all things, of which I have spoken, spiritually, before they were naturally upon the face of the earth.*" (Moses 3:4–5; italics added.) We must keep in mind that the Creation is a past event. These statements are thus, as Elder McConkie wrote, "interpolative; they are inserted in the historical account to give us its true depth and meaning and import. They are not chronological recitations, but are commentary about what [the Lord] had already set forth in its sequential order."[15] Parts of these verses, specifically that which appears in italics above, can apply to the physical-spiritual creation. As we have said, the spiritual creation — the placement of all things in a physical but spiritual state (tangible but immortal, not subject to death) — preceded the natural or mortal creation, that organization and state of things which came as a result of the Fall.

The account continues: "For I, the Lord God, had not caused it to rain upon the face of the earth." Jehovah then makes specific reference to the spirit creation, the premortal creation of man and all forms of life: "And I, the Lord God, had created all the children of men; and not yet a man to till the ground; for in heaven created I them" (Moses 3:5). "Thus, all things have been created," Elder McConkie wrote; "the work is finished; the account is revealed; but it can only be understood if some added truths are set forth. These deal with the premortal existence of all things and with the paradisiacal nature of the earth and of all created things when they first came from their Creator's hand. Both of these concepts are interwoven in the same sentences, and in some instances the words used have a dual meaning and apply to both the premortal life and the paradisiacal creation."[16] And thus the word of the Lord in modern revelation is made clearer. The Lord instructed the early Latter-day Saints that he had created all things "by the word of my power, which is the power of my Spirit. For by the power of my Spirit created I them; yea, all things both spiritual and temporal — first spiritual [the paradisiacal creation], secondly temporal [after the Fall], which is the beginning of my work; and again, first temporal [reference again to this mortal creation], and secondly spiritual [man and all forms of life in and after the resurrection], which is the last of my work." (D&C 29:30–32.)

THE LOCATION OF EDEN

The Prophet Joseph Smith learned early from his translation of the Book of Mormon that the land of America is "a land of promise," a sacred and select site "which is choice above all other lands" (1 Nephi 2:20; see also 2 Nephi 10:19; Ether 2:9–10). Later in his ministry the Prophet came to appreciate, at least in part, why this continent is so highly treasured by the Lord: the drama which we know as Eden was acted out in the land of America. Wilford Woodruff reported that Brigham Young once said: "Joseph, the Prophet, told me that the Garden of Eden was in Jackson County, Missouri. When Adam was driven out he went to the place we now call Adam-ondi-Ahman, Daviess County, Missouri. There he built an altar and offered sacrifices."[17]

Finally, in regard to Eden, we need only add that the scriptural or prophetic word makes no distinction between the state of things in Eden and that of the rest of the earth; that is to say, we have every reason to believe that the entire earth —not a few acres in the Garden of Eden —existed in a physical-spiritual, paradisiacal, terrestrial condition: no death, no decay, no procreation, no development and growth took place anywhere until the universal fall.

THE CREATION OF MAN

Moses called the creative time periods *days*. Abraham called them *times*. "What is a day?" Elder Bruce R. McConkie asked. "It is a specified time period; it is an age, an eon, a division of eternity; it is the time between two identifiable events. And each day, of whatever length, has the duration needed for its purposes." And then, in what is a penetrating insight, he added: "There is no revealed recitation specifying that each of the 'six days' involved in the Creation was of the same duration."[18] As the work of creation progressed, the Gods prepared the heavens and the earth for plant and animal life: they formed the earth from self-existing chaotic matter; divided the light from the darkness; created an expanse or a firmament through dividing the waters on the earth from those in the atmospheric heavens; set the great lights — the sun, moon, and stars — in their proper planetary position, so as to be in place when the earth fell; and prepared animal life in the waters and on earth (see Moses 2; Abraham 4).

The work of the Gods — possibly some of the noble and great ones — had been monumental and their labors extensive; all things were now in readiness for the creation and placement of man on earth. Drawing insights from scriptural and other sacred sources, Elder McConkie has written, "We know that Jehovah-Christ, assisted by 'many of the noble and great ones' (Abraham 3:22), of whom Michael is but the illustration, did in fact create the earth and all forms of plant and animal life on the face thereof. But," he added, "when it came to placing man on earth, there was a change in Creators. That is, the Father himself became personally involved. All things were created by the Son, using the power delegated by the Father, except man. In the spirit and again in the flesh, man was created by the Father. There was no delegation of authority where the crowning creature of creation was concerned."[19] Similarly, Elder McConkie has written elsewhere:

> In the ultimate and final sense of the word, the Father is the Creator of all things. That he used the Son and others to perform many of the creative acts, delegating to them his creative powers, does not make these others creators in their own right, independent of him. He is the source of all creative power, and he simply chooses others to act for him in many of his creative enterprises. But there are two creative events that are his and his alone. First, he is the Father of all spirits, Christ's included; none were fathered or created by anyone else. Second, he is the Creator of the physical body of man. Though Jehovah and Michael and many of the noble and great ones played their assigned roles in the various cre-

ative events, yet when it came time to place man on earth, the Lord God himself performed the creative acts. "I, God, created man in mine own image, in the image of mine Only Begotten created I him; male and female created I them" (Moses 2:27).[20]

Thus we can conclude that scriptural references to Jesus Christ as the creator of man (e.g., Isaiah 45:12; Mosiah 26:23; Ether 3:15–16) are illustrations of the Son speaking for the Father by divine investiture of authority.

Luke, in providing the genealogy of Jesus, spoke of Cainan, who "was the son of Enos, which was the son of Seth, which was the son of Adam, which was the son of God" (Luke 3:38). The Joseph Smith Translation of this passage speaks of "Adam, who was formed of God, and the first man upon the earth" (JST, Luke 3:45). In another account from that same inspired translation, we read of the line of great patriarchs from Adam to Enoch. "And this is the genealogy," the sacred record affirms, "of the sons of Adam, who was the son of God, with whom God, himself, conversed" (JST, Genesis 6:23; Moses 6:22).

A brief treatment of the placement of man and woman on earth is contained in this book in the chapter entitled, " 'Our Glorious Mother Eve.' "

CONCLUSION

The accounts of the creation of man, animals, and all forms of life bear witness of the almighty power of the Father and the Son to organize and orchestrate what is and what is to be. If we could measure their value, these scriptural gems would be worth far more than their weight in gold. But they are fragmentary; they are brief; they weave together the literal and the figurative; and they present the truth in such a manner as to require our greatest exertions to arrive at those transcendent but obtainable realities toward which they but point the honest truth seeker. "The things of God are of deep import," Joseph the Seer declared; "and time, and experience, and careful and ponderous and solemn thoughts can only find them out."[21]

In this chapter we have considered some of the mysteries of creation. We have seen that men and women were begotten as spirits before the physical creation was begun. Further, Jehovah, Michael, and possibly other noble and great ones — all acting by virtue of the power and pursuant to the directions of God the first, the Creator — prepared and organized the earth itself and placed upon it plant and animal life. We hereby come face to face with a creation — a spiritual organization of life on earth — which is almost beyond comprehension. Prior to the Fall and the introduction of the natural or mortal creation, there was no blood, no death, no procreation. All things would have so remained had Adam and Eve not partaken of the forbidden fruit.

Men and women were born and reared in the heavenly mansions as spirit children of God and have the capacity to rise — through the lifting and regenerating powers of the atonement of Christ and by sustained righteousness — to celestial heights and resume their place in the family of the Gods. The Creation thus opened the door to endless and eternal possibilities. And with the Creation as an accomplished task, one of the pillars of eternity was in place.

NOTES

1. In *Journal of Discourses*, 14:300, 302.

2. Joseph Fielding Smith, *Doctrines of Salvation*, comp. Bruce R. McConkie, 3 vols. (Salt Lake City: Bookcraft, 1954–56), 1:75–76.

3. *Teachings of the Prophet Joseph Smith*, comp. Joseph Fielding Smith (Salt Lake City: Deseret Book Co., 1976), p. 190.

4. *Doctrines of Salvation* 1:74–75.

5. Bruce R. McConkie, "Eve and the Fall," in *Woman* (Salt Lake City: Deseret Book Co., 1979), p. 59.

6. *Teachings of the Prophet Joseph Smith*, p. 181.

7. In *Journal of Discourses*, 17:143.

8. In *Journal of Discourses*, 9:317.

9. John Taylor, cited in *The Vision*, comp. N. B. Lundwall (Salt Lake City: Bookcraft, n.d.), p. 146; italics added.

10. *Lectures on Faith* 2:12.

11. *Teachings of the Prophet Joseph Smith*, pp. 248–49.

12. *Doctrines of Salvation* 1:76.

13. In *Journal of Discourses*, 1:281.

14. Joseph Fielding Smith, *Man: His Origin and Destiny* (Salt Lake City: Deseret Book Co., 1954), pp. 362, 376–77.

15. Bruce R. McConkie, "Christ and the Creation," *Ensign* 12 (June 1982): 13.

16. "Christ and the Creation," p. 13.

17. As cited in Matthias F. Cowley, *Wilford Woodruff: History of His Life and Labors* (Salt Lake City: Bookcraft, 1964), p. 481; see also pp. 545–46. Compare John Taylor, *The Mediation and Atonement* (Salt Lake City: Deseret News Co., 1882), pp. 69–70; George Q. Cannon, in *Journal of Discourses*, 11:336–37.

18. "Christ and the Creation," p. 11.

19. Bruce R. McConkie, *The Promised Messiah* (Salt Lake City: Deseret Book Co., 1978), p. 62.

20. Bruce R. McConkie, *A New Witness for the Articles of Faith* (Salt Lake City: Deseret Book Co., 1985), p. 63.

21. *Teachings of the Prophet Joseph Smith*, p. 137.

3

Joseph Fielding McConkie

The Mystery of Eden

What of Eden? Was Eden real or just a universal myth — an allegory to explain the origin of man, an answer for the primitive mind? Was Adam molded from clay and Eve formed from Adam's bone? Was there once a garden in which our first parents lived, blissfully unaware of their nakedness? And if so, what became of that garden when Adam and Eve were no longer there to dress and keep it? Did snakes once stand erect, possessing the power to converse with men and women? Was there once a tree, the fruit of which brought a knowledge of good and evil? Was there yet another tree, the fruit of which brought everlasting life?

What of Eden? Is the story figurative or literal? Is it reality or the shadow of reality, or is it a masterful blend of both? Is it like so much else within the Bible — a parable, a sealed book, a type, a story veiled to the eyes of the spiritually untutored? Is the story of Eden, in fact, a light that reveals the path all must travel to return to the divine presence? Just what is the mystery of Eden?

The confusion of tongues in the city of Babel is no match for the confusion of ideas and doctrines among Bible believers as to

Joseph Fielding McConkie is Professor of Ancient Scripture at Brigham Young University.

the meaning of Eden and the expulsion of Adam and Eve from its paradisiacal splendors. In unfolding that story we make no pretense to being smarter than others. Indeed, answers to spiritual queries have little to do with the powers of intellect alone, while they have much to do with eyes and ears endowed with a capacity to see and hear. Such is the privilege of those of the household of faith, those of believing blood, those who have schooled themselves in the revelations of the Restoration—the Book of Mormon, the Doctrine and Covenants, the book of Moses, and the temple ceremony. Such are the sources to which we turn to obtain an understanding of Eden and the experiences of those who once resided there. This article will confine itself to commentary on scriptural texts.

EDEN: FIGURATIVE OR LITERAL?

The scriptural account of the birth of Adam is a sacred metaphor, as is the account of the birth of his eternal companion, Eve. Indeed, it is Adam and the Lord who are quoted in the discourse by Enoch in which we are told that all mankind are born of the dust of the earth (see Moses 6:49–59). Thus the promise to Adam that in death his body would return to the dust from whence it was taken (Moses 4:25) is extended to all his posterity. "All are of the dust, and all turn to dust again" (Ecclesiastes 3:20; see also Mosiah 2:25).

The imagery used to veil the account of Eve's birth is most beautiful, particularly so in a day when there is so much confusion about the role of women. Symbolically, she was not taken from the bones of Adam's head nor from the bones of his heel, for it is not the place of woman to be either above the man or beneath him. Her place is at his side, and so she is taken, in the figurative sense, from his rib—the bone that girds the side and rests closest to the heart. Thus we find Adam declaring: "This I know now is bone of my bones, and flesh of my flesh; she shall be called Woman, because she was taken out of man" (Moses 3:23). Eve, unlike the rest of God's creations, was of Adam's bone and of his flesh, meaning that she was equal to him in powers, faculties, and rights.

"Therefore," the divine word attests, "shall a man leave his father and his mother, and shall cleave unto his wife; and they shall be one flesh" (Moses 3:24). Thus, because Eve was of his flesh and of his bone —because she was his equal in creation and in divine endowment — Adam was to leave his father and his mother, as all men were to do after him, and cleave unto his wife and none else (see Matthew 19:5–6). All men and women are commanded to do likewise; that is, they (the newly formed couple), like their first earthly parents, are to be "one flesh"; they are to be as if they had one body, thus suggesting that they cannot properly have separate cares or concerns, different rights or varied privileges. The phrase also suggests that as Adam and Eve were in the image and likeness of their parents, so their posterity would be in their image and likeness.

How literally do we take the story of the Garden of Eden? This we know: Adam was real. He was as real as Christ. For if Adam was not real the Fall was not real; and if the Fall was not real the Atonement was not real; and if the Atonement was not real Jesus the Christ is not and was not necessary. Of some parts of the Eden story it matters little if we choose to view them as figurative or literal, but of others it is not so. The testimony of Christ, of necessity, embraces the testimony of Adam. Had there been no Eden there could be no Gethsemane; had there been no Eve there could be no Mary; if we have not inherited death from Adam, we have no claim on everlasting life through Christ.

What then became of Eden? This we know: it constituted sacred space when mother earth resided in her paradisiacal state, for it was here that Adam and Eve walked and talked with God, and it was from the confines of Eden that they were cast following their transgression. Further, we know that it existed after the Fall for a period of time and that God continued to instruct Adam and Eve from its sacred groves. (Moses 5:4; 6:4.) In likening Tyrus to Eden, Ezekiel made use of the term "mountain of God" (Ezekiel 28:13–14), a phrase used throughout the scriptures to depict a place where one went to commune with God, to worship, to make sacrifices, and to enter into sacred covenants. Mountains were most suited for such purposes and thus became symbols for the temple, the place where heaven and earth meet. Perhaps Ezekiel was implying that Eden was a mountain or at least had a high place suited for worship.

As to what became of Eden, the scriptures are silent. Perhaps, after Adam and his righteous posterity had built the city of Adam-

ondi-Ahman — which undoubtedly would have had a temple —
Eden was no longer needed as a place of God's presence. A place of
sacrifice and of covenant, Eden thus could either be taken into
heaven or be allowed to be assimilated into the earth.

What of the trees of Eden? Was there actually a tree whose fruit
would make one wise, and another whose fruit would assure everlasting life? The scriptural account, for instance, tells us that the
Lord planted "the tree of knowledge of good and evil" in the midst
of the garden (Moses 3:9). He then gave Adam and Eve the command: "Of every tree of the garden thou mayest freely eat, but of
the tree of the knowledge of good and evil, thou shalt not eat of it,
nevertheless, thou mayest choose for thyself, for it is given unto
thee; but, remember that I forbid it, for in the day thou eatest
thereof thou shalt surely die" (Moses 3:16–17). "Again," wrote
Elder Bruce R. McConkie, "the account is speaking figuratively.
What is meant by partaking of the fruit of the tree of the knowledge of good and evil is that our first parents complied with
whatever laws were involved so that their bodies would change
from their state of paradisiacal immortality to a state of natural
mortality."[1] Elder McConkie also wrote elsewhere: "We do not
know how the fall was accomplished any more than we know how
the Lord caused the earth to come into being and to spin through
the heavens in its paradisiacal state."[2]

If we were to reason that it was the fruit itself that brought
about this change in the bodies of Adam and Eve, we would then
have to suppose that our first parents fed some of the fruit to all
the other living things upon the whole earth. Had they not done
so, "all things which were created must have remained in the same
state in which they were after they were created; and they must
have remained forever, and had no end" (2 Nephi 2:22; see also
Moses 3:9). Every plant and animal, including all sea life and the
fowls of the air, would have been required to eat some of this fruit
(and must also have been precluded from partaking of it either by
design or accident before this point of time).

What of the serpent that beguiled Eve into partaking of the forbidden fruit? Did animals in Eden have the capacity to converse in
the language of men, as some ancient traditions suggest? Was it
then a natural thing for Eve to have a conversation with a serpent?
And what of the curse which consigned the serpent to crawl upon

its belly and eat of the dust of the earth? Does this suggest that snakes once stood upright, having legs and arms, as they are so commonly depicted in ancient Egyptian drawings? The key question is, Did Satan actually possess the body of a serpent and speak to Eve through that medium, or did Moses choose to describe Eve's confrontation with the father of lies as a discussion with a snake because a snake is such a vivid metaphor to dramatize the subtle, crafty, and dangerous nature of the devil?

Whether a serpent was actually the agent of deception in the Eden story or merely a metaphorical representation of the devil, it matters little. Neither point of view changes or tampers with the integrity of the story. If, however, we assume the partaking of the fruit to have been a figurative representation of what actually brought about the transformation of the earth from a paradisiacal to a natural or mortal sphere, then it might follow that the speaking serpent would also have been figurative.

What, then, do we conclude of the Eden story? Was it figurative or literal? We answer by way of comparison. It, like the temple ceremony, combines a rich blend of both. Our temples are real, the priesthood is real, the covenants we enter into are real, and the blessings we are promised by obedience are real; yet the teaching device may be metaphorical. We are as actors on a stage. We role-play and imagine. We do not actually advance from one world to another in the temple, but rather are taught with figurative representations of what can and will be.

EDEN AS AN ALLEGORY

Should it ever be our privilege to call upon father Adam and ask him to share with us his treasured memories of Eden, can we not confidently suppose that he would speak in reverent terms of walking with God and being instructed by him? Would he not speak of hands that were laid upon his head to convey the priesthood and its keys? Would he not tell of his marriage with his beloved companion, Eve, and the charge given to them to multiply and fill the earth with their posterity? Would he not recount that instruction given him and his eternal companion by which they could obtain the fulness of heavenly knowledge and power? Would he not rehearse how he had been taught the law of sacrifice

(Moses 5:1–8) and how he and Eve had been clothed in the garments of salvation preparatory to their entering the lone and dreary world, where they were to be tried and tested in all things?

A rehearsal of the key events of Eden brings the realization that we too are privileged to leave the lone and dreary world and enter the sacred sanctuaries of the Lord, where we participate in essentially the same experiences known to our first parents before the Fall. The temple is to us as Eden was to Adam and Eve. It is in the temple that we, like Adam and Eve, are invited to walk with God; it is in the temple that we are instructed in those things that we must do to return to his holy presence; it is in the temple that we are married for eternity and commanded to multiply and replenish the earth; it is within these sacred walls that we are taught the law of sacrifice, placed under covenant to be true and faithful, and clothed in a garment of protection.

After Adam and Eve had partaken of the forbidden fruit, but before they were expelled from the garden, the Father taught them the law of sacrifice. Animals were slain that Adam and Eve might be clothed in "coats of skins" (Moses 4:27) that were to be a protection to them in our fallen world. Adam and Eve subsequently learned that the shedding of the animals' blood was in similitude of the atoning blood of Christ (Moses 5:7). Thus the garments given them in Eden were to serve as a constant reminder that through the atoning blood of Christ they could be protected from all the effects of a fallen world. Through his blood they could obtain a remission of sins, be born again, and return to the divine presence.

Adam and Eve were further instructed by an angel of the Lord that they were to take upon them the name of Christ and that all they did was to be done in his name (Moses 5:8). Thus as God had clothed them in coats or garments of skin as a token of the protection provided them through Christ, a protection from the effects of a fallen world, so they were to clothe themselves in his name by faith, and in that name they were to do all that they did that pertained to salvation or to things of the Spirit. Thus they were assured that they could overcome.

"He that hath an ear, let him hear," John wrote unto the seven churches in Asia, "what the Spirit saith unto the churches; To him that overcometh will I give to eat of the tree of life" (Revelation

2:7). The fruit is the gospel of Jesus Christ and is described by Lehi as being "desirable to make one happy" and as filling the soul with "exceedingly great joy" (1 Nephi 8:10–12). To Nephi it was revealed that the tree of life — that tree which stood in the midst of Eden — represented the love of God, and by extension, the eternal life made possible by the atonement of the Son of God (see 1 Nephi 11:4–21).

EFFECTS OF THE FALL

After Adam and Eve had partaken of the forbidden fruit — thus becoming mortal and imposing mortality upon the earth and all forms of life — they were driven out of the Garden of Eden to till the earth, which is to say that the whole earth was destined to lose its paradisiacal splendor. The change of the earth from its incorruptible state to that of a fallen world is symbolized by Adam and Eve's expulsion from the garden. The garden — earth that once was — became the lone, dreary, and often hostile earth that now is. The "cherubim and a flaming sword, which turned every way to protect the tree of life" (Moses 4:31), constituted a symbolic announcement that the earth could not return to its paradisiacal state while death reigned. Until the great millennial day, the earth would be subject to corruption.

As to the procreation that attends mortality, Lehi said: "They [Adam and Eve] have brought forth children; yea, even the family of all the earth" (2 Nephi 2:20). Eve is truly the mother of all living; every living soul on earth is a descendant of Adam and Eve. "God . . . hath made of one blood all nations of men for to dwell on all the face of the earth" (Acts 17:24–26). All of earth's inhabitants share a common father.

The days of the children of men were prolonged, according to the will of God, that they might repent while in the flesh. The day within which their destined mortal death came was a thousand of our years (Abraham 3:4; 5:13). "Wherefore, their state became a state of probation, and their time was lengthened, according to the commandments which the Lord God gave unto the children of men. For he gave commandment that all men must repent; for he showed unto all men that they were lost, because of the transgression of their parents." (2 Nephi 2:21.) The effects of the Fall pass upon all men; all must repent; all must be reconciled to God; all must be redeemed from death, hell, and endless torment.

"And now, behold, if Adam had not transgressed he would not have fallen, but he would have remained in the garden of Eden." He would be there today, nearly six thousand years later, because there was no death before the Fall. "And all things which were created" — all things: the earth, all forms of life, vegetation, trees, grass, herbs, everything that comes from the ground; the fowl and fish and creeping things in all their varieties; animals of every sort; the field mouse and the dinosaur — "all things which were created must have remained in the same state in which they were after they were created" — that is, in a paradisiacal state — "and they must have remained forever, and had no end." (2 Nephi 2:22.) There was no death — not for man, not for fowl, not for fish, not for animals, not for any form of life — until Adam fell.

"And they would have had no children; wherefore they would have remained in a state of innocence, having no joy, for they knew no misery; doing no good, for they knew no sin" (2 Nephi 2:23). Until Adam and Eve transgressed they were innocent. There was no righteousness because there was no wickedness; there was no good because there was no evil. Hence, as we have seen, Adam needed to transgress in order to be put on probation and be subject to sin, that he might reject sin, overcome, and embrace righteousness.

"But behold, all things have been done in the wisdom of him who knoweth all things." Contrary to the beliefs of traditional Christianity, Adam conformed to the will of the Lord when he partook of the forbidden fruit. "Adam fell that men might be; and men are, that they might have joy." (2 Nephi 2:24–25.) And joy is available only because of misery, its opposite. If there were no misery, which could not exist in the state of innocence before the Fall, there could be no joy. This is why Eve said that if she and Adam had not transgressed, they "never should have had seed, and never should have known good and evil, and the joy of [their] redemption, and the eternal life which God giveth unto all the obedient" (Moses 5:11).

As to the doctrine of the Fall, and the philosophical basis upon which it rests, Alma tells us that "our first parents" were cast out of Eden; that man became like God in the sense that he knew good from evil; that cherubim and a flaming sword kept the way of the tree of life; and that had fallen man partaken of the tree of life, he would have lived forever in his sins. "And thus we see, that there was a time granted unto man to repent, yea, a probationary time, a time to repent and serve God." (Alma 42:2–4.) The creation of a mortal state of probation was the very reason for the Fall, and it was a state that could not come into being without the transgression of the first man and the first woman.

If, after the Fall, "Adam had put forth his hand immediately, and partaken of the tree of life, he would have lived forever, according to the word of God, having no space for repentance; yea, and also the word of God would have been void, and the great plan of salvation would have been frustrated" (Alma 42:5). Again we learn that Adam's transgression brought probation, the necessity of repentance, the opportunities to do good, and the possibility of salvation. "But behold, it was appointed unto man to die — therefore, as they were cut off from the tree of life they should be cut off from the face of the earth — and man became lost forever, yea, they became fallen man" (Alma 42:6). Adam and Eve's being cut off from the tree of life means they became mortal and would not continue to live without death. The mortal state, being lower than the immortal state, is thus a fallen state.

"And now, ye see by this that our first parents were cut off both temporally and spiritually from the presence of the Lord; and thus we see they became subjects to follow after their own will." Temporal death is the natural death, the separation of body and spirit; spiritual death is to die as pertaining to the things of the Spirit, which are the things of righteousness. "Now behold, it was not expedient that man should be reclaimed from this temporal death, for that would destroy the great plan of happiness." (Alma 42:7–8.) Death is essential to the plan of salvation. Only in death do we have hope of a glorious resurrection and of eternal life. Fulness of joy is available only when body and spirit are inseparably connected in immortality (see D&C 93:33–34).

"Therefore, as the soul [the spirit] could never die, and the fall had brought upon all mankind a spiritual death as well as a temporal, that is, they were cut off from the presence of the Lord, it was expedient that mankind should be reclaimed from this spiritual death." Those who are reclaimed from spiritual death become alive to the things of righteousness and are thereby qualified to return to the presence of the Lord. "Therefore, as they had become carnal, sensual, and devilish, by nature, this probationary state became a state for them to prepare; it became a preparatory state." (Alma 42:9–10.) And thus the foundation was laid and the need established for the great and eternal plan of redemption.

CONCLUSION

From Genesis to Revelation no story in scripture has been the source of more theological mischief than the story of Eden. It is the prime example of scriptural misuse and abuse. The errors that have come from the perversions of this story have given birth in turn to a thousand more. In no story have the figurative and the literal been so thoroughly confused, and in no other story has the absence of "plain and precious" parts caused more to stumble. In the mystery of Eden we have a classic case study of the dangers and difficulties with which uninspired scriptural exegesis is fraught, and the manner in which the scriptures remain a sealed book to all save those who know that same Spirit by which they were originally given.

Sexual desire is evil; infants are infected from the moment of conception with the stain of original sin; infants that die without baptism are everlastingly lost; our paradisiacal state was unnecessarily lost —each of these beliefs claims to be a fruit of Eden; each is bitter to the taste. Yet those who partook of Eden's fruits declared them to be "most sweet" and to bring "great joy" (1 Nephi 8:11–12). Our promise is of fruits sweet above all that is sweet, white above all that is white, pure above all that is pure, fruits upon which we may feast until we know hunger and thirst no more (see Alma 32:42).

Indeed the story of Eden has remained a mystery. Too often the picture that is painted is that of Adam, bent and bowed in his new world of thorns and thistles, with the weak and gullible Eve dutifully following behind. Revealed religion exults in the Fall and rejoices in the blessings that flow from it (2 Nephi 2:25). The Adam we see is one who "blessed God and was filled, and began to prophesy concerning all the families of the earth, saying: Blessed be the name of God, for because of my transgression my eyes are opened, and in this life I shall have joy, and again in the flesh I shall see God. And Eve, his wife, heard all these things and was glad, saying: Were it not for our transgression we never should have had seed, and never should have known good and evil, and the joy of our redemption, and the eternal life which God giveth unto all the obedient. And Adam and Eve blessed the name of God, and they made all things known unto their sons and their daughters." (Moses 5:10–12.)

In the story of man's earthly origin we find the rich blend of figurative and literal that is so typical of the Bible, of the teachings of Christ, and of our daily experience — this that the story might unfold according to the faith and wisdom that we bring to it. Like all scriptural texts, its interpretation becomes a measure of our maturity and our spiritual integrity. Such is the mystery of Eden.

NOTES

1. Bruce R. McConkie, "Christ and the Creation," *Ensign* 12 (June 1982): 15.

2. Bruce R. McConkie, *A New Witness for the Articles of Faith* (Salt Lake City: Deseret Book Co., 1985), pp. 85–86.

4

Robert J. Matthews

The Fall of Man

This chapter is written from the vantage point of a belief in the four standard works of the Church as sacred, revealed scripture. We start with the assurance that these scriptures are correct and convey an accurate impression as to the purposes of God in the creation of the earth, the divine origin of man, the reality of the fall of man, and the provision for redemption from the Fall.

It is not the aim of this chapter to seek to harmonize conflicting views generated by those who look to nonscriptural, secular, or philosophical sources for information on the subject of the Fall, or who desire to rationalize or compromise in order to make the pieces fit a nonscriptural frame of reference. It is my conviction that the scriptures are consistent within themselves, and even though all the details are not made known, there is sufficient information in them to enable us to understand what caused the Fall, what its effects have been, and what its role is in the purposes of God. Enough has been revealed to enlighten us on the practical

Robert J. Matthews is Dean of Religious Education and Professor of Ancient Scripture at Brigham Young University.

and useful purposes that the Fall serves in man's progress toward salvation, and to help us realize that neither Adam nor God regretted that the Fall occurred — in fact, this event is a matter for ultimate rejoicing. Since the point of view in this chapter is that the scriptural account is accurate (if not complete), our energies will not be spent on trying to determine the correctness of the record, but only to learn what the scriptures really say and the interpretation placed upon them by the latter-day prophets.

There is a good reason why we should look to and rely upon the scriptures as our chief source of information about the origin of things, including man's roots. Until we know just what these origins are, it is impossible to gain a perspective. None of us remembers being present at the creation of the earth, or at the creation of Adam, or at the Fall. None of us remembers from our own experience what the conditions were, or what discussions took place previous to, during, or after the Creation or the Fall. We are totally dependent on sources outside ourselves for information about these things. Since no other human being on earth has any personal recollection of these things, a revelation from someone who does remember is absolutely necessary if we are to have reliable information on the subject.

There is a story that Diogenes of Sinope, the Greek educator of about 300 B.C., once listened to a philosopher talk with overmuch certainty about eternal things, whereupon Diogenes approached him and asked, "When did you come back from heaven?"[1] Likewise, the Prophet Joseph Smith, commenting on our need for revelation if we want correct information, said: "Men of the present time [speak] of heaven and hell, and have never seen either; and I will say that no man knows these things without [revelation]." And he also said: "We never can comprehend the things of God and of heaven, but by revelation. We may spiritualize and express opinions to all eternity; but that is no authority." The Prophet further declared: "Could you gaze into heaven five minutes, you would know more than you would by reading all that ever was written on the subject."[2]

Our purpose, therefore, in this chapter is to present and comment upon what the Lord, who was present and who remembers the situation, has revealed about the fall of man and its effects on man and the entire creation.

THE PLAN OF SALVATION:
A DOCTRINAL FRAMEWORK OF FIXED PRINCIPLES

A special contribution of latter-day revelation is the concept that there is a plan of salvation that has existed in the mind of God from before the creation of the world, a concept about which the present biblical record makes no definitive statements. While there is not enough in the Bible alone to learn that God does indeed have such a plan, after learning about the plan from latter-day scriptures one can then discern traces of it in the Bible.

The Father's plan calls for the fall of man as an indispensable step and process in His purpose to "bring to pass the immortality and eternal life of man" (Moses 1:39). Thus the Creation, the Fall, and the Redemption are all necessary parts of the Lord's grand design; all were planned, and each is essential to the success of the others.

That God has a plan for mankind is mentioned at least twenty-eight times in latter-day scripture. These scriptures give various names for the divine plan, such as the following:

"Great and eternal plan" (Alma 34:16)
"Great plan of happiness" (Alma 42:8)
"Great plan of redemption" (Jacob 6:8; Alma 34:31)
"Plan of deliverance" (2 Nephi 11:5)
"Plan of mercy" (Alma 42:15, 31)
"Plan of our God" (2 Nephi 9:13)
"Plan of redemption" (Alma 12:25, 26, 30, 32, 33; 17:16;
      18:39; 22:13–14; 29:2; 39:18; 42:11, 13)
"Plan of restoration" (Alma 41:2)
"Plan of salvation" (Jarom 1:2; Alma 24:14; 42:5; Moses 6:62)
"Plan of the Eternal God" (Alma 34:9)
"Plan of the great Creator" (2 Nephi 9:6)
"Their [the Gods'] plan" (Abraham 4:21)

The plan of God calls for a creation, a fall that brings two kinds of death, a probationary period, a set of commandments and ordinances, an infinite atonement by a God, a resurrection, a judgment, and an assignment to one's everlasting destiny. It would destroy the plan if any part or any step were changed or omitted (see Alma 42:8). The plan is a package—none of it is superfluous, none is optional. The whole of it is "fitly joined together" by that which "every joint supplieth" (Ephesians 4:16).

The Prophet Joseph Smith taught that there are immutable laws that govern the premortal, mortal, and postmortal existences. He called these laws "fixed principles."

> We are only capable of comprehending that certain things exist, which we may acquire by certain fixed principles. If men would acquire salvation, they have got to be subject, before they leave this world, to certain rules and principles, which were fixed by an unalterable decree before the world was. . . .
>
> The organization of the spiritual and heavenly worlds, and of spiritual and heavenly beings, was agreeable to the most perfect order and harmony: their limits and bounds were fixed irrevocably, and voluntarily subscribed to in their heavenly estate by themselves, and were by our first parents subscribed to upon the earth. Hence the importance of embracing and subscribing to principles of eternal truth by all men upon the earth that expect eternal life.
>
> I assure the Saints that truth, in reference to these matters, can and may be known through the revelations of God.[3]

And again from the Prophet:

> God has made certain decrees which are fixed and immovable; for instance, God set the sun, the moon, and the stars in the heavens, and gave them their laws, conditions and bounds, which they cannot pass, except by His commandments; they all move in perfect harmony in their sphere and order, and are as lights, wonders and signs unto us. The sea also has its bounds which it cannot pass. God has set many signs on the earth, as well as in the heavens; for instance, the oak of the forest, the fruit of the tree, the herb of the field, all bear a sign that seed hath been planted there; for it is a decree of the Lord that every tree, plant, and herb bearing seed should bring forth of its kind, and cannot come forth after any other law or principle.[4]

WHY WE SHOULD LEARN ABOUT THE FALL

The reason why it is important for us to know that God has a plan for the salvation of man, and that the plan includes the fall of man, is such knowledge dignifies the Fall and gives man a sense of security by removing the idea of chance or happenstance. The idea of a plan of God directs us to the conclusion that the Fall (1) was necessary, (2) was not a surprise to God, (3) was not an outright rebellion, (4) was an actual occurrence, and (5) is an essential part of the journey of man toward perfection. There may be other dimensions to the Fall, but the above conclusions are philosophically and doctrinally of basic importance for man to know while he lives on the earth as a mortal. If it were not for the concept that a comprehensive, intelligent plan of God is being carried out in behalf of the earth and man, it would not be possible for us to gain the necessary perspective and to have the necessary faith in the atonement of Jesus Christ. The revelations unfold to us a doctrinal framework of understanding so that we can have faith in the right things.

President Ezra Taft Benson has given us a very good reason why we should understand the Fall:

> The Book of Mormon Saints knew that the plan of redemption must start with the account of the fall of Adam. In the words of Moroni, "By Adam came the fall of man. And because of the fall of man came Jesus Christ . . . and because of Jesus Christ came the redemption of man." (Mormon 9:12.)
>
> Just as a man does not really desire food until he is hungry, so he does not desire the salvation of Christ until he knows why he needs Christ. No one adequately and properly knows why he needs Christ until he understands and accepts the doctrine of the Fall and its effect upon all mankind. And no other book in the world explains this vital doctrine nearly as well as the Book of Mormon.[5]

STATEMENTS ABOUT THE FALL

There are many evidences in the world that mankind is in a fallen condition. We understand that the human family is the offspring of Deity—not just one of his creations, but literally his spirit children—his sons and his daughters. Man therefore has a different relationship to God than do the animals, the earth, and the planets and stars. Those things are the work of his hands; man is his offspring. Yet surprisingly, despite this divine lineage, man has displayed much hatred, selfishness, greed, war, sickness, and other traits far beneath the majesty and high moral character of an all-wise, all-knowing, perfect, and benevolent God. A little reflection on the history of mankind, and the nature of man's society, will lead one to conclude either that man is not the offspring of a noble Deity or that man has departed from the ways of God and fallen from any position of holiness and righteousness that he once had. At any rate, mortal man, past and present, has not consistently displayed the traits of virtue or the physical, moral, spiritual, and intellectual perfection that naturally one would expect to be found in the family of a perfect, glorious God.

The Lord has given an explanation through his prophets as to how these conditions were brought about. They are the results of the fall of Adam, or the fall of man. In the Doctrine and Covenants we read: "We know that there is a God in heaven, who is infinite and eternal, from everlasting to everlasting the same unchangeable God . . . ; and that he created man, male and female, after his own image and in his own likeness, created he them; and gave unto them commandments that they should love and serve him, the only living and true God. . . . But by the transgression of these holy laws man became sensual and devilish, and became fallen man." (D&C 20:17–20.)

This same doctrine was taught by Aaron, son of Mosiah:

> And it came to pass that when Aaron saw that the king would believe his words, he began from the creation of Adam, reading the scriptures unto the king—how God created man after his own image, and that God gave him commandments, and that because of transgression, man had fallen.
>
> And Aaron did expound unto him the scriptures from the creation of Adam, laying the fall of man before him, and their carnal state and also the plan of redemption, which was prepared from the foundation of the world, through Christ, for all whosoever would believe on his name.
>
> And since man had fallen he could not merit anything of himself; but the sufferings and death of Christ atone for their sins, through faith and repentance. (Alma 22:12–14.)

There are many other statements in the scriptures, particularly in latter-day scriptures, that delineate the effects of the Fall. The story of the fall of Adam is given in Genesis, chapter 3, and in Moses, chapter 4. An account of the Fall also was contained on the plates of brass, for the Book of Mormon record tells us that Lehi, having received the plates, read "of Adam and Eve, who were our first parents" (1 Nephi 5:10–11; see also 2 Nephi 2:17–20). In addition, the Book of Mormon contains a great many references to Satan's temptation of Adam and Eve in the Garden of Eden. It is clear that the Nephite prophets were well acquainted with the scriptural account of the Creation and of Adam, Eve, the tree of life, the tree of knowledge, Lucifer, the temptation, the transgression, the expulsion from Eden, and the effects of the Fall on Adam and Eve and their entire posterity. These particular items are spoken of in detail by Lehi, Jacob, Benjamin, Abinadi, Alma, Amulek, Aaron, Ammon, Samuel the Lamanite, and Moroni. Even the apostate Antionah shows some acquaintance with the content of the Nephite scripture when he questions Alma about the flaming sword, the Garden of Eden, and the tree of life (see Alma 12:20–21).

From the details given in the Book of Mormon, we can discern that the account of the Fall given on the plates of brass was more complete than the one given in our present book of Genesis. The plates of brass evidently contained a record very much like that found in the book of Moses, which is an extract from the Prophet Joseph Smith's inspired translation and restoration of the Genesis account. Obviously the biblical account of the Fall has suffered from the removal of many plain and precious things, which has resulted in a clouding and weakening of the message.

THE FALL WAS AN ACTUAL OCCURRENCE

In order to be of eternal value, it is essential that the fall of Adam be a historical event that actually happened at a specific time and place. We accept Adam and Eve as real persons who lived, transgressed, and brought about their own fall and the consequent fall of all mankind. If we had a complete record it would be possible to mark on the calendar the actual time that the Fall occurred. Likewise, if we had an adequate map it would be possible to mark the exact spot where the transgression occurred. The Fall is just that real and absolute. A real man and a real woman did, at a particular time and geographical location, transgress a commandment which brought about the fall of man, an event which has affected not only all of mankind but also the whole creation. The Fall is a historical event, an actual fact, an absolute occurrence, and is not simply a philosophical or so-called "religious" truth.

Conditions of Life in the Garden of Eden

What was the type of life experienced by man and the animals in the Garden of Eden before the Fall? According to the scriptures, and the interpretations made by many of the Brethren, the conditions were as follows:

1. *There was no death for man or the animals in the garden.* Father Lehi states that there was no death among all the creations God had made on this earth until Adam ate the forbidden fruit: "And now, behold, if Adam had not transgressed he would not have fallen, but he would have remained in the garden of Eden. And all things which were created must have remained in the same state in which they were after they were created; and they must have remained forever, and had no end." (2 Nephi 2:22.)

Similarly we read in the book of Moses: "And out of the ground made I, the Lord God, to grow every tree, naturally, that is pleasant to the sight of man; and man could behold it. And it became also a living soul. For it was spiritual in the day that I created it; *for it remaineth in the sphere in which I, God, created it*, yea, even all things which I prepared for the use of man; and man saw that it was good for food." (Moses 3:9; italics added.)

We note that the above statements do not pertain to man alone, but to the whole creation. Lehi speaks of "all things which were created," and the passage from the book of Moses refers to "all things which I [the Lord] prepared for the use of man." Thus the message of these two passages is clear: when God created the earth, man, and all things in the earth, there was no death, and all of these things would have remained forever and had no end if death had not entered by the transgression of Adam. This brings to mind the declaration in the Doctrine and Covenants that to God all things are spiritual, and that he has given no temporal or mortal commandment (D&C 29:34–35). That is, God is everlasting and endless; he is a spiritual being, and that which he does is spiritual, not mortal and not temporal. According to the scriptures it was

Adam, not God, that brought death. Death was not part of the Lord's original creation of this earth or of anything in the earth.

2. *There would have been no children born in the garden.* Lehi is forthright in his explanation that without the Fall Adam and Eve would not have had children (2 Nephi 2:23). And Lehi is not the only one who mentions that Adam and Eve would have had no children if there had been no fall. Eve herself realized the situation and spoke forth with gladness, "Were it not for our transgression we never should have had seed" (Moses 5:11). This marvelous declaration is not found in our present Bible and was made known through the translation of the Bible by the Prophet Joseph Smith. It no doubt was upon the plates of brass, which seems to be the source for Lehi's understanding. In addition, we have the confirming words of the prophet Enoch: "Because that Adam fell, we are; and by his fall came death" (Moses 6:48).

3. *There was no blood in the bodies of Adam and Eve in the garden.* That there was no blood in the bodies of Adam and Eve before the Fall, and that blood came as a result of the Fall, is not categorically stated in any one passage of scripture, but leading doctrinal teachers such as President Joseph Fielding Smith and Elder Bruce R. McConkie have declared that such was the case.[6] This conclusion is scripturally based and takes into account that blood is the mortal life of the body (see Genesis 9:2-6; Leviticus 17:10-15).

A further point supporting the conclusion that Adam and Eve had no blood in their premortal, non-death bodies is that we are assured by the Prophet Joseph Smith that resurrected beings do not have blood but possess bodies of flesh and bones "having spirit in their bodies, and not blood." The Prophet also said, "When our flesh is quickened by the Spirit, there will be no blood in this tabernacle." In speaking of the place where God dwells, the Prophet said, "Flesh and blood cannot go there; but flesh and bones, quickened by the Spirit of God, can."[7] (See also 1 Corinthians 15:50.)

This much we know about blood: (a) it is a vital part of our mortal lives and is basic to the reproductive process of mortals; (b) it was the agent of redemption in the atonement of Jesus Christ, he shedding his blood to redeem all people from the effects of the Fall and, upon the condition of repentance, from their personal sins; and (c) blood will not exist in the bodies of resurrected beings.

With these known facts it becomes evident that blood is the badge of mortality, and since it will not exist in the deathless bodies of Adam, Eve, and their posterity in the resurrection, it is therefore reasonable to conclude that blood did not exist in the deathless, premortal bodies of Adam and Eve prior to the Fall.

4. *There was no sin in the Garden of Eden until the transgression of Adam and Eve.* This fact seems to be without controversy. The whole concept of the Fall is based upon it. Lehi declared that without the Fall Adam and Eve "would have remained in a state of innocence, . . . doing no good, for they knew no sin" (2 Nephi 2:23).

5. *Adam and Eve were in the presence of God in the Garden of Eden.* Although the Father was not constantly in the garden with Adam and Eve, he visited them from time to time, and they could see him and talk with him. However, after the Fall occurred and they were cast out of the garden, they were able to hear God's voice, but "they saw him not; for they were shut out from his presence" (Moses 5:4).

The five conditions outlined above, which were characteristic of Eden, no longer exist on the earth. They have been taken away and replaced by physical death, reproduction, blood, sin, and separation from God. This is the mortal, temporal, fallen world into which we were born. Since the Fall, mankind has, by the birth process, come directly from the premortal spirit world into a world of mortality. However, Adam, Eve, and the animals — those beings placed first upon the earth — went from the premortal condition, into the Garden, and then into mortality.

Definitions of Key Words

It will be helpful at this point to examine and define some terms that are frequently used in the scriptures and that relate to the subject of the Fall.

Soul

A *soul* is defined in scripture as being the combination of a spirit body and a physical body (D&C 88:15; see also Genesis 2:7; Moses 3:7, 9, 19; Abraham 5:7). Man, trees, animals, and the earth itself are all living souls. All are created first as spirits and become living souls upon receiving tabernacles — tabernacles which have been mortal, or temporal, since the fall of Adam.

Spirit and Spiritual

A *spirit* is a personage, composed of spirit material too refined and subtle for the mortal eye to perceive naturally or the mortal hand to touch (D&C 129:6-8; 131:7-8). All things pertaining to this earth were created as spirits before anything was created physically. This would properly be spoken of as the *spirit* creation. Then God created all things physically, but there was no death and no sin attached. Therefore the physical creation (as described in Genesis 1 and 2) was tangible in nature, but *spiritual* in its conditions. A resurrected body is a physical, tangible tabernacle, as much so as our bodies are at this time in mortality; but a resurrected body is not subject to death, and so it is called a *spiritual* body (not a *spirit* body). In this sense, physical, tangible resurrected bodies are spoken of as spiritual in the scriptures (see Alma 11:45; D&C 88:26-28; 1 Corinthians 15:42-49). There can be no doubt from the context of these scriptural passages that a physical body is being spoken of, as contrasted to a spirit body, even though the word *spiritual* is used.

Having thus determined how the word *spiritual* is used in various scriptures that speak of death and resurrection, we can gain a most important understanding of the condition of the earth and everything in the earth when they were first created. The six-day accounts of creation in Genesis, Moses, and Abraham are records of the spiritual creation, which was a physical creation under deathless conditions. We have no detailed account, however, of the spirit creation — that creation which occurred before the spiritual creation — other than to know that there was one.

Flesh

The word *flesh* has several connotations in the scriptures, one of which is mortality. We are warned repeatedly not to trust in the "arm of flesh" (2 Nephi 4:34; 28:31; Jeremiah 17:5), and are reminded that all "flesh is grass" (Isaiah 40:6). The scriptures also speak of the "lusts of the flesh" (1 Nephi 22:23; Galatians 5:19; 1 John 2:16). These all refer to man in his mortal, fallen condition. There are also references pertaining to the flesh of resurrected beings, such as in the Gospel of Luke where Jesus says, "A spirit hath not flesh and bones, as ye see me have" (Luke 24:39). However, in the majority of cases the word *flesh* has reference to man in his fallen, mortal state. Therefore, when Adam is spoken of as the "first flesh upon the earth," it has reference to his being the first to become mortal (Moses 3:7). *Flesh* in this case means mortal. In the physical creation, man was placed on the earth after the animals. But in the process of the Fall, man became mortal before the animals. This being the case, man could not have evolved from the animals, since there was no mortality before Adam's fall, and without mortality there was neither birth nor death on the earth.

The three-step process by which man and the earth became mortal is illustrated on the accompanying chart.

Death

Death literally means "separation" or to be "separated from." Thus the physical death is the separation of the body from the spirit. Spiritual death means to be out of the presence of, or alienated or separated from, God or righteousness.

THE EFFECTS OF THE FALL

Having defined the relevant terms, we are now prepared to discuss the effects of the Fall. One of the clearest statements about these effects was made by Jacob, son of Lehi:

> I know that ye know that our flesh must waste away and die; nevertheless, in our bodies we shall see God. . . .
>
> For as death hath passed upon all men, to fulfil the merciful plan of the great Creator, there must needs be a power of resurrection, and the resurrection must needs come unto man by reason of the fall; and the fall came by reason of transgression; and because man became fallen they were cut off from the presence of the Lord. (2 Nephi 9:4, 6.)

In this passage Jacob touches on the two deaths that came as a consequence of the Fall. The penalty affixed by the Lord to partaking

Creation, Fall, and Atonement

Our present mortal world is the result of a three-step process:

1. SPIRIT CREATION

- No detailed account given; we only know it occurred.
- Earth, plants, animals, and mankind all created as spirits — "In heaven created I them" (Moses 3:5).

2. PHYSICAL-SPIRITUAL CREATION

- Accounts given in Genesis 1; Moses 2–3; Abraham 4–5.
- Consisted of six creative periods.
- A physical, tangible creation, but no blood, no death, no reproduction, and no sin.
- Animals and plants created and placed on earth *prior* to man.

3. THE MORTAL, TEMPORAL, FALLEN WORLD

- Accounts of Fall given in Genesis 3; Moses 4–5.
- The physical, tangible world with blood, death, reproduction, and sin.
- Man the first to fall, become mortal; other forms of life became mortal *after* man.

The Fall brought two kinds of death:
  1. Temporal—physical death.
  2. Spiritual—separation or alienation from things of God.

The Atonement rescues man from these two deaths.

of the forbidden fruit was that "in the day that thou [Adam] eatest thereof thou shalt surely die" (Genesis 2:17). First to take effect was a spiritual death, or in other words, being cut off from the presence of God. This is, as Alma describes it, a "death as to things pertaining unto righteousness" (Alma 12:32). Adam experienced this death after partaking of the tree of the knowledge of good and evil. How fast the process was we do not know, but it came as a direct result of partaking of the fruit, and the impression given is that it was relatively soon.

The physical death did not come so quickly. The record states that Adam lived 930 years after becoming mortal (Moses 6:12). Even so, Adam's physical death occurred within a Lord's day — which is one thousand of our years — for, as Abraham observes, at the time the penalty of death was announced Adam and the earth were still functioning on the Lord's time (see Abraham 5:13; 3:4).

Thus the first judgment which came upon man was death, both kinds of death, according to the warning of the Lord. In the context of discussing the Atonement, Jacob carefully defines the effects of the Fall:

> Wherefore, it must needs be an infinite atonement — save it should be an infinite atonement this corruption could not put on incorruption. Wherefore, the first judgment which came upon man must needs have remained to an endless duration. And if so, this flesh must have laid down to rot and to crumble to its mother earth, to rise no more.
>
> O the wisdom of God, his mercy and grace! For behold, if the flesh should rise no more our spirits must become subject to that angel who fell from before the presence of the Eternal God, and became the devil, to rise no more.
>
> And our spirits must have become like unto him, and we become devils, angels to a devil, to be shut out from the presence of our God, and to remain with the father of lies, in misery, like unto himself. (2 Nephi 9:7-9.)

These deaths, the physical and the spiritual, are so real, so terrible, and, without Christ's redemption, so destructive to the happiness of mankind — the separation from God being especially dreadful — that Jacob calls them an "awful monster": "O how great the goodness of our God, who prepareth a way for our escape from the grasp of this awful monster; yea, that monster, death and hell, which I call the death of the body, and also the death of the spirit." And later he says again: "O the greatness of the mercy of our God, the Holy One of Israel! For he delivereth his saints from that awful monster the devil, and death, and hell, and that lake of fire and brimstone, which is endless torment." (2 Nephi 9:10, 19.)

Because of the fall of Adam the approach of physical death is inevitable for everyone. Decay and death are the literal inheritance of every living thing on this earth. Medical science and proper physical care may postpone the day of physical death, but nothing can prevent it. If an accident or disease does not cause death, the unremitting march of time and "wasting away" of the flesh will eventually bring it. Even those who are translated will eventually experience a kind of death, a change, albeit an instantaneous one. They will not "taste" death, but they will have to undergo this change in order to be resurrected. (See 3 Nephi 28:6–8, 17, 36–40; John 21:21–23.)

The other death, which also is inherited from Adam by all mankind, is separation from God. None of us reading this page has experienced the physical death, but every one of us has already experienced the spiritual death. Just by being born as a descendant of Adam we have experienced spiritual death, at least in the sense that we are out of the presence of God. This condition begins at mortal birth, and it increases after we pass the beginning of accountability at eight years of age, unless or until we receive the rebirth of the Spirit.

Jacob graphically describes what the effect of the Fall would be on all mankind if there were no atonement: there would be no resurrection of our dead bodies, and our spirits would all become devils, forever miserable, shut out from the presence of God to dwell everlastingly with the devil. This is the legal, just, and ultimate extension of the Fall if there were no redemption — in Jacob's words, "The first judgment which came upon man must needs have remained to an endless duration." What was the first judgment? It was "Thou shalt surely die" (Genesis 2:17; Moses 4:17).

The reason why there are two kinds of death is the Fall affects both body and spirit. Jacob explained the situation more pointedly than perhaps any other person in scripture. We could not appreciate Jesus as our Savior unless we knew what was lost and what he saved us from, and Jacob provides us with this important information.

Samuel the Lamanite also taught that there were two deaths as the result of the Fall: "All mankind, by the fall of Adam being cut off from the presence of the Lord, are considered as dead, both as to things temporal and to things spiritual" (Helaman 14:16). The brother of Jared, humbly expressing his sense of weakness and unworthiness, pleaded with the Lord for mercy, saying, "Because of the fall our natures have become evil continually" (Ether 3:2).

In our dispensation also the Lord has spoken concerning the effect of the Fall upon Adam and his posterity. Note that both kinds of death are discussed in the following:

> Wherefore, it came to pass that the devil tempted Adam, and he partook of the forbidden fruit and transgressed the commandment, wherein he became subject to the will of the devil, because he yielded unto temptation.
>
> Wherefore, I, the Lord God, caused that he should be cast out from the Garden of Eden, from my presence, because of his transgression, wherein he became spiritually dead, which is the first death, even that same death which is the last death, which is spiritual, which shall be pronounced upon the wicked when I shall say: Depart, ye cursed.
>
> But, behold, I say unto you that I, the Lord God, gave unto Adam and unto his seed, that they should not die as to the temporal death, until I, the Lord God, should send forth angels to declare unto them repentance and redemption, through faith on the name of mine Only Begotten Son. (D&C 29:40–42.)

Paul, as recorded in the New Testament, succinctly states that "as in Adam all die, even so in Christ shall all be made alive" (1 Corinthians 15:22). Other scriptural passages help us understand clearly that Paul's statement has reference to more than the physical death alone; it also has application to the spiritual death. Every being dies the spiritual and the mortal death because of Adam. Likewise, because of Christ (as will be demonstrated in the next chapter) every being shall be redeemed from the spiritual death and the physical death, both of which were inherited from Adam. Man will thereafter be judged for his own sins and not for Adam's transgression. (See Helaman 14:15–18.)

WHEN ADAM FELL THE WHOLE CREATION FELL

Thus far, in discussing the effects of the fall of Adam, we have emphasized primarily the effect on mankind. However, we noted earlier that the scriptures apply the Fall to "all things which were created" (2 Nephi 2:22; Moses 3:9). It has been the teaching of many of the Brethren over the years that when Adam fell the whole creation fell. We see evidence of the universal fall in the death and mortal, temporary nature of all plants, animals, and birds. Death is the order of this creation in which we live.

The scripture says that even the earth shall die and be renewed again: "The earth abideth the law of a celestial kingdom . . . wherefore, it shall be sanctified; yea, notwithstanding it shall die, it shall be quickened again" (D&C 88:25–26). This gives added meaning to the tenth article of faith, which states that the earth "will be renewed and receive its paradisiacal glory."

Among the Brethren who have taught the doctrine that the whole creation fell was Elder Orson Pratt, who said: "The heavens and the earth were thus polluted, that is, the material heavens, and everything connected with our globe; all fell when man fell, and became subject to death when man became subject to it."[8]

Similarly, Elder Parley P. Pratt wrote:

It now becomes my painful duty to trace some of the important changes which have taken place and the causes which have conspired to reduce the earth and its inhabitants to their present state.

First, man fell from his standing before God by giving heed to temptation, and this fall affected the whole creation, as well as man, and caused various changes to take place. He was banished from the presence of his Creator; a veil was drawn between them, and man was driven from the Garden of Eden to till the earth, which was then cursed for his sake and should begin to bring forth thorns and thistles, and with the sweat of his face he should earn his bread, and in sorrow eat of it all the days of his life, and finally return to dust. . . .

Now, reader, contemplate the change. This scene, which was so beautiful a little before, had now become the abode of sorrow and toil, of death and mourning: the earth groaned with its production of accursed thorns and thistles; man and beast at enmity; the serpent slyly creeping away, fearing lest his head should get the deadly bruise; and man startling amid the thorny path, in fear lest the serpent's fangs should pierce his heel; while the lamb yields his blood upon the smoking altar. Soon man begins to persecute, hate, and murder his fellow, until at length the earth is filled with violence, all flesh becomes corrupt, the powers of darkness prevail.[9]

In more recent years Elder Bruce R. McConkie wrote of the universal fall: "To Adam the decree came: 'Cursed shall be the ground for thy sake; in sorrow shalt thou eat of it all the days of thy life. Thorns also, and thistles shall it bring forth to thee.' Thus the paradisiacal earth was cursed; thus it fell; and thus it became as it now is."[10] Another statement from this same Apostle reads, "Radical changes were in the offing for man, the earth, and all forms of life when the fall came." And he further declared, "When Adam fell, the earth fell also and became a mortal sphere, one upon which worldly and carnal people can live."[11]

From a discourse of President Brigham Young we note the following:

[Adam and Eve] transgressed a command of the Lord, and through that transgression sin came into the world. The Lord knew they would do this, and He had designed that they should. Then came the curse upon the fruit, upon the vegetables, and upon our mother earth; and it came upon the creeping things, upon the grain in the field, the fish in the sea, and upon all things pertaining to this earth, through man's transgression.[12]

And finally from President Joseph Fielding Smith we have this succinct statement regarding the effect of Adam's fall on all creation: "After Adam's fall, the Lord declared that he placed a 'curse' upon the earth, and this mortal condition then passed upon the earth and all upon its face."[13]

Animals, plants, and the earth evidently do not have the moral responsibility that man has, but all other effects of the Fall seem to pertain to the whole creation and not to man alone. The significance of realizing that Adam's fall brought mortality to the whole creation is that it denies the concept that man evolved from lower forms of life by organic evolution. Adam was the first to become mortal — the first to have the power to reproduce.

The Question of Original Sin

Since the effects of the fall of Adam have been passed on to all of Adam's posterity through birth into mortality, every one of Adam's descendants, except Jesus Christ, has fully partaken of the fall of Adam and will experience both physical and spiritual death. Jesus came into the world as the Only Begotten of the Father in the flesh, and therefore death did not dominate him as it does the rest of Adam's posterity. Jesus had ancestry through the Father outside of or beyond the descent from Adam, and therefore Jesus had "life in himself" because he was the Son of God in the flesh (John 5:26; 10:17–18). Thus he was able to atone for the Fall and pay the debt occasioned by Adam; hence what we lost in Adam we regain by Christ. Although all must die, Jesus will raise all of Adam's descendants in the resurrection, so that they will never die a physical death again (Alma 11:45). All of Adam's posterity has been shut out of the presence of God by virtue of the Fall, but because of the Atonement — made by Jesus Christ who had no sin — all of Adam's posterity will be rescued from the spiritual death and be brought back into the presence of God for a judgment of individual deeds (Alma 42:23; Helaman 14:17). If an individual at that time has unremitted sins, he may be sent away again from the presence of God permanently — for his own sins, not for Adam's transgression.

Because man inherits the effects of the fall of Adam, it raises the question of original sin and whether or not children are born sinners, having inherited sin from Adam. Advocates of original sin, a concept taught for centuries throughout Christendom, rely on their interpretation (or misinterpretation) of Paul's writings for justification of their opinions.

Paul is more specific than other biblical writers in discussing the Fall, and he testifies that Adam's fall has descended upon man's nature. For example, to the Corinthians he wrote, "In Adam all die" (1 Corinthians 15:22), and to the Roman Saints he declared: "Wherefore, as by one man sin entered into the world, and death by sin; and so death passed upon all men, for that all have sinned. . . . For if through the offence of one many be dead, much more the grace of God, and the gift by grace, which is by one man, Jesus Christ, hath abounded unto many. . . . For as by one man's disobedience many were made sinners, so by the obedience of one shall many be made righteous." (Romans 5:12, 15, 19.)

Even though Paul discusses the relationship of Adam to Christ better than any other writer in the Bible, his writings in their present form do not approach the clarity of the Book of Mormon, the Doctrine and Covenants, or the Pearl of Great Price. Because of the particular wording of the above passage from Romans, theologians have concluded that infants actually inherit the sin of Adam. This they call "original sin."

"Original sin" is the concept that, since Adam's fall brought death and alienation to all of the human family, little children are born in sin, or under the penalty of sin, and are out of favor with God: therefore, should they die in their infancy without baptism, they would be forever shut out from the presence of the face of God. This belief seems to stem from an awareness of the effects of the Fall without a complete awareness of the results of the Atonement. This concept of original sin is indeed a false doctrine, because it recognizes the Fall and the consequent death and sin but fails to acknowledge the work of the Savior in redeeming mankind from the Fall. The doctrine of original sin would be partly true if there had been no atonement wrought by Jesus Christ, and it would apply not only to children but also to the whole human family. But since Christ did perform an atonement, the doctrine of original sin, as it has been traditionally taught, is not correct.

The doctrine of original sin, as held throughout portions of Christianity, is based on the reasoning of various philosophers who lived during the era of the Apostasy. It arose among these philosophers as early as the second and third centuries A.D., and was more fully developed by Augustine in the fifth century. This reasoning held that the posterity of Adam actually sinned by Adam's transgression. Proponents of this concept would cite Romans 5:12, 15, 19 (quoted above), which they interpreted to mean that through Adam sin entered into the world, and so in the trespass of Adam all men sinned themselves. We should note at this point that there is a difference between a child's inheriting the actual sin itself and his inheriting only the *consequences* of the sin. It appears that the church fathers of the second to fourth centuries A.D. were teaching that children actually sinned in Adam. Latter-day revelation teaches that man inherits only the consequences, not the sin itself.

Since children were regarded as actual sinners from birth, it was but a short intellectual journey for the uninspired philosophers to suppose that children would therefore be denied a place in heaven if they died before receiving baptism. Hence the concept of infant baptism was developed to accommodate this particular view of the fall of Adam.

This mistaken view of original sin —holding that little children are born in sin— also led to the development in Catholicism of the doctrine of the "immaculate conception." This doctrine is not, as many have supposed, a reference to Jesus' own conception; rather, it is the belief that Mary, mother of Jesus, was conceived miraculously in her mother's womb so that she (Mary) would not be born with the taint of original sin, and thus she could be free to conceive the holy child Jesus.

There is nothing in our present Old or New Testaments that clearly and unequivocally explains just how the fall of Adam applies to children —whether mankind actually *sinned* in Adam, or whether man only suffers the *consequences* of the Fall. Nor does there appear in the Bible a statement that clearly defines how the Atonement specifically relates to children. There is just such a statement, however, in the book of Moses, which was revealed as part of the Prophet Joseph Smith's translation of Genesis.

In this particular passage the prophet Enoch teaches the people about Adam and how death and sin came into the world. Enoch reminds his hearers just what was taught to Adam and how the plan of salvation was explained to the first man:

And he [God] called upon our father Adam by his own voice, saying: I am God; I made the world, and men before they were in the flesh.

And he also said unto him: If thou wilt turn unto me, and hearken unto my voice, and believe, and repent of all thy transgressions, and be baptized, even in water, in the name of mine Only Begotten Son, who is full of grace and truth, which is Jesus Christ, the only name which shall be given under heaven, whereby salvation shall come unto the children of men, ye shall receive the gift of the Holy Ghost, asking all things in his name, and whatsoever ye shall ask, it shall be given you.

And our father Adam spake unto the Lord, and said: Why is it that men must repent and be baptized in water? And the Lord said unto Adam: Behold I have forgiven thee thy transgression in the Garden of Eden.

Hence came the saying abroad among the people, that *the Son of God hath atoned for original guilt, wherein the sins of the parents cannot be answered upon the heads of the children,* for they are whole from the foundation of the world. (Moses 6:51–54; italics added.)

We are fully assured by this passage that Adam stands forgiven of his transgression in the garden and that his posterity is free from all responsibility for that transgression. We are held accountable only for our own sins. If this passage had remained in the book of Genesis, or if the correct doctrine had survived in our present New Testament, the whole mistaken concept of original sin and infant baptism as taught and practiced by much of Christianity for the past eighteen hundred years could have been avoided.

In a discourse recorded in the Book of Mormon, King Benjamin explains that man inherits his fallen condition from Adam, but he also says that the atonement of Christ shields the untaught and the little children from the full force of the Fall. "For behold," he says, "and also his blood atoneth for the sins of those who have fallen by the transgression of Adam, who have died not knowing the will of God" (Mosiah 3:11). And further on he states, "I say unto you they [little children] are blessed; for behold, as in Adam, or by nature, they fall, even so the blood of Christ atoneth for their sins" (Mosiah 3:16).

Likewise the Lord has spoken in our day on this subject: "Every spirit of man was innocent in the beginning; and God having redeemed man from the fall, men became again, in their infant state, innocent before God" (D&C 93:38). Implicit in the foregoing passage is this: Every man, upon being born into mortality, is fallen through being a descendant of Adam, but because of the atonement of God (Christ) all little children in their infant mortal state are innocent before God.

In our sophisticated and "enlightened" age many religious peoples reject the idea of original sin and the guiltiness of little children. But they do it for the wrong reasons. They do not reject it because they have a better understanding of the atonement of Jesus Christ, but because they have also rejected the fall of Adam and the fall of mankind. Taking a humanistic approach they have discarded the story of Adam and thus have dissolved the necessity for an atonement. Instead of being theologians, they are ecclesiastical sociologists and teachers of ethics. The gospel of Jesus Christ provides the only correct answers to the great questions and problems concerning life, and death, and sin, and innocence. These answers are found in the true doctrine of the fall of Adam and the atonement of Jesus Christ.

We thus see the power and importance of the Book of Mormon and the other doctrinal revelations that were given to us through the Prophet Joseph Smith. Furthermore, we come to appreciate the energy with which Mormon testified against the baptism of little children, as recorded in the Book of Mormon. Having "inquired of the Lord" regarding this very practice, Mormon wrote to Moroni, his son:

> The word of the Lord came to me by the power of the Holy Ghost, saying:
> Listen to the words of Christ, your Redeemer, your Lord and your God. . . . Little children are whole, for they are not capable of committing sin; *wherefore the curse of Adam is taken from them in me*, that it hath no power over them; and the law of circumcision is done away in me.
> And after this manner did the Holy Ghost manifest the word of God unto me; wherefore, my beloved son, I know that it is solemn mockery before God, that ye should baptize little children. . . .
> But little children are alive in Christ, even from the foundation of the world. . . .
> Little children cannot repent; wherefore, it is awful wickedness to deny the pure mercies of God unto them, for they are all alive in him because of his mercy.
> And he that saith that little children need baptism denieth the mercies of Christ, and setteth at naught the atonement of him and the power of his redemption. (Moroni 8:7–9, 12, 19–20; italics added.)

Mormon did not deny the effects and reality of the Fall; rather, he astutely placed the Fall and the Atonement in proper perspective.

WHY THE LORD DID NOT SIMPLY CREATE MAN MORTAL

Perhaps our treatment of the fall of man would not be adequate without an attempt to deal with a question often raised during discussions about the Fall: Why didn't the Lord simply create man mortal in the first place and avoid all the trauma and experience of a fall brought to pass through transgression and seemingly conflicting commands?

There are in the scriptures no one-sentence answers to this question, but we have been given enough knowledge concerning God's plan to think through a possible response. In the plan of salvation God does for mankind only what they cannot do for themselves. Man must do all he can for himself. The doctrine is that we are saved by grace, "after all we can do" (2 Nephi 25:23). We recognize this principle both in the salvation of the living and in the work for the dead. We must do all we can do for ourselves. If Adam and Eve had been created mortal, they would have been denied one of the steps in the process that they were capable of performing themselves. As we read in the Book of Mormon, man "brought upon himself" his own fall (Alma 42:12). Since the Fall was a necessary part of the plan of salvation, and since man was capable of bringing about the fallen condition himself, he was required—or rather it was his privilege—to take the necessary steps.

If God had created man mortal, then death, sin, and all the circumstances of mortality would be God's doing and would be eternal and permanent in their nature; whereas if man brings the Fall upon himself, he is the responsible moral agent, and God is able to rescue and redeem him from his fallen state. Moreover, Adam and Eve's having brought about the Fall themselves made them subject to punishment or reward for their actions. A little reflection upon these matters leads one to conclude that the Fall was accomplished in the very best possible way. As Lehi said about the Fall and the Atonement, "All things have been done in the wisdom of him who knoweth all things" (2 Nephi 2:24). Furthermore, the Lord has explained to us that he does not create temporal or mortal conditions nor function on a mortal level (D&C 29:34–35).

We can benefit from the observation of Elder Orson F. Whitney, who said, "The fall had a twofold direction—downward, yet forward."[14] It is as the Prophet Joseph Smith said: "Adam was made to open the way of the world."[15] Adam and Eve had the privilege of getting things under way by their own actions. This is far better than their being created mortal and sinful.

THE FALL OF ADAM WAS A BLESSING

How should we regard the Fall? How did Adam and Eve feel about it? We do not know their immediate reaction, but after they were enlightened with the gospel and had eternal insight, they rejoiced in the Fall because of its ultimate benefits. Of Adam we read: "And in that day Adam blessed God and was filled, and began to prophesy concerning all the families of the earth, saying: Blessed be the name of God, for because of my transgression my eyes are opened, and in this life I shall have joy, and again in the flesh I shall see God" (Moses 5:10).

And of Eve it is written: "And Eve, his wife, . . . was glad, saying: Were it not for our transgression we never should have had seed, and never should have known good and evil, and the joy of our redemption, and the eternal life which God giveth unto all the obedient. And Adam and Eve blessed the name of God, and they made all things known unto their sons and their daughters." (Moses 5:11–12.)

President Brigham Young spoke with much favor toward Adam and Eve and the Fall:

> Some may regret that our first parents sinned. This is nonsense. If we had been there, and they had not sinned, we should have sinned. I will not blame Adam or Eve, why? Because it was necessary that sin should enter into the world; no man could ever understand the principle of exaltation without its opposite; no one could ever receive an exaltation without being acquainted with its opposite. How did Adam and Eve sin? Did they come out in direct opposition to God and to His government? No. But they transgressed a command of the Lord, and through that transgression sin came into the world. The Lord knew they would do this, and He had designed that they should.[16]

And again from President Brigham Young:

> Mother Eve . . . [partook] of the forbidden fruit. We should not have been here today if she had not; we could never have possessed wisdom and intelligence if she had not done it. It was all in the economy of heaven, and we need not talk about it; it is all right. We should never blame Mother Eve, not the least. I am

thankful to God that I know good from evil, the bitter from the sweet, the things of God from the things not of God. When I look at the economy of heaven my heart leaps for joy, and if I had the tongue of an angel, or the tongues of the whole human family combined, I would praise God in the highest for His great wisdom and condescension in suffering the children of men to fall into the very sin into which they have fallen, for He did it that they, like Jesus, might descend below all things and then press forward and rise above all.[17]

President Joseph Fielding Smith declared that the fall of Adam was a blessing: "When Adam was driven out of the Garden of Eden, the Lord passed a sentence upon him. Some people have looked upon that sentence as being a dreadful thing. It was not; it was a blessing. I do not know that it can truthfully be considered even as a punishment in disguise." He also explained that "the transgression of Adam did *not* involve sex sin as some falsely believe and teach. Adam and Eve were married by the Lord while they were yet immortal beings in the Garden of Eden and before death entered the world."[18]

Again in praise of Adam and Eve, President Smith stated:

Now, I can open the Bible, almost any Bible—maybe I can this one—and find written here that Adam [in the headings at the top of the page], not the words of the scriptures but man's interpretation, that he committed a dreadful sin. No, he didn't. Adam did not commit a sin. He came to do the thing that he was called upon to do, that he was assigned to do before he ever came here. . . .

I think I have said in this room before that I am very, very grateful for Mother Eve. If I ever get to see her, I want to thank her for what she did and she did the most wonderful thing that ever happened in this world and that was to place herself where Adam had to do the same thing that she did or they would have been separated forever. . . .

. . . Adam and Eve did the very thing they had to. I tell you, I take my hat off to Mother Eve and I rejoice and I want to read what she said. When Eve learned what the full condition was, the result of that fall, she preached this discourse. It is the first discourse ever recorded—that is, that we have. [Cites Moses 5:11.][19]

President Smith also gave an enlightening definition and application to the idea of the "forbidden fruit." He indicated that the "forbidden" aspect was not in the partaking, but instead had reference to Adam and Eve's not being able to remain in the garden if they partook. This explanation suggests that the Lord wanted the Fall to occur. President Smith expressed these ideas as follows:

> Why did Adam come here? Not subject to death when he was placed upon the earth, there had to come a change in his body through the partaking of this element —whatever you want to call it, fruit —that brought blood into his body; and blood became the life of the body instead of spirit. And blood has in it the seeds of death, some mortal element. Mortality was created through the eating of the forbidden fruit, if you want to call it forbidden, but I think the Lord has made it clear that it was not forbidden. He merely said to Adam, if you want to stay here [in the garden] this is the situation. If so, don't eat it.[20]

CONCLUSION

In this chapter we have presented some of the major doctrinal and historical factors relating to the fall of man. Special emphasis has been given to the need for the Fall and to the concept that the fall of Adam affected the whole creation. Because of the Fall, man and all created things became mortal and stood in need of a redemption. The Fall is an integral and necessary part of the plan of salvation, and Adam and Eve are heroes, deserving our praise. If the account of the Fall is correct as given in the scriptures, and we believe it is, then Adam could not have come into existence on this earth through the process of organic evolution from lower forms of life, for Adam and Eve were the first to become mortal and the first to have the power to reproduce.

NOTES

1. Quoted in Frits Staal, *Exploring Mysticism: A Methodological Essay* (Berkeley: University of California Press, 1975), p. 59.

2. *Teachings of the Prophet Joseph Smith*, comp. Joseph Fielding Smith (Salt Lake City: Deseret Book Co., 1976), pp. 160, 292, 324.

3. *Teachings of the Prophet Joseph Smith*, pp. 324–25.

4. *Teachings of the Prophet Joseph Smith*, pp. 197–98.

5. Ezra Taft Benson, *The Teachings of Ezra Taft Benson* (Salt Lake City: Bookcraft, 1988), p. 28.

6. See Joseph Fielding Smith, *Man: His Origin and Destiny* (Salt Lake City: Deseret Book Co., 1954), pp. 362–64; Bruce R. McConkie, *Mormon Doctrine*, 2d ed. (Salt Lake City: Bookcraft, 1966), p. 268.

7. *Teachings of the Prophet Joseph Smith*, pp. 200, 367, 326.

8. In *Journal of Discourses*, 1:291.

9. Parley P. Pratt, *A Voice of Warning* (Salt Lake City: Deseret Book Co., 1978), pp. 85–86.

10. Bruce R. McConkie, *A New Witness for the Articles of Faith* (Salt Lake City: Deseret Book Co., 1985), p. 86.

11. *Mormon Doctrine*, pp. 268, 211.

12. In *Journal of Discourses*, 10:312.

13. Joseph Fielding Smith, *Doctrines of Salvation*, comp. Bruce R. McConkie, 3 vols. (Salt Lake City: Bookcraft, 1954–56), 1:92.

14. Forace Green, comp., *Cowley and Whitney on Doctrine* (Salt Lake City: Bookcraft, 1963), p. 287.

15. *Teachings of the Prophet Joseph Smith*, p. 12.

16. In *Journal of Discourses*, 10:312; *Discourses of Brigham Young*, sel. John A. Widtsoe (Salt Lake City: Deseret Book Co., 1971), p. 103.

17. In *Journal of Discourses*, 13:145; *Discourses of Brigham Young*, p. 103.

18. *Doctrines of Salvation* 1:113, 114–15; italics in original.

19. Joseph Fielding Smith, *Take Heed to Yourselves*, comp. Joseph Fielding Smith, Jr. (Salt Lake City: Deseret Book Co., 1966), pp. 291–92.

20. Unpublished address given at the LDS Institute of Religion, Salt Lake City, Utah, 14 January 1961. Typescript approved by President Smith.

5

Robert J. Matthews

The Revelation of the Gospel to Adam: The Meaning of the Atonement

How long it was after Adam and Eve were cast out from the Garden of Eden, and out of the Lord's presence, before the gospel was made known to them we do not know. It seems unlikely that it was a long time. The particular way that events are chronicled in Moses 5 and 6 could give the impression that Adam and Eve were grandparents before the gospel was taught to them (see Moses 5:1–12). However, that impression may only be the result of the way the account is written. I, for one, do not see the account's sequence of events as decisive evidence for an insistence on a long period of ignorance for father Adam.

We learn from the scriptures that Adam and his posterity were all shut out of the presence of the Lord and made subject to physical death as a result of the Fall. If there were no infinite atonement wrought by Jesus Christ, Adam and Eve and all of their posterity to the latest generation would be everlastingly subject to physical death with no hope of resurrection. Their bodies would rot and crumble into dust, never to be reclaimed; worse, the spirits of all men would become devils, forever miserable, with no hope of re-

Robert J. Matthews is Dean of Religious Education and Professor of Ancient Scripture at Brigham Young University.

demption or release (2 Nephi 9:6–9). The fall of Adam is that powerful!

We are indebted to latter-day revelation for clarification of these matters. The Bible tells us *what* happened as regards the Fall and the Atonement, but latter-day revelation gives the reasons *why* these events are so important. Because of this clarity of latter-day revelation, in addition to the wonderful information in the Bible, Latter-day Saints ought to have the greatest appreciation of all people for Adam and for Jesus Christ. We are everlastingly indebted to both of them.

VALUE OF THE BOOK OF MOSES
IN TEACHING ABOUT ADAM

In this chapter we will emphasize certain aspects of the Atonement that are particularly made clear in the book of Moses in the Pearl of Great Price and that pertain primarily to the revelation of the gospel to father Adam. There is a certain expansion and elaboration of these matters in the Pearl of Great Price not found in the other standard works. For example, we learn from every standard work that the gospel was taught to the ancient patriarchs and that they knew of Christ. But the book of Moses is an actual record of the way in which it was done and provides details and concepts not found in any other account. The book of Moses is an excerpt from Joseph Smith's translation of Genesis and therefore more nearly presents what Moses wrote originally (see Moses 1:40–41). It also more nearly offers what the Nephites had on the plates of brass (1 Nephi 5:10–11) than any other document available to us today.

In treating the subject of the revelation of the gospel to Adam, with particular emphasis on what that revelation teaches us about the Atonement, we will focus mainly upon Moses 5:1–12 and 6:51–62. The first of these passages deals with the words of an angel to Adam and the meaning of animal sacrifice as it pertains to the mission and person of Jesus Christ. It also records Adam's response to the teaching he received. The second deals with the teaching of Enoch seven generations after Adam. But it is from Enoch, who appears to have been recounting and quoting from Adam's ancient "book of remembrance," that we learn of a further revelation to Adam about why men must repent, be baptized, and receive the gospel of Jesus Christ in order to be saved.

In both of the above passages the situation is particularly focused upon Adam himself. This is especially meaningful because Adam (after his fall) is the prototype of all other mortal men, but since he is the very one (along with Eve) through whom mortality was introduced into the world, special notice is made of his unique status and historical situation. And thus the book of Moses provides for us a more detailed account of the gospel as taught to Adam than any other record to which we have access at the present time. As noted above, it probably reads like the plates of brass. The book of Moses not only attests to the antiquity of the gospel but also teaches a particular concept about the Atonement as it relates to Adam that is nowhere else available in such detail, especially as it pertains to Adam's unique situation before and after his transgression in the Garden of Eden.

The Plan of Salvation Is Always the Same

In order to properly appreciate that the fulness of the gospel was taught to Adam and the early patriarchs of the earth, we must understand that the gospel and the plan of salvation are older than the earth. The plan was known and talked about among the hosts of heaven ages ago, existing in the mind of God and in the minds of millions of his sons and daughters long before the earth was created. In fact, we see that the earth was created in compliance with the plan. Creations, foreordinations, promises, ordinances, agencies, and all that pertains to the fall and redemption of the earth were all known and provided for even before the earth was formed. It was therefore no surprise to heaven when Adam and Eve partook of the forbidden fruit and became mortal. The Fall was foreordained from before the foundation of the world. Certainly we know that Jesus was called and foreordained before the world was formed to make an atonement, as noted in the following passages:

> Christ [is] a lamb without blemish and without spot:
> Who verily was foreordained before the foundation of the world (1 Peter 1:19–20).
>
> [Jesus is] the Lamb slain from the foundation of the world (Revelation 13:8; see also Moses 7:47).

Behold, I am he who was prepared from the foundation of the world to redeem my people. Behold I am Jesus Christ. (Ether 3:14.)

They would not . . . believe on his Only Begotten Son . . . who was prepared from before the foundation of the world (Moses 5:57).

The Fall and the Atonement go hand in hand. Both were known in the premortal world, and both are necessary for the advancement of mankind from the spirit state to the final resurrected state. The Fall made the Atonement necessary, and as the atonement of Christ was foreordained so also was the fall of Adam.

The plan of salvation is older than the earth and has not been added to or changed since that early time. This is attested in the following passages:

There is a law, irrevocably decreed in heaven before the foundations of this world, upon which all blessings are predicated—
And when we obtain any blessing from God, it is by obedience to that law upon which it is predicated (D&C 130:20–21).

For all who will have a blessing at my hands shall abide the law which was appointed for that blessing, and the conditions thereof, as were instituted from before the foundation of the world (D&C 132:5).

And will I appoint unto you, saith the Lord, except it be by law, even as I and my Father ordained unto you, before the world was? (D&C 132:11.)

Along this same line, the Prophet Joseph Smith taught: "Everlasting covenant was made between three personages before the organization of this earth, and relates to their dispensation of things to men on the earth; these personages, according to Abraham's record, are called God the first, the Creator; God the second, the Redeemer; and God the third, the Witness or Testator."[1]

Elder Orson Pratt expressed his understanding of the antiquity and unchangeableness of the plan as follows: "The dealing of God toward his children . . . is a pattern after which all other worlds are dealt with. . . . The creation, fall, and redemption of all future worlds with their inhabitants, will be conducted upon the same general plan. . . . The Father of our spirits has only been doing what his Progenitors did before Him." Elder Pratt further explained that when new worlds are formed, their inhabitants "are redeemed after the pattern by which more ancient worlds have been redeemed."[2]

The reason that Elder Pratt's statements make doctrinal sense is that the plan of God is perfect, and perfection is unchanging. If the plan of redemption varied from time to time, from world to world, or from person to person, men would be saved by different means, and salvation would have its bargain days. The "sameness" of the plan of salvation does not mean that every world is an exact, monotonous, and unimaginative copy of every other, or that there are the same number of inhabitants on each. It means that the same eternal principles, the same kind of mortality, and the same kind of salvation are in effect wherever there are gods and devils and men.

JESUS THE PERFECT EXAMPLE OF A SAVED BEING

At this point we might well ask, What constitutes true salvation? Salvation in its fullest sense means to become like God. Those things that lead to godhood are saving principles. Jesus is the prototype or best example of a "saved" person. We read in the *Lectures on Faith:*

> In order to have this subject clearly set before the mind, let us ask what situation must a person be in in order to be saved? or what is the difference between a saved man and one who is not saved? . . . But to be a little more particular, let us ask — Where shall we find a prototype into whose likeness we may be assimilated, in order that we may be made partakers of life and salvation? or, in other words, where shall we find a saved being? for if we can find a saved being, we may ascertain without much difficulty what all others must be in order to be saved. We think that it will not be a matter of dispute, that two beings who are unlike each other cannot both be saved; for whatever constitutes the salvation of one will constitute the salvation of every creature which will be saved; and if we find one saved being in all existence, we may see what

all others must be, or else not be saved. We ask, then, where is the prototype? or where is the saved being? We conclude, as to the answer of this question, there will be no dispute among those who believe the Bible, that it is Christ: all will agree in this, that he is the prototype or standard of salvation; or, in other words, that he is a saved being.

And if we should continue our interrogation, and ask how it is that he is saved? the answer would be—because he is a just and holy being; and if he were anything different from what he is, he would not be saved; for his salvation depends on his being precisely what he is and nothing else; for if it were possible for him to change, in the least degree, so sure he would fail of salvation and lose all his dominion, power, authority and glory, which constitute salvation; for salvation consists in the glory, authority, majesty, power and dominion which Jehovah possesses and in nothing else; and no being can possess it but himself or one like him. Thus says John, in his first epistle, third chapter, second and third verses: "Beloved, now are we the sons of God, and it doth not yet appear what we shall be; but we know that, when he shall appear, we shall be like him, for we shall see him as he is. And every man that hath this hope in him, purifieth himself, even as he is pure." Why purify themselves as he is pure? Because if they do not they cannot be like him.[3]

IMPORTANCE OF KNOWING THAT THE PLAN IS OLDER THAN THE EARTH

Continuing our discussion on the antiquity of the gospel plan, we turn to one of the clearest explanations in scripture, given by Alma, of why the entire plan of salvation had to be known before the creation of the world. When his son was concerned as to why the gospel should be known so long before the mortal advent of Jesus, Alma said:

> And now I will ease your mind somewhat on this subject. Behold, you marvel why these things should be known so long beforehand. Behold, I say unto you, is not a soul at this time as precious unto God as a soul will be at the time of his coming?
>
> Is it not as necessary that the plan of redemption should be made known unto this people as well as unto their children?

Is it not as easy at this time for the Lord to send his angel to declare these glad tidings unto us as unto our children, or as after the time of his coming? (Alma 39:17–19.)

When we contemplate the antiquity and eternal nature of the plan of salvation, we can conclude that the Grand Council in Heaven, as it is sometimes called, was not a single meeting but rather a series of meetings — an entire education, so to speak — in which we, as the sons and daughters of God, were taught the gospel and became acquainted with eternal principles and with the great and noble personages who would be the future leaders of the kingdom of God on the earth. We first met Jesus and the great prophets and patriarchs in the premortal life, and we are learning again those same principles and laws we knew in that ancient sphere but have forgotten because of our mortality. The Savior, the prophets, the wives and mothers of the prophets, and other noble and great ones were all selected in that premortal world according to their obedience to the plan of salvation, the same plan that is now taught to us on the earth through the scriptures and the living prophets.

THE WAR IN HEAVEN HAS NEVER ENDED

In studying the revelation of the gospel to Adam, it will be helpful to have a brief background of what preceded that revelation. Not only had the plan of salvation been presented to the spirit children of God and the prospect of eternal life been shown, but also a war had broken out among the spirits on the principle of how the human family would be saved. The Prophet Joseph Smith explained: "The contention in heaven was — Jesus said there would be certain souls that would not be saved; and the devil said he could save them all."[4] And Elder Bruce R. McConkie has written: "Lucifer wanted to . . . impose salvation upon all men without effort on their part — an impossible thing since there can be no progression except by the upward pull of obedience to law."[5]

As a result of Lucifer's rebellion in seeking to obtain as his personal reward the very throne and power of God, he and the spirits who followed him were cast out and thrust down to the earth without the privilege of being born and obtaining mortal bodies of flesh and bones and blood (Moses 4:1–4; JST, Revelation 12:1–17). "And thus came the devil and his angels" (D&C 29:37).

Lucifer has continued the war on this earth among mankind. The same issues, the same participants, and the same inevitable results prevail, only on a different battleground.[6]

WHAT IF THERE HAD BEEN NO CHRIST?

An explanation of the Atonement would not be adequate if it did not consider the consequences if there were no atonement wrought by Christ. What if there were a fall but no redemption? What would have been the condition and the fate of the human family, including Adam, if there were no atoning sacrifice to pay for the transgression in the Garden of Eden and also for man's own sins? Could any individual or group of individuals have saved themselves? The teaching of the scriptures is a resounding no to this vital question. We read the following from the teachings of Jacob:

> Wherefore, it must needs be an infinite atonement—save it should be an infinite atonement this corruption could not put on incorruption. Wherefore, the first judgment which came upon man must needs have remained to an endless duration. And if so, this flesh must have laid down to rot and to crumble to its mother earth, to rise no more.
>
> O the wisdom of God, his mercy and grace! For behold, if the flesh should rise no more our spirits must become subject to that angel who fell from before the presence of the Eternal God, and became the devil, to rise no more.
>
> And our spirits must have become like unto him, and we become devils, angels to a devil, to be shut out from the presence of our God, and to remain with the father of lies, in misery, like unto himself. (2 Nephi 9:7–9.)

This same doctrine is taught by Lehi as recorded in 1 Nephi 10:6 and in 2 Nephi 2:8; by King Benjamin as recorded in Mosiah 3:11–17; and by Aaron as found in Alma 21:9. It is also implicit in the words of Jesus: "For God so loved the world, that he gave his only begotten Son, that whosoever believeth in him should not perish, but have everlasting life" (John 3:16).

This total dependence on the atonement of Jesus Christ was no doubt known in the premortal world by the spirits who would be coming to earth to gain mortal bodies and was a trial to those who had not strong faith in and a testimony of Jesus Christ. It was no doubt a factor in causing some to align themselves with the "guaranteed," "no-risk," "no-effort," "no-individual-responsibility" seduction of Lucifer.

Our relationship to Jesus Christ is just that vital and critical. He is our Redeemer, and without him we could do nothing (see John 15:1-6). True it is that, in order to receive all the blessings offered through the Atonement, we must give our best efforts; but without him, no one could ever attain to even a particle of salvation. Thus the meaning of the word *gospel*—the good news! Jesus is good news to all mankind.

Offering Sacrifice a Test of Adam's Faith

When Adam and Eve were in the Garden of Eden, the devil, Satan, tempted them and was successful in getting them to eat of the forbidden fruit and to be cast out of the garden into the world. Having now become mortal, Adam and Eve needed to be taught the gospel, the same plan of salvation they had known beforehand but had forgotten now that they were here upon the earth.

Adam was commanded by the Lord to offer sacrifices. The account in the book of Moses is as follows:

> And Adam and Eve, his wife, called upon the name of the Lord, and they heard the voice of the Lord from the way toward the Garden of Eden, speaking unto them, and they saw him not; for they were shut out from his presence.
>
> And he gave unto them commandments, that they should worship the Lord their God, and should offer the firstlings of their flocks, for an offering unto the Lord. And Adam was obedient unto the commandments of the Lord. (Moses 5:4-5.)

In this passage it is made clear that Adam and Eve were fallen, for they were "shut out" of God's presence. The information about animal sacrifice is especially instructive because of the command to offer the "firstlings of their flocks."

The word *firstlings* puts certain qualifications and restrictions and even determines the quality of faith that is used in offering the sacrifice. *Firstling* does not necessarily denote the oldest of the flock but the firstborn of its particular mother. A firstling is a male, the first "that openeth the matrix" of its mother (Exodus 34:19; 13:2). Each mother in her lifetime could produce only one firstling, but a flock of sheep could have several firstlings born each year. In order to know which lambs were acceptable for sacrifice, the owner would have to know his flock. Some notice would have to be made of mothers and of young. Otherwise, how could anyone know which mothers had produced offspring for the first time? There is no way that a man, Adam or anyone else, could know which males were firstlings unless a record and some identification of mothers and offspring were kept. This requirement removes the element of chance and of haphazard or sometime obedience. Not only is one's faith shown in the willingness to offer a sacrifice but also in the care required and the preparation needed beforehand in making the selection of the proper animal.

This particular passage of scripture illustrates the concept that the commandments of God require the intelligent and deliberate attention of those who are seeking salvation. It gives a reason for Paul's observation that "without faith it is impossible to please" God (Hebrews 11:6), for without faith one would not have kept a record and marked (at least mentally) which animals were proper for sacrifice.

The passage in Moses continues:

> And after many days an angel of the Lord appeared unto Adam, saying: Why dost thou offer sacrifices unto the Lord? And Adam said unto him: I know not, save the Lord commanded me.
>
> And then the angel spake, saying: This thing is a similitude of the sacrifice of the Only Begotten of the Father, which is full of grace and truth.
>
> Wherefore, thou shalt do all that thou doest in the name of the Son, and thou shalt repent and call upon God in the name of the Son forevermore. (Moses 5:6–8.)

Adam acted by faith, not by full understanding, and because of his obedience an angel of the Lord came and explained the future sacrifice of Jesus Christ. The symbolic nature of the sacrifice is emphasized in the words: "This thing is a similitude of the sacrifice of the Only Begotten of the Father, which is full of grace and truth." Surely the shedding of the blood of animals cannot remit man's sin except it be done in imitation of something such as the shedding of the blood of Jesus Christ.

One of the most important concepts of this passage is the clear declaration that Adam was to do all that he did "in the name of the Son," to repent and "call upon God in the name of the Son forevermore." This is the same doctrine taught in many other scriptural passages, of which the following are a few:

> Neither is there salvation in any other: for there is none other name under heaven given among men, whereby we must be saved (Acts 4:12).

> Jesus Christ [is] the only name which shall be given under heaven, whereby salvation shall come unto the children of men (Moses 6:52).

> There shall be no other name given nor any other way nor means whereby salvation can come unto the children of men, only in and through the name of Christ, the Lord Omnipotent (Mosiah 3:17; see also 2 Nephi 31:20–21).

> And there is none other salvation save this which hath been spoken of; neither are there any conditions whereby man can be saved except the conditions which I have told you (Mosiah 4:8).

> Behold, Jesus Christ is the name which is given of the Father, and there is none other name given whereby man can be saved;
> Wherefore, all men must take upon them the name which is given of the Father (D&C 18:23–24).

Thus we see that this most fundamental of all doctrines — that there is only one plan of salvation with only one Savior — was taught to Adam right from the start. These passages also specify that there were no alternate plans nor alternate saviors. We note that in the passages cited above only two (Acts 4:12 and D&C 18:23–24) were uttered after Jesus had accomplished the Atonement. All the other passages were uttered centuries before his birth, showing that there *never* was an alternate plan or person.

The Holy Ghost subsequently bore record to Adam: "And in that day the Holy Ghost fell upon Adam, which beareth record of the Father and the Son, saying: I am the Only Begotten of the Father from the beginning, henceforth and forever, that as thou hast fallen thou mayest be redeemed, and all mankind, even as many as will" (Moses 5:9). The foregoing is the earliest recorded direct mention to Adam in his mortal state that he was *fallen* and that he could be redeemed—not only he but also all mankind—through the intercession of the Only Begotten Son. Again the Fall and the Atonement are linked together. It was apparently the Holy Ghost that caused Adam and Eve to understand more fully the consequences of their fall and the means of their redemption.

The passage continues to record the history of Adam and Eve and how they rejoiced to learn of the prospect of their redemption:

> And in that day Adam blessed God and was filled, and began to prophesy concerning all the families of the earth, saying: Blessed be the name of God, for because of my transgression my eyes are opened, and in this life I shall have joy, and again in the flesh I shall see God.
>
> And Eve, his wife, heard all these things and was glad, saying: Were it not for our transgression we never should have had seed, and never should have known good and evil, and the joy of our redemption, and the eternal life which God giveth unto all the obedient.
>
> And Adam and Eve blessed the name of God, and they made all things known unto their sons and their daughters. (Moses 5:10–12.)

The expression of Adam's joy and also of Eve's realization that she and Adam could not have had seed if it were not for their transgression are corollaries to Lehi's explanation that without the Fall "they [Adam and Eve] would have had no children" and that "Adam fell that men might be; and men are, that they might have joy" (2 Nephi 2:23, 25). When Lehi uttered these words, he was expressing a concept he had read in the plates of brass (see 2 Nephi 2:17). Evidently the account on those plates is similar to what we now have in the Joseph Smith Translation of the Bible, of which the book of Moses is an extract. This same doctrine of the childless condition of Adam and Eve if there had been no fall is borne out by Enoch, who seems to have learned this concept from Adam's book of remembrance: "Because that Adam fell, we are; and by his fall came death" (Moses 6:48).

We thus have three passages on which to base the teaching that without the fall of Adam the human family would not have been born — 2 Nephi 2:23, 25; Moses 5:11–12; and Moses 6:48 — a doctrine, by the way, of which the whole Christian and non-Christian world is totally unaware, but which is basic to a proper understanding of life and of mankind's origin and purpose for being on the earth. The book of Moses and the Book of Mormon support each other in teaching this important and fundamental truth, and both clarify the biblical account.

We see, then, that in the initial revelation of the gospel to Adam this much was accomplished: the offering of sacrifice was taught, Adam learned to be obedient, the doctrine of the atonement of the Son of God was made known unto him, and the Holy Ghost taught Adam and Eve the consequences of their fall and the joy of a redemption.

The Plan of Salvation Revealed to Adam

Sometime after the initial revelation to Adam by the angel and by the workings of the Holy Ghost, Adam received further instructions, as Enoch later explained:

> And he [God] called upon our father Adam by his own voice, saying: I am God; I made the world, and men before they were in the flesh.
>
> And he also said unto him: If thou wilt turn unto me, and hearken unto my voice, and believe, and repent of all thy transgressions, and be baptized, even in water, in the name of mine Only Begotten Son, who is full of grace and truth, which is Jesus Christ, the only name which shall be given under heaven, whereby salvation shall come unto the children of men, ye shall receive the gift of the Holy Ghost, asking all things in his name, and whatsoever ye shall ask, it shall be given you. (Moses 6:51–52.)

The foregoing is a very revealing passage and details something concerning Adam which is not as clearly specified anywhere else.

We are familiar with Adam's singular transgression in the Garden of Eden, which was the cause of his fall into mortality. However, in this passage the Lord directed Adam to "repent of all [his] transgressions [plural]," not having reference to the event in the garden but to any other transgressions that Adam may have committed after he became mortal. We do not have an account of any of these, but we could confidently expect that since he was mortal there might be some. This passage seems to say that Adam was not without transgressions.

That these plural transgressions of which Adam was to repent deliberately did not include the original transgression in the Garden of Eden is borne out in the following verses:

> And our father Adam spake unto the Lord, and said: Why is it that men must repent and be baptized in water? And the Lord said unto Adam: Behold I have forgiven thee thy transgression in the Garden of Eden.
>
> Hence came the saying abroad among the people, that the Son of God hath atoned for original guilt, wherein the sins of the parents cannot be answered upon the heads of the children, for they are whole from the foundation of the world. (Moses 6:53–54.)

It appears from this passage that Adam was not required to repent of the transgression that he had committed in the garden. In verse 52 the Lord was promising future forgiveness to Adam, whereas in verse 53 the Lord tells Adam that He had already forgiven him his "transgression in the Garden of Eden." Hence the saying that the Son of God "hath atoned for original guilt." We might have reasoned from other scriptures that Adam did not have to repent of his transgression committed in the garden, but this scripture categorically says it in one sentence.

In other words, this passage, probably more than any other scripture, shows that Adam was, after his fall, in the same position as all mankind now is. The Atonement unconditionally covers Adam's original sin (covers it for Adam as well as for us) and also covers our own sins on condition of our repentance and baptism, which ordinance brings with it the promise of the Holy Ghost to come upon us.

The Lord subsequently explained to Adam the process of spiritual rebirth and its parallel to the mortal birth involving spirit, water, and blood (Moses 6:58–61). Then the Lord said: "And now, behold, I say unto you: This is the plan of salvation unto all men, through the blood of mine Only Begotten, who shall come in the meridian of time" (Moses 6:62).

We thus are treated in the book of Moses to a very clear, lucid, and extensive account of how the fulness of the gospel, with the plan of salvation and the doctrine of the atoning blood of Jesus Christ, was made known to our father Adam, how he taught it to his children, and how it was handed down from generation to generation. We learn of these great truths and historical events from the writings of Moses, who recorded the teachings of Enoch, who seems to have read of these things in the "book of remembrance" which was begun in the days of Adam himself. This important revelation of the gospel to Adam is alluded to in other scriptures (see, for example, 2 Nephi 2:15–26; Alma 12:22–37; D&C 20:17–29; 29:40–44), but it is delineated only in the account given in the Joseph Smith Translation as found in the book of Moses in the Pearl of Great Price.

We would also understand from various other scriptures and statements by the Prophet Joseph Smith that the fulness of the plan of salvation —all of the ordinances that pertain to the temple, the endowment, the covenants, the full understanding of everything that leads to exaltation —was made known to Adam and to Eve.

The Prophet Joseph Smith taught that Adam stands next to Christ and presides over the human family and the spirits of all mankind and holds the keys of all dispensations.[7]

There is nothing about the gospel and its ordinances and blessings, as we have them today, that Adam did not have.

TRUE REPENTANCE THROUGH THE ATONEMENT

We have noted that Adam was commanded to "call upon God" and also to "repent of all [his] transgressions." These two things are inseparable. To be effective, repentance must be directed toward one's relationship to God. A person may be sorry he has lost a blessing, or he may be unhappy that he is not permitted to continue "to take happiness in sin" (Mormon 2:13; see also Alma 41:10). His sorrow may be brought on only by the embarrassment of being caught. That type of "repentance" will not cleanse a soul of its unrighteousness. Indeed, Paul indicated that some repentance itself needs to be repented of:

> Now I rejoice, not that ye were made sorry, but that ye sorrowed to repentance: for ye were made sorry after a godly manner. . . .
> For godly sorrow worketh repentance to salvation not to be repented of: but the sorrow of the world worketh death.
> For behold this selfsame thing, that ye sorrowed after a godly sort, what carefulness it wrought in you, yea, what clearing of yourselves! (2 Corinthians 7:9–11.)

True repentance follows when a person has deep remorse that he has offended God by breaking his laws and being disobedient. He is sorry because of the alienation from God that the sin has brought into his life. His repentance then is "of the godly sort," and he learns that "wickedness never was happiness" (Alma 41:10). Because repentance requires a broken heart and a contrite spirit, nothing less will bring permanent relief. Mormon lamented that the Nephites were sorrowful for the wrong reason: "Their sorrowing was not unto repentance, because of the goodness of God; but it was rather the sorrowing of the damned" (Mormon 2:13). Even though the scripture says the blood of Jesus Christ "was shed for the remission of [our] sins" (D&C 27:2), yet, because nothing but genuine remorse on our part for having offended God can bring forgiveness, the Lord has also said: "My blood shall not cleanse them if they hear me not" (D&C 29:17).

A Payment for a Debt

One of the dimensions to the Atonement that was emphasized in the revelation of the gospel to Adam and that must be understood is that the shedding of the Savior's blood was more than an evidence of his total dedication and commitment (see Moses 6:59–60). It was a payment, and the medium of exchange was the blood of Jesus Christ —the blood of one who had no sin and who was not himself totally subject to the fall of Adam. The shedding of

Jesus' precious blood was a payment so that mercy would not rob justice. It was a ransom so that he could be our Savior and Redeemer — to rescue all mankind from the grasp of the law that was broken in the Garden of Eden and to rescue as many as repent from the effects of their personal sins. Thus the gospel becomes a means of redemption, of salvation, and of exaltation. Amulek, as recorded in the Book of Mormon, expressed it this way:

> For it is expedient that an atonement should be made; for according to the great plan of the Eternal God there must be an atonement made, or else all mankind must unavoidably perish; yea, all are hardened; yea, all are fallen and are lost, and must perish except it be through the atonement which it is expedient should be made.
>
> For it is expedient that there should be a great and last sacrifice; yea, not a sacrifice of man, neither of beast, neither of any manner of fowl; for it shall not be a human sacrifice; but it must be an infinite and eternal sacrifice.
>
> Now there is not any man that can sacrifice his own blood which will atone for the sins of another. Now, if a man murdereth, behold will our law, which is just, take the life of his brother? I say unto you, Nay.
>
> But the law requireth the life of him who hath murdered; therefore there can be nothing which is short of an infinite atonement which will suffice for the sins of the world. . . .
>
> And behold, this is the whole meaning of the law, every whit pointing to that great and last sacrifice; and that great and last sacrifice will be the Son of God, yea, infinite and eternal.
>
> And thus he shall bring salvation to all those who shall believe on his name; this being the intent of this last sacrifice, to bring about the bowels of mercy, which overpowereth justice, and bringeth about means unto men that they may have faith unto repentance.
>
> And thus mercy can satisfy the demands of justice, and encircles them in the arms of safety, while he that exercises no faith unto repentance is exposed to the whole law of the demands of justice; therefore only unto him that has faith unto repentance is brought about the great and eternal plan of redemption. (Alma 34:9–12, 14–16.)

This payment is the theme of one of our hymns, wherein we sing:

> Behold the great Redeemer die,
> A broken law to satisfy.
> He dies a sacrifice for sin,
> That man may live and glory win.
>
> .   .   .   .
>
> He died, and at the awful sight
> The sun in shame withdrew its light!
> Earth trembled, and all nature sighed
> In dread response, "A God has died!"[8]

When Jesus died there were great quakings of the earth, even so much that on the American continent "the whole face of the land was changed" (3 Nephi 8:12). In 1 Nephi 19:12 we read that the prophet Zenos, predicting the event, said that "kings of the isles of the sea shall be wrought upon by the Spirit of God, to exclaim: The God of nature suffers."

The idea of Christ's payment for us was also suggested by Peter in his words to the early Church: "Ye are a chosen generation, a royal priesthood, an holy nation, a peculiar people" (1 Peter 2:9). *Peculiar* in this instance is not used in the sense of being odd but of being unusual, beyond ordinary, and a special treasure. The word used in the Greek manuscripts from which the English translation was made was *peripoiēsis*, which means an acquisition. A similar instance in Exodus 19:5 uses the Hebrew *segullâ*, meaning a treasure or special possession. This purchase of us by Jesus was spoken of by Paul: "Know ye not that . . . ye are not your own? For ye are bought with a price." (1 Corinthians 6:19–20.) Also Peter, when speaking of false teachers, said that they even deny "the Lord that bought them" (2 Peter 2:1). Inasmuch as *redeemed* means "to be recovered for a price," Peter was teaching the same doctrine when he said, "Ye know that ye were not redeemed with corruptible things, as silver and gold . . . but with the precious blood of Christ" (1 Peter 1:18–19).

The ransom, or redemption, has to do with the just payment of a debt incurred by the transgression against divine law. The debt was incurred at a time and a place by a person or persons. The payment must be as stable and real and substantial as the debt. The Atonement, the payment of the blood, was made at a time and a place by a person as real as the debtor. Anything less than this would rob the gospel of its power and legitimacy. To deny that Jesus made the payment is to deny the legal basis for salvation, and chaos would reign in the universe!

WHY PAYMENT HAD TO BE BY BLOOD

That there was a broken law to be paid for in order to satisfy justice is plainly taught in the scriptures. What might not be quite so evident is that the payment required blood and could not be done in any other way. It is important to note that in every instance when the plan of salvation is explained in holy writ, whether it be to Adam, Enoch, Noah, Abraham, Moses, the meridian Twelve, or to those who recorded the doctrines of the plan in the Book of Mormon or in the Doctrine and Covenants, the blood of Jesus Christ is always mentioned in connection with the Atonement (see Mosiah 3:11–16; D&C 45:4; 76:69).

Early in this article we noted passages from the Doctrine and Covenants that indicate that the plan of salvation was in full existence and operation even before the world was created and that nothing has been added to it since that time (D&C 130:20–21; 132:5, 11). It was also shown that Jesus is called the Lamb slain from before the foundation of the world. Since Jesus came not to do his own will but the will of the Father who sent him, and since sacrifices by the shedding of blood were inaugurated in the earliest revelation of the gospel to Adam as a similitude of Christ, it seems inescapable that the plan of salvation always called for the shedding of the blood of Jesus Christ and that it therefore could be done in no other way.

We are familiar with the scenes in the Garden of Gethsemane, when Jesus pleaded with the Father, "If it be possible, let this cup pass from me" (Matthew 26:39). The "cup" was the excruciating experience through which Jesus would take upon him the sins of all mankind and, as a result, would suffer and bleed at every pore (see Luke 22:44; Mosiah 3:7; D&C 19:16–20). Jesus cried aloud, "Father, all things are possible unto thee; take away this cup from me: nevertheless not what I will, but what thou wilt" (Mark 14:36). This was the Father's Chosen and Beloved Son, his Only Begotten, pleading for an escape from the experiences that resulted in his blood oozing through the pores of his skin. Yet the Father did not excuse him nor devise another way. If there were another way, this would have been the time to put it into operation. The fact that no other system was used, even at the Son's pleading, suggests in the strongest terms that no other way was possible. Surely, if there had been any other way, the Father would have hearkened when his Son thus pleaded.

But why blood? Why not some other substance? Blood is thought of as the substance of the Fall. Blood is the "life of the flesh," meaning mortal flesh (see Leviticus 17:11–14). It is the "red badge," so to speak, of mortality. It will not exist in resurrected beings, for they are immortal (see 1 Corinthians 15:50).[9] In blood are the seeds of mortal life and death. The scripture says: "As in Adam all die, even so in Christ shall all be made alive" (1 Corinthians 15:22). In other words, as by Adam's sin came blood which brings death, so by Christ's blood came redemption from sin and death.

Luke recorded that in the Garden of Gethsemane Jesus "kneeled down and prayed. . . . And there appeared an angel unto him from heaven, strengthening him. And being in an agony he prayed more earnestly: and he sweat as it were great drops of blood falling down to the ground." (JST, Luke 22:41–44.) Elder Bruce R. McConkie postulated that this angel was likely Adam.[10]

If this angel was Adam (and there seems to be no reason to doubt it), here was the Messiah in the Garden of Gethsemane in his greatest of all trials, shedding his blood to redeem mankind from the effects of Adam's transgression in the Garden of Eden and also from the results of each person's own sins. There appeared from heaven to strengthen him the very person of Adam himself — he who brought mortality and blood and death and sin into the world. The parallel issue is unmistakable! The plan of salvation to which both Adam and Jesus subscribed in the premortal world was being worked out in the world of Adam's posterity. Each had fulfilled his foreordained part, and now the two principals were together as Jesus triumphed over sin and mortality. The next day Jesus would die upon the cross, and three days later he would rise from the grave, totally triumphant, not only over the death of the body but also over the death of the spirit — which is alienation from God.

He who was slain from before the foundation of the world is alive forevermore, and the doctrine of the blood atonement that was so long beforehand revealed to Adam has become an accomplished fact. Adam and all of the children of men between Adam and the final generation are on the road to immortality and eternal life, just as had been anticipated in the plan of salvation as discussed in the councils of God before the world was.

NOTES

1. *Teachings of the Prophet Joseph Smith*, comp. Joseph Fielding Smith (Salt Lake City: Deseret Book Co., 1976), p. 190.

2. Orson Pratt, "The Pre-existence of Man," *The Seer* 1 (September 1853): 134–35.

3. *Lectures on Faith* 7:9.

4. *Teachings of the Prophet Joseph Smith*, p. 357.

5. Bruce R. McConkie, "Who is the Author of the Plan of Salvation?" *The Improvement Era* 56 (May 1953): 323.

6. See the entry under "War in Heaven" in the Bible Dictionary of the LDS edition of the Bible, p. 788.

7. *Teachings of the Prophet Joseph Smith*, pp. 157, 158, 167–69.

8. "Behold the Great Redeemer Die," *Hymns*, no. 191.

9. See also *Teachings of the Prophet Joseph Smith*, pp. 326, 367.

10. Bruce R. McConkie, *The Mortal Messiah*, 4 vols. (Salt Lake City: Deseret Book Co., 1979–81), 4:125.

6

Vivian M. Adams

"Our Glorious Mother Eve"

Adam we know. In the premortal life he was Michael, meaning one "who is like God"; he presumably stood second only to Christ in governing power; he sat in council with the Gods in planning and executing the creations of the earth; he led the righteous in the War in Heaven; he was foreordained to come to earth as the father of the human family; he holds the keys of salvation over all his posterity; he will reign as Michael, our prince, to all eternity. He was set at the head of the human family to mark the way. As he was the pattern for Seth his son, who was in his likeness and after his image, he is the pattern to all his sons after him who seek salvation in the kingdom of God.

Adam we know; but what of "our glorious Mother Eve" (D&C 138:39)? The doctrine of Adam is the doctrine of Eve; their mission and purpose are one. "As she was at Michael's side before the foundations of the earth," wrote Elder Bruce R. McConkie, "so she came with him into Eden."[1] Together they performed the mission of the Fall, making the probation of life available to all. Chosen as the first wife and the first mother, her role in the salvation of their posterity is as vital as his. She is Adam's counterpart and his

Vivian M. Adams is a homemaker in Salt Lake City, Utah.

crown. She is our glorious mother. With Adam she was set at the head to mark the way.

To achieve the same salvation which she has achieved, we must seek her path and walk as she has walked. Shall we not take counsel from all that she has done? Should we not ask, then, Who was Eve in her premortal existence, and how did she achieve her preeminence there? What was her part in the councils of heaven, her role in the great war of spirits, her part in the earth's creation? What was her condition in the Garden of Eden, her place as the wife of Adam, and her part in the Fall? What was her experience as the first earthly mother? What of her growth in the world? And what is her destiny?

The true story of Eve is known only through the restoration of the gospel through the Prophet Joseph Smith. We must look to scripture for commentary on scripture, to the sermons and writings of the prophet who established the great latter-day work. From these sources we know that the gospel is always the same, dispensation by dispensation, before the world and after. These principles are the principles which teach us of Eve. We learn that the story of Eve is a story of many levels and endless truths. While speaking of Eve we cannot separate her from Adam. They are not to be separated. To do so would deprive Eve of her rightful place. This we must learn: Adam and Eve are one, bone of bone and flesh of flesh. Their journey is the pattern of faith.

Eve Was Prepared from the Foundation of the World

Eve was born in the premortal life to heavenly parents, an eternal Father and an eternal Mother, in an eternal family unit. Intelligence was organized through a birth process to become her spirit body (see D&C 93:29; 131:7–8). She was born a female spirit in the similitude of the universal mother in heaven, and her nature by divine inheritance was feminine.[2] We may surmise that she was radiant and beautiful, and that her spirit was in the likeness of her heavenly mother and would mold the likeness of her mortal person yet to be (see D&C 77:2; Ether 3:14–17). Eve was endowed with every capacity to become, in time, exalted as her heavenly parents. She was literally a daughter of Deity.

Eve, we may suppose, was cherished, nurtured, and tutored by her heavenly parents in the heart of the celestial family. As a spirit she had agency; she had complete capacity to comprehend, reason, act, and grow. Eve would come to be numbered among the noble and great.

Presumably the tutelage for her earthly mission came not only through the family but also through the premortal Church, for it is reasonable to assume such an organization existed in the premortal life.[3] The Church would have taught the gospel and administered the ordinances of salvation pertaining to that sphere. Eve and all the Father's children who covenanted to serve and keep his commandments were "blessed . . . with all spiritual blessings in heavenly places," apparently meaning they received all covenants and ordinances of the premortal Church (Ephesians 1:3–4).

The heavenly Church was perfectly arranged with every blessing and administration, and no doubt Eve was a full participant in that premortal organization. Perhaps she was given teaching and administrative responsibility in the family and the Church, particularly among her sisters. Through these experiences she was tested, and grew, and developed increasing capacity. As with the Lord and all who conformed to truth, she grew from grace to grace, until she became a leader among female spirits.

In this infinite period of schooling, Eve learned the gospel in its fulness and came to an extensive understanding of the plan of salvation. Though she assuredly developed strengths in many fields, we infer that she was particularly receptive to the principles of salvation, and that her spiritual proclivities became chief among her abilities. She had placed her trust in the word of God, and her faith in his word became the principle of action and power in each stage of her being.[4]

We would assume that the daughters of God were taught that on earth they were to marry and "to multiply and replenish the earth . . . to fulfil the promise which was given by [their] Father before the foundation of the world . . . that they [might] bear the souls of men," a blessing and labor through which they would achieve exaltation and continue the works of the Father (D&C 132:63). From the beginning Eve was one who, having chosen good, exercised exceeding great faith, doing good works which prepared her for the holy calling to come (compare Alma 13:3). Eve's preparation to become "the mother of all living" would be the hinge upon which mortality would turn.

Eve in the Grand Council in Heaven

No doubt there were many heavenly councils in which the plan of salvation was taught to the spirit offspring of the Father. Apparently the Grand Council in Heaven was the solemn assembly called by the Father to formally announce that the provisions of the plan would now be put into place. In this council, as the Prophet Joseph Smith explained, "every man who has a calling to minister to the inhabitants of the world was ordained to that very purpose."[5] In the Grand Council, with all the spirits present, Jesus Christ, the firstborn spirit son of the Father, "Beloved and Chosen from the beginning" (Moses 4:2), became the appointed Redeemer and Savior of mankind. He became the "author" or cause of salvation (Hebrews 5:9). The gospel of God the Father became the gospel of Jesus Christ, the Son.[6] Christ became the great High Priest, and salvation centered in his atonement. He would reclaim mankind from sin and death. He was now the ordained "Lamb slain from the foundation of the world" (Revelation 13:8).

As the plan of redemption was laid before the foundation of the world, so was the plan of the Fall. As there was a Redeemer chosen and ordained from the beginning, there was also one chosen to fall. Michael, perhaps second only to Christ in intellect and might, was called to assume this role. As Christ was appointed to bring life, Michael was appointed to open the world and bring mortality to himself and the spirit children of the Father (see Alma 12:25–27).

The name *Michael* signified one "who is like God." "He is Michael," the Prophet said, "because he was the first and father of all" and because he was "the first to hold the spiritual blessings."[7] Michael was one like unto God, the Eternal Father of spirits, one who understood the priestly office to teach, lead, and guide his posterity to salvation. Michael was in the pattern or image of his Father. Pursuant to his call, Michael received the keys of presidency and salvation over the spirits who would follow him into mortality. "Christ is the Great High Priest; Adam next," Joseph Smith taught.[8]

Michael could not come to fall to mortality alone, neither could he multiply as commanded alone. Mortality had to come upon the first man and woman by the same means; posterity would come through a man and his wife. Michael was to receive a companion equal in stature, dignity, and preparation — one preeminent in station and character, fit to become the mother of all living, and one he would love as his own being.

Eve was chosen to stand at Michael's side. She was a companion of "like stature, capacity, and intelligence," as Elder McConkie wrote.[9] Through the extended schooling of eternity, Eve had proven herself worthy in every particular. Though we have not been given her premortal name, we know she was one like unto or after the pattern of the heavenly mother. We conclude, then, that Eve, by endowment and preparation, corresponded in all things to Michael. She was his completion.

We would suppose that the Grand Council in Heaven was a work of long duration, a conference with many sessions. Michael's further work in the council may have been to assist in organizing the "nations of men" according to "the times before appointed, and the bounds of their habitation" (Acts 17:26). In other words, Michael assisted in the organizing of the dispensations of man. He was to preside, under Christ, over the dispensations of men, sending salvation forth continually to his posterity. In the words of the Prophet Joseph Smith, he was "made" for his work,[10] a work he would perform with Eve at his side. It was according to their natures, the substance of their faith, and it was the whole of their desire.

Michael and Eve in the War in Heaven

While Michael and Eve rejoiced in Christ, Lucifer rebelled. While Michael and Eve exercised faith in the plan to create and people the world, Lucifer sought kingship and glory. Having a comprehensive knowledge (of his Father and his laws) Lucifer, a son of the morning and one in authority, waged open rebellion. War raged in heaven — a combat of distortion, deceit, and slander on the one hand and a combat of faith on the other.

From the beginning Christ had adopted, advocated, and sponsored the Father's plan.[11] But Lucifer's aspiration was unholy. He had said in his heart, "I will exalt my throne above the stars of God: . . . I will be like the most High" (Isaiah 14:13–14). In the council Lucifer rose in rebellion to the Father's plan, seeking to replace Christ as Savior and Son. "Behold," he declared, "here am I, send me, I will be thy son . . . ; wherefore give me thine honor" (Moses 4:1).

Refused the lordship he so desired, Lucifer sought to take the kingdom of his Father and of Christ (D&C 76:28). He established his opposition against the Father, the Son, and the plan of atonement which they espoused.[12] He labored expressly to destroy faith in a fall and atonement to come, and in a Michael and a Christ who had not yet performed their missions. He waged systematic warfare for the souls of men, drawing after him one-third of the hosts of heaven — and truly were they devils who rebelled against their God. He became Satan, the "great dragon," "that old serpent" (Revelation 12:9), titles denoting the fierceness of his wrath and the fatality of his venom.

Lucifer contested authority and doctrine. It was a war of words, a tumult of opinions — "Lo, here" and "Lo, there." Lucifer, a liar and a murderer "from the beginning," unleashed the wrath of blasphemy, the hiss of slander and perjury, subtlety and deceit (D&C 93:25; John 8:44). He was the accuser of his brethren (Revelation 12:10), and he commissioned his prophets and servants the same.

His violence rose in great swelling tidal waves against Michael, who led the forces of the Lord. Under Jehovah, Michael held directing powers for the Church and the family of man. All spirits worked under his leadership, and all, except the minions of Satan, believed his voice and obeyed his counsel as he received it from the Father and the Son. Michael made no railing accusation. His was the voice of truth and of testimony, which cannot be controverted. (Compare Jude 1:9; Revelation 12:11.) He was one who taught the ordinances and laws, and showed men "the way wherein they must walk, and the work that they must do" (Exodus 18:20). He commissioned the future prophets the same.

Eve surely knew the peril of defiance to eternal law and the urgency of battle; it was a war of salvation for her promised seed. Her intellect and capacity were as Michael's. Eve undoubtedly raised the standard of truth to family and Church; she taught, worked, and did all she could to further the Father's plan.

Great were the works and the words of Michael and of Eve.

They engendered faith and testimony in God's spirit children, and thus these spirits believed in things which were not yet seen which were true (see Alma 32:21). These were the faithful works and the words of the war. The blood of the war was that of the Lamb, through which all promises would take effect.

Thus it was as described by John the Beloved: "And I heard a loud voice saying in heaven, Now is come salvation, and strength, and the kingdom of our God, and the power of his Christ: for the accuser of our brethren is cast down, which accused them before our God day and night. And they overcame him by the blood of the Lamb, and by the word of their testimony; and they loved not their lives unto the death." (Revelation 12:10–11.)

MICHAEL AND EVE IN CREATION

In the beginning the Father, as Joseph Smith taught, "called together the Gods and sat in grand council to bring forth the world."[13] This work was one of planning and delegation, possibly embracing some of those designated as noble and great (Abraham 3:22). As with the War in Heaven, the Creation was an exercise of great and abiding faith. To Michael the Creation was a priesthood work for which he held appropriate authority; to Eve it was the creation of a home for their posterity.

Michael received the keys of the universe and creation.[14] With Jehovah, and under the direction of the Father, he accomplished the work of creation through the priesthood, which priesthood is, as Elder Bruce R. McConkie wrote, the power and authority "by which all things exist; by which they are created, governed, and controlled; by which the universe and worlds without number have come rolling into existence."[15] This was the priesthood power of the Father and the Son, and the priesthood power of heaven. The Creation, as the war, was a work of authority and delegation. Michael, at the side of Christ, commanded the noble and great through the creative labor, each serving according to his assigned labor. These were the rulers in heaven who would become the rulers on earth (Abraham 3:23). Surely this group of spirits was the same hierarchy set over the family of man in the Grand Council and the same body of servants and prophets who led the great war. Presumably these spirits were now termed "Gods" because of the creative commission they received through the word of God (see Abraham 3:22–24; 4:1).

Their work was no doubt the labor of many councils and much learning. "The grand councilors," the Prophet said, "sat at the head in yonder heavens and contemplated the creation of the worlds which were created at the time."[16] The Creation was accomplished according to the same eternal and immutable laws governing the creation of all earths, endless eons past and into the infinite future (Abraham 5:3; Moses 1:28–35).

The Creation was an exercise of faith in the laws of creation, or in other words, faith exercised in the word of God. "Through faith we understand that the worlds were framed by the word of God," Paul said, "so that things which are seen were not made of things which do appear" (Hebrews 11:3). Apparently the creators, relying on the word of God, took of existing materials, not seen by man, and organized an earth.[17]

The earth came into being through three stages: first, in planning; second, by spirit creation; and third, as the paradisiacal world which would fall. Each successive work, or day, was accomplished according to the law of the generation of earths. During the creative enterprise, the creators, councilors, noble and great, or "Gods," as they were termed, "counseled among themselves." The work was completed, we read, "according to all that which they had said." (Abraham 5:3–5.)

Elder McConkie suggested that Eve was among these "Gods" who labored upon the creation of the earth:

Christ and Mary, Adam and Eve, Abraham and Sarah, and a host of mighty men and equally glorious women comprised that group of "the noble and great ones," to whom the Lord Jesus said: "*We* will go down, for there is space there, and *we* will take of these materials, and *we* will make an earth whereon these may dwell." (Abraham 3:22–24. Italics added.) This we know: Christ, under the Father, is the Creator; Michael, his companion and associate, presided over much of the creative work; and with them, as Abraham saw, were many of the noble and great ones. Can we do other than conclude that Mary and Eve and Sarah and myriads of our faithful sisters were numbered among them? Certainly these sisters labored as diligently then, and fought as valiantly in the war in heaven, as did the brethren, even as they in like manner stand firm today, in mortality, in the cause of truth and righteousness.[18]

These noble and great labored for the immortality and eternal life of their children to come. Michael and Eve perhaps labored together, preparing a sphere where their assigned posterity might further their salvation. This work of surpassing magnitude was the labor of love and testimony. They had created the earthly home "whereon these may dwell," and it was a work the Father pronounced "very good" (Abraham 3:24; Moses 2:31).

In describing the placement of man and woman on earth, Elder Bruce R. McConkie has written:

> How did Adam and Eve gain their temporal bodies? Our revelations record Deity's words in this way: "And I, God, said unto mine Only Begotten, which was with me from the beginning: Let us make man in our image, after our likeness." (Moses 2:26.) Man on earth — Adam and Eve and all their descendants — was to be created in the image of God; he was to be in his image spiritually and temporally, with power to convert the image into a reality by becoming like him. Then the scripture says: "And I, God, created man in mine own image, in the image of mine Only Begotten created I him; male and female created I them." (Moses 2:27.) Also: "And I, the Lord God, formed man from the dust of the ground, and breathed into his nostrils the breath of life; and man became a living soul, the first flesh upon the earth, the first man also." (Moses 3:7.)
>
> For those whose limited spiritual understanding precludes a recitation of all the facts, the revealed account, in figurative language, speaks of Eve being created from Adam's rib. (Moses 3:21–25.) A more express scripture, however, speaks of "Adam, who was the son of God, with whom God, himself, conversed." (Moses 6:22.) In a formal doctrinal pronouncement, the First Presidency of the Church (Joseph F. Smith, John R. Winder, and Anthon H. Lund) said that "all who have inhabited the earth since Adam have taken bodies and become souls in like manner," and that the first of our race began life as the human germ or embryo that becomes a man. (See *Improvement Era*, November 1909, p. 80.)
>
> Christ is universally attested in the scriptures to be the Only Begotten. At this point, as we consider the "creation" of Adam,

and lest there be any misundertanding, we must remember that Adam was created in immortality, but that Christ came to earth as a mortal; thus our Lord is the Only Begotten in the flesh, meaning into this mortal sphere of existence. Adam came to earth to dwell in immortality until the fall changed his status to that of mortality.

Those who have ears to hear will understand these things. All of us, however, must know and believe that when Adam and Eve were placed in the Garden of Eden, there was no death. They were immortal. Unless some change occurred they would live forever, retaining all the bloom, beauty, and freshness of youth. Joseph Smith, Brigham Young, Orson Pratt, and our early brethren preached many sermons on this.

Also, though they had been commanded to multiply and fill the earth with posterity, Adam and Eve, in their then immortal state, could not have children. Nor could they be subject to the tests, trials, and probationary experiences of mortality. Hence, came the need—the imperative, absolute need—for the fall, for the change in status that would bring children, death, and testing into the world.[19]

MARRIAGE IN EDEN

In my mind the story of the rib is a love story of unparalleled beauty, enacted in the dawn of time and meant to be repeated by the posterity of Adam and Eve ever after. It is the story of our first parents joined in the covenant of eternal marriage by their Father, who was God. The story is prelude to the Fall and the basis of all future promise. I would like to suggest a meaning to this story which has deep significance to me.

Adam and Eve were placed in the Garden of Eden separately at the Father's discretion. God placed Adam in the garden before Eve as a matter of governance and preparation. Adam was to preside or govern over the earth and over the family yet to be. (Moses 3:15; 1 Corinthians 11:3, 8–9.) He was charged to dress or cultivate, keep or protect the garden, in which all things had been prepared for the use of man (Moses 3:9). This stewardship was the initiation of his foreordained work—he had been commanded to multiply and fill the earth, and yet Adam was companionless, alone and solitary in all his labors.

"It was not good," God declared, "that the man should be alone" (Moses 3:18), or, as the Hebrew suggests, "separate," "divided," or "desolate." The personal implication is that Adam could not prosper without his beloved companion. God announced that he would provide Adam with his foreordained consort, companion, and friend. The Father's words are his preface to the doctrine of eternal union here taught.

"I will make," God said "an *help meet* for him" (Moses 3:18; italics added) —not one word, but two, meaning the Lord would bring forth "a helper, aid, or partner" who was "suited to, worthy of, or corresponding to" Adam.[20] Eve was the prepared companion who was suited to Adam, a "full partner . . . in both temporal and spiritual things," as Elder McConkie expressed it.[21] She was to be, in the Hebrew, the indispensable "help, aid, succor," and "protection," which "strengthens, girds, or saves the onward course."

Let me now more specifically suggest an interesting interpretation of the rib story. We read that the Lord caused, or designed in the natural scheme of things, a "deep sleep" to fall upon Adam (Moses 3:21), an emphatic phrase that in the Hebrew suggests perhaps that Adam became lifeless and despondent. While Adam languished, the Lord took from him his rib, literally his "side," and made Eve. Eve *is* the rib, we learn, a metaphor telling us that Eve is the side, support, and stay to Adam, and that she is intrinsic to his being, the most intimate and inseparable companion. She is to be called *woman*, meaning "wife of man," because she was "taken out of man" (see Moses 3:22–24). Eve was not a mysterious extension of man, as some have supposed, but the companion who came in answer to his longing and was placed at his side.

Through his need the man gave the woman being; in return she gave purpose and being to him. There was now reason to survive, love, and labor, and in course of time there would come issue, the most precious gift, each to each. And thus the Lord closed the flesh in the stead of Adam's wound (Moses 3:21), suggesting that he closed or repaired the wound of Adam's yearning. "For as the woman is of the man," Paul said, "even so is the man also by the woman; but all things of God" (1 Corinthians 11:12).

Each was now entire. "This [my companion]," Adam exulted, "I know now is bone of my bones"; that is, she is of my same order or genesis. The term *bone* also connotes power and strength. Eve, continued Adam, is "flesh of my flesh," indicating a proper physical union drawing husband and wife together. "Therefore," Adam realized, "shall a man leave his father and his mother, and shall cleave unto his wife" in faithful union. (Moses 3:23–24.)

Now, the record says, "they were both naked, the man and his wife, and were not ashamed" (Moses 3:25). Jewish legends suggest a fascinating alternative explanation for *naked*—a "symbol of their guiltless relation to God and to one another."[22] Borrowing a metaphor from the prophet Jacob, we might say that they were free of guilt and uncleanness, "being clothed with purity, yea, even with the robe of righteousness" (2 Nephi 9:14). The idea that they wore sacred robes in their union corresponds to Jewish traditions that, while in the garden, Adam and Eve were clothed in garments of light.[23]

In that day God "blessed them, and called their name Adam," a name which Eve esteemed as one of honor and which betokened Adam's willingness to love, protect, and provide for her. The taking of Adam's name fully symbolized their perfect unity. They were one in purpose and destiny, commanded to remain together forever. (Moses 6:9.)

Adam and Eve, described in apocryphal literature as supreme in intellect,[24] and matchless in beauty,[25] were in the likeness of their heavenly parents —the Hebrew word *image* ordinarily meaning an exact reproduction,[26] and the word *likeness* meaning in similitude. Eve would have been much like Mary, "a virgin, most beautiful and fair above all other virgins" (1 Nephi 11:14). Not only were Adam and Eve in the beauty and likeness of their heavenly parents, but they also walked in their footsteps, marking the path for the generations to come.

In Eden, Adam was given priesthood and keys, and here Adam and Eve received sacred instruction and ordinances. The marriage performed by God in the garden was an ordinance intended to endure forever. In the words of Joseph Smith, "Marriage was an institution of heaven, instituted in the garden of Eden; . . . it was necessary it should be solemnized by the authority of the everlasting Priesthood."[27]

Adam and Eve understood and believed in the ordinances performed for them in the garden. They understood the power of the priesthood as its purposes had been revealed to Adam in the garden. They knew their marriage covenant entitled them to posterity in the world and offered the promise of exaltation or life in the eternal family as the Father knew it. Their inheritance and aspiration were to become like God.

To my mind, then, this is the story concealed within the account of the rib, a story of eternal love and beauty. When Adam was ready to receive her, then God brought Eve into Eden's flowering vales and woods. Adam received the companion he had longed for, a help meet for him. Eve would assist and sustain him in his work and mission, for her mission was his. Bound together by an eternal ordinance, they would choose to obey the Father's command: they would remain as one, and they would open the world for the family of man.

THE FALL

Everything in the eternal scheme is planned and executed in accordance with divine law. God ordained the fall of Adam according to eternal principles. As the redemption was prepared in the eternal councils, so was the plan of the Fall, upon which that redemption was predicated. Adam and Eve were placed in the garden to bring the earth from the Edenic state the Father had pronounced good into its mortal duration, or span. By faith they accomplished their mission.

To facilitate the Fall, God placed two trees in the midst of the garden, the tree of life and the tree of the knowledge of good and evil. The significance of the trees extended beyond that of natural or physical fruit: their importance lay in the figures provided. The trees, with their spreading branches and fruit, represented essential doctrines.

The tree of the knowledge of good and evil, for example, was the tree of mortal probation. To partake would bring mortality, sin, and death into the world (Moses 3:17; 4:9). Man would fall from the presence of God in the garden to the proving ground of mortality, where he would become subject to sin. He would be tried and tested to the fullest, continually challenged in the struggle of good over evil, acquiring wisdom, should he so choose, through the schooling provided by encounters with the bitter and the sweet. Procreative powers would become his natural inheritance, and the dissolution of the physical body would be the certain fate of all. The effects of the Fall would pass upon the earth and all forms of life upon its face. (Abraham 3:24–25; 2 Nephi 2:22.)

The tree of life was basically the representation of eternal life. All scriptural references to the tree of life speak of the same tree of immortality and eternal life. Nephi identifies the tree as the love of God as beautifully manifest in the mission of his Son, and the fruit as the eternal life coming through Christ's atonement (1 Nephi 11:4–23). As Joseph Fielding McConkie and Robert L. Millet have written, the scriptural tree of life is "the symbol, even from the time of paradise, of the central and saving role of Jesus Christ."[28]

Adam and Eve enjoyed a free association with the Father and the Son. As the Prophet Joseph Smith explained, "Adam . . . received instruction from, and walked, talked and conversed with him [God], as one man talks and communes with another."[29] Adam and Eve were spiritually alive in the garden, yet they did not enjoy the full blessings of eternal life. They were not as God, possessing eternal life as saved beings. They understood the promise was theirs by covenant. How were they to achieve it?

"To bring about his [God's] eternal purposes in the end of man, after he had created our first parents," Lehi said, " . . . it must needs be that there was an opposition; even the forbidden fruit in opposition to the tree of life; the one being sweet and the other bitter" (2 Nephi 2:15). God had sent Adam and Eve into the world to multiply and fill the earth with their posterity. This was the great commandment given to Adam and Eve in the day of their creation and again in the garden. It was the purpose of their marriage union. Procreation was a function of mortality. Procreation could come only through the tree of the knowledge of good and evil (2 Nephi 2:22–23; Moses 5:11).

On the other hand, God forbade Adam and Eve to partake of the tree of the knowledge of good and evil, which seems to symbolize mortality. God would not create the imperfect state, nor would he instruct man to fill the earth with sin and sorrow. "Of the tree of the knowledge of good and evil, thou shalt not eat of it," the Lord told Adam, "nevertheless, thou mayest choose for thyself, for it is given unto thee; but, remember that I forbid it, for in the day thou eatest thereof thou shalt surely die" (Moses 3:17).

"The Lord God gave unto man that he should act for himself," father Lehi said again. "Wherefore, man could not act for himself save it should be that he was enticed by the one or the other." (2 Nephi 2:16.) Thus they were required to use their agency in the matter of the Fall: the opposition provided the means of choice, the choice provided the means of agency, and the power was theirs. The Fall could not be a matter of coercion on the part of the Father. Man must assume mortality by conscious decision; he must of his own will become subject to death, sin, and corruption. Of his own will he must bring this condition upon the earth and all forms of life thereon.

It is possible that the decision to partake was a process. Adam and Eve were enticed by the one fruit and the other, leading them to reason, weigh, and ponder. The two trees were in the midst of the garden as a continual reminder of the principles they represented. In the most propitious moment, "that Satan," who was cast out of the Father's presence for rebellion (Moses 4:3), interjected himself into the process of decision. Satan, who "knew not the mind of God" (Moses 4:6), became the increased opposition, the impetus in the process. He tempted both Adam and Eve (D&C 29:40).

Satan is again the serpent, a creature of stealth, subtlety, and venom. Satan spoke by the mouth of the serpent, which, from the Hebrew, might indicate the continual hiss and whisper of his deception. His motive was the destruction of mankind; he must gain access to the spirits of men, and the earth as his dominion. (Moses 4:6; 2 Nephi 2:18.) Satan used their understanding to tempt them. To Eve he said, "Ye shall not surely die," but "ye shall be as gods" (Moses 4:10–11). How craftily Satan laid his snare! Contrary to what Satan told Eve, spiritual death would be the immediate result of the Fall, and physical death would ensue. Truly they would gain wisdom, as Satan indicated, but Satan offered the wisdom of the world, the philosophies and priesthoods over which he reigns, and not the wisdom of God to which Adam and Eve rightfully aspired. Though Adam and Eve understood principles of exaltation, Satan intended to deceive and lead the first parents and their posterity captive.

Through the natural process of enticement and through the temptation of Satan, the tree of knowledge "*became* pleasant to the eyes" (Moses 4:12; italics added). The phrase "pleasant to the eyes" is a Hebrew idiom meaning "a desirable thing." Eve saw the tree was, in the Hebrew, "desirable as a means to wisdom, insight," and that man must know the evil to prize the good.[30] Eve knew the tree of life was a great tree, with a fruit precious above all others, yet she discerned the tree of knowledge was also "good for food," meaning nourishment and growth.

With deliberation Eve partook of the fruit—an irretrievable step which she knew to be such. She "also gave unto her husband *with her*, and he did eat" (Moses 4:12; italics added). We may assume that the processes of the Fall had already begun to operate in Eve, before such was the case with Adam, for she was the first to partake of the forbidden fruit. Eve offered the fruit to Adam, not "in malice, but with a sincere view to his advantage."[31] Elder Bruce R. McConkie explained: "Eve partook without full understanding; Adam partook knowing that unless he did so, he and Eve could not have children and fulfill the commandment they had received to multiply and replenish the earth."[32]

We do not know the real meaning of the term *forbidden fruit*. We do know that Adam and Eve transgressed, literally meaning to step over, in systematic fashion, the law of continuance in the garden. They "complied with the law which enabled them to become mortal beings," Elder McConkie wrote, "and this course of conduct is termed eating the forbidden fruit."[33] What Adam and Eve knew, and what they had to know in the designs of the Father, was sufficient to produce the faith to choose the Fall. In this connection, it is interesting to note that the prophet Alma said that God *drew* them from the garden (Alma 42:2). Of one thing we may be assured: to gain the fulness of either tree Adam and Eve could not stay in the garden; they must partake of the one to gain the fulness of the other. The two trees together comprised the eternal plan of salvation.

We might say, then, that it was their faith in the teachings symbolized by the trees that enabled them again to "hope for things which are not seen, which are true" (Alma 32:21). To partake of the tree of knowledge, they must trust in the tree of atonement. They knew enough to do so. The faith exercised by Adam and Eve was greater than we may have ever supposed. "Faith is not only the principle of action, but of power also, in all intelligent beings whether in heaven or on earth," the Prophet taught. Hence he concluded that without faith "there is no power, and without power there could be no creation nor existence!"[34]

Through faith, they had opened the floodgates of heaven; man would come forth and have opportunity for salvation. "And now, behold," father Lehi proclaimed,

> if Adam had not transgressed he would not have fallen, but he would have remained in the garden of Eden. And all things which were created must have remained in the same state in which they were after they were created; and they must have remained forever, and had no end.
>
> And they would have had no children; wherefore they would have remained in a state of innocence, having no joy, for they knew no misery; doing no good, for they knew no sin.
>
> But behold, all things have been done in the wisdom of him who knoweth all things.
>
> Adam fell that men might be; and men are, that they might have joy. (2 Nephi 2:22–25.)

ADAM AND EVE PREPARE TO ENTER THE WORLD

Why has the scripture placed such emphasis on the fall of Eve while the story of Adam is almost subsidiary? Through the Restoration we realize that history has misread the account of Eve's fall. The scriptural account is in no way intended to be an aspersion on mother Eve. We simply do not know how much Adam and Eve understood in the garden. The emphasis placed by scripture on Eve's actions signals the paramount importance of her mission.

Eve, we might say, is the wellspring of life. All creation was dependent upon her motherhood. God breathed the breath of life into Adam, the Prophet Joseph Smith taught, but to Eve he gave the breath of lives.[35] While Adam came to govern and provide, Eve came to bear and nurture children. The gift of children was the burden Eve carried in her heart and brought to Eden.

With Eve's fall, the Father, besides setting forth the consequences that would surely follow, administered comfort to her. Though Satan would, in the course of mortality, bruise the heel of man, through her lineage was to come the Christ, who would crush the serpent's head (Genesis 3:15; Moses 4:21; Hebrews 2:14).

Satan—and his power of sin, corruption, and death—would, through the atonement of Christ, be destroyed. The Father's words gave testimony that Adam and Eve, in the Fall, had done as they ought.

The Father explained to Eve the nature of her motherhood in the world (Moses 4:22). Her conception would be multiplied: Eve was to be given many children. She would bring them forth in *sorrow*, a term that in the Hebrew seems to indicate that Eve would experience physical and mental labor in her role, and not that she was to be punished for her part in the Fall. This was the nature of the tree of the knowledge of good and evil, the field of learning and growth. But more significant, this was the beginning of the race of man.

That Adam hearkened to his wife in the matter of the Fall suggests his willingness to accept fatherhood. The Father, therefore, charged Adam to labor by the sweat of his brow. In sorrow—that is, through physical and mental toil—Adam brought his abundance from the reluctant earth. His labor was, to a certain degree, for his own sake, and this, in the province of the tree of the knowledge of good and evil, was a part of his schooling and development. All that Adam did he did for his wife and the children they were to bring into the world. "Adam called his wife's name Eve, because she was the mother of all living." *Eve* was a title as well as a personal name: Eve, the first of all women, the beginning mother. (Moses 4:26.) In announcing her name, Adam revealed his understanding of her call and acknowledged his responsibility to protect and provide for Eve in her role.

With the Fall their work became reality. Therefore, the Lord sent them "forth from the Garden of Eden, to till the ground" from whence they were taken (Moses 4:29). The scriptural language is that of mission. The Lord clothed Adam and Eve in coats or garments of skins prior to their leaving the garden. These garments would serve as protection in their sojourn, through righteousness and obedience to their covenants.[36] They were to enter the world rightly clothed, anointed, and instructed. Their judgment and wisdom, knowing good and evil, would be according to their faith in God, and not according to the wisdom Satan contrived. "Behold," the Father said, "the man is become as one of us," meaning Adam and Eve had stepped forward on the path to exaltation (Moses 4:28).

Adam and Eve had walked and talked with the Father and the Son in Eden's garden. Neither sin, nor disbelief, nor misunderstanding had raised any barrier between them. To walk and talk with no veil between them was a great blessing. But the full blessing was to be as the Father, an exalted being. Adam and Eve partook of the tree of death in order to eventually gain eternal life. In the world they would again reach out to the tree of life. In their choosing, Adam and Eve gained the nourishment of salvation. The sustenance of Satan was the dust of the earth, which held no reward. Relying upon the word of God, Adam and Eve entered the world of briar and thorn. Such was their faith.

ADAM AND EVE IN THE WORLD

Adam and Eve came into the world and dwelt somewhere on the plains of Olaha Shinehah (D&C 117:8). Together they labored; together they brought forth children; together they called upon the name of the Lord; and together they heard his voice from the way toward the Garden of Eden. They rejoiced in the gospel and together they taught their children. (Moses 5:1–12.) Together Adam and Eve laid the pattern of salvation for their children.

Adam was a prince, patriarch, and governing father over his family. He stood first over his immediate family unit and then as father to the vast human family. The name *Adam*, meaning man or mankind, also signified "first father" and "many," indicating the posterity that was to flow from him. He became the father of all. Undoubtedly, his administration to his family was one of persuasion, long-suffering, gentleness, meekness, and love unfeigned (D&C 121:41). He placed his name upon his wife and family as a shield and cover. We read that Adam, who held the priesthood of God, begot a son who grew to be in his likeness and image, and that he "called his name Seth," a phrase suggesting the possibility that the child received a name and blessing through ordinance (Moses 6:10). The ordinance signified the parental acknowledgment of obligation and accountability in the child's upbringing.

We assume that Adam baptized his children at the age of accountability, that he gave his righteous sons the priesthood, and that he blessed his posterity with patriarchal blessings (see Moses 6:51–68; 7:1; D&C 107:42–50; 84:16). Surely he taught them to do all that they did "in the name of the Son," to "repent and call upon

God in the name of the Son forevermore" (Moses 5:8). He was a living witness, and he spoke by the power of the Holy Ghost, even predicting all things that would befall his posterity (Moses 5:10). His fatherhood was the demonstration of faith.

Eve, the Mother of All Living

Eve, in like manner, undoubtedly exercised great faith to perform her mission as the mother of all living. The word *mother* as applied to Eve, translated from the Hebrew, implies "bond of the family." Eve became the bonding, uniting force which secures and saves in the onward course. Now, more than ever, Eve provided the support and stay taught by the imagery of the rib, and through her labors her love assuredly became that of a true mother — a kind of love that, in the words of Joseph F. Smith, "comes nearer being like the love of God than any other kind."[37]

The literal Hebrew meaning for *Eve* was "lifegiver," or, as the Prophet Joseph said, "lives," signifying the posterity that would flow from her. This crucial work of creation was uniquely hers. It placed her at the very center of her children's existence, as she bore and cradled each new human life. Eve was to be saved through childbearing; that is, not only would she be preserved through physical travail, but also her salvation would come through her sacrifice and labor (see JST, 1 Timothy 2:15). Her willingness to tender life into the world might be thought of as a gentle similitude of the sacrifice of the Lord.

Eve received her children as gifts from God. "I have gotten a man from the Lord," she said; and she prayed for the faith of her children, "wherefore he may not reject his words" (Moses 5:16). Eve certainly felt the obligation to train and instruct her children. Undoubtedly she also was a teacher who taught with power, having walked in Eden with the Father and the Son (Moses 5:11–12).

Eve would be mother to a priestly line; prophets and "preachers of righteousness" would come through her (Moses 6:23). The promise given her in Eden was that the Redeemer would be of her seed, and Eve labored in the hope of these things (Moses 4:21). Thus, Eve was faithful to her charge as first and beginning mother.

Adam and Eve in the Organization of the Church

It was Michael, or Adam, who was given the keys of First Presidency. It was Michael, or Adam, who, under Christ, led the armies of heaven. It was Michael, or Adam, who went down with Jehovah day after creative day to make the earth and the heavens. It was Adam who opened the world for the spirits of men, providing them with the opportunity for a mortal probation. And now it was Adam, serving under Christ, who would regulate and govern all the affairs of the Lord's work on earth.

"That he [Adam] received revelations, commandments and ordinances at the beginning is beyond the power of controversy," declared the Prophet Joseph Smith.[38] Adam was given, the Prophet taught, the "keys of the dispensation of the fullness of times; i.e., the dispensation of all the times have been and will be revealed through him from the beginning to Christ, and from Christ to the end of the dispensations that are to be revealed." Adam's stewardship was thus to work for the salvation of all mankind.

Adam's keys of presidency authorized him to organize the Church in his day and, as Joseph Smith said, to watch over the ordinances and "to reveal them from heaven to man, or to send angels to reveal them," in all subsequent ages. The Prophet further observed, "Adam received commandments and instructions from God: this was the order from the beginning."[39] Apparently the Church was organized line upon line, as Adam received direction: "And thus the Gospel began to be preached, from the beginning, being declared by holy angels sent forth from the presence of God, and by his own voice, and by the gift of the Holy Ghost" (Moses 5:58).

The Church was patriarchal. It was a time when all things, secular and spiritual, sprang from the family. Surely Eve was a support to her husband as the Church grew to accommodate their extensive posterity. "After the fall," Elder McConkie wrote, "Eve continued to receive revelation, to see visions, to walk in the spirit."[40] Eve, as the first and head, would have been first to lead and teach her faithful daughters in particular. Eve's knowledge of the gospel, her capacity, and her intelligence must have been, as with father Adam, unexcelled.

Though Adam and Eve grieved for their children who "loved Satan more than God" (Moses 5:13), they found joy in that portion of their posterity who served the Lord. These were the faithful members of the family and the Church who gathered at Adam-ondi-Ahman, where "the Lord administered comfort unto Adam." This was a posterity who knew the mission accomplished by the first parents and blessed them for it. These righteous children "rose up and blessed Adam, and called him Michael, the prince, the archangel." (D&C 107:53–56.)

Adam and Eve understood the process of mortality. They had withstood the worldly test. No longer did they have direct, personal, face-to-face communion with the Father. Christ was the Mediator who conveyed the Father's words to them, who interceded on their behalf, who advocated their cause in the courts above — on conditions of repentance. In the day of Adam's baptism the Lord declared, "Behold I have forgiven thee thy transgression in the Garden of Eden," meaning that through the atonement of Christ the breach of sin and death was healed (Moses 6:53). Through repentance and baptism Adam and Eve were again alive in Christ. Christ's redemptive act, the greatest manifestation of God's love, was the tree of life. Adam and Eve had followed the same counsel that Alma would later give to those in Zarahemla: "Come and be baptized unto repentance, that ye . . . may be partakers of the fruit of the tree of life" (Alma 5:62).

THE HOUR OF REDEMPTION

It is the hour of redemption. It is the moment between the Crucifixion and the empty tomb. Eve, our mother, glorious and faithful, stands confirmed in all that she has done. She is, as ever, at the side of Michael, the prince and father of all, to receive the atoning Lord into the world of waiting spirits, into the congregation of the just. (D&C 138:38–39.)

The spirit hosts assembled to see the face of the Lord and to hear his voice are the righteous dead, those who were faithful in the testimony of Jesus and who suffered tribulation in his name. They are the faithful children from the days of Adam and Eve to the meridian of time. These have followed the prophets and now accept direction from Adam's hand. (D&C 138:12–13.)

It is an interval of glad hosannas, the moment of joy to which Eve prophesied nearly four millennia before, saying, "Were it not for our transgression we never should have had seed, and never should have known good and evil, and the joy of our redemption, and the eternal life which God giveth unto all the obedient" (Moses 5:11). In this moment the Lord appears, preaching the everlasting gospel, declaring the doctrine of resurrection and the redemption of mankind from the Fall. It is the moment when the bands of death shall be broken, when the faithful captives shall go free. (D&C 138:18–19.)

To those assembled, the Lord gives power to come forth after His own resurrection, each in his own order (D&C 138:51; 1 Corinthians 15:23). Adam, holding the keys of salvation and presidency over all his children would surely be among the first to rise, followed by Eve, his eternal companion.

It is at this juncture that Adam and Eve shall follow the risen Lord into the Father's kingdom to be crowned with immortality and eternal lives. They have become as the gods. They, in turn, shall draw their faithful children after them, those for whom they opened the world and the way of salvation. (D&C 138:51.) This is the moment of efficacy, force, and validity—the moment in which creation, fall, and atonement meet. Adam our father and Eve our mother have been intimate participants through it all.

CONCLUSION

Adam and Eve are the mirror for those seeking full salvation. They are the first, the example, the pattern, the archetype, or the figure of salvation unto their children. They are the first of a kind or group of persons seeking and receiving salvation. What they have obtained they have achieved through faith in the word of God.

By faith, Eve sought the knowledge of God before the world came into being; by "exceedingly great faith," Eve was called with a holy calling as first wife and first mother, mother of the family of all the earth; by faith she labored to teach the Father's spirit children of the Redeemer and his salvation; by faith she, with the Gods, assisted in the creation of the world; by faith Eve made sacred covenants in Eden; by faith Eve bore and nurtured children and filled the earth with many; by faith she partook of eternal life and was crowned with glory.

As she knew principle, her daughters must know principle. As she conformed to truth, her daughters must conform to truth. As she exercised faith in the plan of God and Christ, we must exercise faith. As she and her husband worshipped, we must worship. The faithful children of Adam and Eve in every age must struggle and obtain according to the same principles if they are to achieve the same reward. This pattern is after the example of the Father and the Son. To walk where God and his prophets have walked is the nature of salvation.[41]

NOTES

1. Bruce R. McConkie, "Eve and the Fall," in *Woman* (Salt Lake City: Deseret Book Co., 1979), p. 67.

2. See Joseph Fielding Smith, *Man: His Origin and Destiny* (Salt Lake City: Deseret Book Co., 1954), p. 351.

3. See Joseph Fielding Smith, *The Way to Perfection* (Salt Lake City: Deseret Book Co., 1972), p. 51.

4. See *Lectures on Faith* 1:13.

5. *Teachings of the Prophet Joseph Smith*, comp. Joseph Fielding Smith (Salt Lake City: Deseret Book Co., 1976), p. 365.

6. See Bruce R. McConkie, *The Promised Messiah* (Salt Lake City: Deseret Book Co., 1978), p. 51.

7. *Teachings of the Prophet Joseph Smith*, p. 167.

8. *Teachings of the Prophet Joseph Smith*, p. 158.

9. "Eve and the Fall," p. 58.

10. *Teachings of the Prophet Joseph Smith*, p. 12.

11. See McConkie, *The Promised Messiah*, p. 51.

12. See *Teachings of the Prophet Joseph Smith*, p. 365.

13. *Teachings of the Prophet Joseph Smith*, p. 348.

14. See *Teachings of the Prophet Joseph Smith*, p. 157; Bruce R. McConkie, *The Millennial Messiah* (Salt Lake City: Deseret Book Co., 1982), p. 119.

15. Bruce R. McConkie, *Mormon Doctrine*, 2d ed. (Salt Lake City: Bookcraft, 1966), p. 594.

16. *Teachings of the Prophet Joseph Smith*, pp. 348–49.

17. See Bruce R. McConkie, *Doctrinal New Testament Commentary*, 3 vols. (Salt Lake City: Bookcraft, 1965–73), 3:193–94.

18. "Eve and the Fall," p. 59.

19. "Eve and the Fall," pp. 60–61.

20. See footnote to Genesis 2:18, LDS edition of the Bible.

21. "Eve and the Fall," p. 65.

22. *The Oxford Annotated Bible*, eds. Herbert May and Bruce Metzger (New York: Oxford University Press, 1962), p. 2.

23. See Louis Ginzberg, *The Legends of the Jews*, 7 vols. (Philadelphia: Jewish Publication Society, 1909), 5:97.

24. See *Encyclopedia Judaica* (Jerusalem, New York: Macmillan, 1971), 1:240.

25. See "The Book of the Revelation of Abraham," reproduced in *Improvement Era* 2 (August 1898): 57.

26. See Raymond E. Brown, ed., *The Jerome Biblical Commentary* (Prentice Hall), p. 11.

27. *History of the Church*, 2:320.

28. Joseph Fielding McConkie and Robert L. Millet, *Doctrinal Commentary on the Book of Mormon*, 4 vols. (Salt Lake City: Bookcraft, 1987–), 1:76.

29. *Teachings of the Prophet Joseph Smith*, p. 345.

30. See footnotes to Genesis 3:6, LDS edition of the Bible.

31. J. R. Dummelow, ed., *The One Volume Bible Commentary* (Macmillan), p. 9.

32. Bruce R. McConkie, *A New Witness for the Articles of Faith* (Salt Lake City: Deseret Book Co., 1985), p. 86.

33. *Mormon Doctrine*, p. 289.

34. *Lectures on Faith* 1:13, 24.

35. *Teachings of the Prophet Joseph Smith*, p. 301.

36. See Joseph Fielding McConkie, *Gospel Symbolism* (Salt Lake City: Bookcraft, 1985), pp. 32, 202.

37. Joseph F. Smith, *Gospel Doctrine* (Salt Lake City: Deseret Book Co., 1966), p. 315.

38. *Teachings of the Prophet Joseph Smith*, pp. 168–69.

39. *Teachings of the Prophet Joseph Smith*, pp. 167–68.

40. "Eve and the Fall," p. 68.

41. See *Lectures on Faith* 7:9–16.

7

Larry E. Dahl

Adam's Role from the Fall to the End — and Beyond

With the Fall, Adam entered a new phase of his ongoing stewardship of helping to bring to pass the immortality and eternal life of man. His mortal ministry lasted nine hundred thirty years. After that, he continued his close involvement with his posterity on the earth, directing through successive dispensations the restoration of the priesthood and its keys. Undoubtedly he also presided over the spirits in the post-earth spirit world, supervising their efforts to prepare for the Savior's mortal ministry and subsequent personal visit to that spirit realm, with all that those events would entail for them. In addition he maintained, and will continue to maintain, a constant vigil against the power of the devil and his angels as they "maketh war with the saints of God, and encompasseth them round about" (D&C 76:29). In making war with the Saints of God, the devil and his angels not only apply directly their trade upon the Saints but also employ other mortals whose hearts they can capture and who "love darkness rather than light, because their deeds are evil" (D&C 10:20–21). At pivotal points

Larry E. Dahl is Professor and Chairman of the Department of Church History and Doctrine at Brigham Young University.

throughout earth's history Adam has had to confront the devil personally, or reveal his deceit to others when the devil has appeared pretending to be an angel of light. Hence the war that began in heaven continues on earth. That war will continue to rage until its final battle, what the scriptures call the "battle of the great God," which will take place at the end of the Millennium (D&C 88:110-15). In the meantime Adam will keep the devil in check and one day preside at a special council at Adam-ondi-Ahman in preparation for the Lord's second coming. Furthermore, he will play a key role in the judgment and resurrection of all mankind and then continue in a presiding role—in the patriarchal order of the priesthood—in the eternities to come.

ADAM'S MORTAL MINISTRY

The Fall brought death—both spiritual and temporal. Spiritual death involved Adam's being cast out of the Garden of Eden and out of God's immediate presence; becoming subject to the temptations and weaknesses associated with that fallen, mortal condition; and being estranged from God and in need of reconciliation. Temporal death for Adam was to come later—nine hundred thirty years later (Genesis 5:5)—but still within the "day" spoken of by God when he instructed Adam and Eve concerning the tree of knowledge of good and evil (Moses 3:16-17).[1] The atonement of Jesus Christ provided the means for Adam and his posterity to overcome both of these deaths—to be resurrected and to be reconciled to God (see D&C 29:40-43; Alma 42; 2 Nephi 9).

Adam Had the Fulness of the Gospel

For man to become reconciled to God requires that man be obedient to the principles and ordinances of the everlasting covenant, or the fulness of the gospel (D&C 22:1; 66:2; 133:57). The gospel is the same in all ages for all men. Adam had the fulness of the gospel. He was baptized by water. He was "baptized with fire, and with the Holy Ghost." He was given the priesthood "after the order of him who was without beginning of days or end of years," becoming "a son of God." (Moses 6:64-68.) What does it mean to enter into this order? President Ezra Taft Benson explained: "To enter into the order of the Son of God is the equivalent today of entering into the fullness of the Melchizedek Priesthood, which is only received in the house of the Lord. Because Adam and Eve had complied with these requirements, God said to them, 'Thou art after the order of him who was without beginning of days or end of years, from all eternity to all eternity.' "[2]

Indeed, "all things were confirmed unto Adam, by an holy ordinance, and the Gospel preached, and a decree sent forth, that it should be in the world, until the end thereof" (Moses 5:59).

Adam's Language — Pure and Undefiled

"The first man placed upon this earth was an intelligent being," President Joseph Fielding Smith explained, "created in the image of God, possessed of wisdom and knowledge, with power to communicate his thoughts in a language, both oral and written, which was superior to anything to be found on the earth today."[3] Adam and Eve had sons and daughters who "began to divide two and two in the land, and to till the land, and to tend flocks, and they also begat sons and daughters" (Moses 5:3). A goodly number of these children rejected the gospel when their parents taught it to them. They "loved Satan more than God" and "began from that time forth to be carnal, sensual, and devilish." (Moses 5:12–13.) But "Adam hearkened unto the voice of God, and called upon his sons to repent" (Moses 6:1). More children were born, among them Seth, who, like his father Adam, was a handsome, righteous man.[4] With Seth there began a line of faithful patriarchs for many generations — Seth, Enos, Cainan, Mahalaleel, Jared, Enoch, Methuselah (all seven of whom were ordained high priests in the patriarchal order of the priesthood by Adam himself), Lamech (who was ordained by Seth), and Noah (who was ordained by Methuselah). Speaking of Adam, Seth, and Enos the scriptural record says:

> And then began these men to call upon the name of the Lord, and the Lord blessed them;
> And a book of remembrance was kept, in the which was recorded, in the language of Adam, for it was given unto as many as called upon God to write by the spirit of inspiration;

And by them their children were taught to read and write, having a language which was pure and undefiled. . . .

. . . And a genealogy was kept of the children of God. And this was the book of the generations of Adam, saying: In the day that God created man, in the likeness of God made he him;

In the image of his own body, male and female, created he them, and blessed them, and called their name Adam, in the day when they were created and became living souls in the land upon the footstool of God. (Moses 6:4-9.)

Oh, that we had that book of remembrance! Portions of it, perhaps only fragments, have been preserved in the Bible. What appear to be additional parts have been restored through the instrumentality of the Prophet Joseph Smith and are found in latter-day scriptures—the Book of Mormon, the Doctrine and Covenants, the Pearl of Great Price, and the Joseph Smith Translation of the Bible. Perhaps if we had access to the full record as kept by Adam and other righteous patriarchs, we would have an understanding of the Creation, the Fall, and the works of God in the earliest generations of Adam's posterity as "pure and undefiled" as the language in which the record was written. Someday we will have it.

Adam's Government—A Patriarchal Theocracy

The first government on earth was patriarchal and theocratic. That is, it was administered through families, with fathers presiding, and was directed by God. The keys of the kingdom were held by the oldest righteous patriarch. He ordained and presided over other faithful patriarchs according to the revelations of the Lord to him. The Prophet Joseph Smith taught: "The Priesthood was first given to Adam; he obtained the First Presidency, and held the keys of it from generation to generation. . . . He had dominion given him over every living creature."[5] That dominion was both civil and religious. About this early government, Elder Bruce R. McConkie has written:

Adam, our father, the first man, is the presiding high priest over the earth for all ages. The government the Lord gave him was patriarchal, and from the expulsion from Eden to the cleansing of the earth by water in the day of Noah, the righteous portion of mankind were blessed and governed by a patriarchal theocracy.

This theocratic system, patterned after the order and system that prevailed in heaven, was the government of God. He himself, though dwelling in heaven, was the Lawgiver, Judge, and King. He gave direction in all things both civil and ecclesiastical; there was no separation of church and state as we now know it. All governmental affairs were directed, controlled, and regulated from on high. The Lord's legal administrators on earth served by virtue of their callings and ordinations in the Holy Priesthood and as they were guided by the power of the Holy Ghost.

"This order was instituted in the days of Adam, and came down by lineage." It was designed "to be handed down from father to son." It came down in succession; it is priesthood government; it is the government of God both on earth and in heaven. And even today, it "rightly belongs to the literal descendants of the chosen seed, to whom the promises were made." (D&C 107:40–41.) That it is not now in full operation simply means that fallen men have departed from the ancient ways and are now governing each other as they choose.

But in the beginning the Lord's true system prevailed. The successive sons who held rulership of one kind or another in the original earthly kingdom were Adam, Seth, Enos, Cainan, Mahalaleel, Jared, Enoch, Methuselah, Lamech, and Noah. In their respective days there were, of course, apostate peoples who set up governments of their own. But those who believed the gospel and sought salvation remained subject to the patriarchal order revealed and established by the Eternal Patriarch.[6]

Adam presided over his righteous posterity under this patriarchal theocracy for nine hundred thirty years, receiving revelation, keeping a book of remembrance, teaching, ordaining, crying repentance, offering sacrifices in anticipation of the Savior's infinite and eternal atoning sacrifice, and otherwise faithfully exercising First Presidency keys as head of the initial gospel dispensation on the earth. As the end of his mortal ministry drew near, Adam called his righteous posterity together to give them his last blessing.

A Farewell Council at Adam-ondi-Ahman

In March of 1835, a revelation received by the Prophet Joseph Smith was recorded that included some interesting and important information originally recorded in the book of Enoch, a book that was probably a part of that ancient book of remembrance:

> Three years previous to the death of Adam, he called Seth, Enos, Cainan, Mahalaleel, Jared, Enoch, and Methuselah, who were all high priests, with the residue of his posterity who were righteous, into the valley of Adam-ondi-Ahman, and there bestowed upon them his last blessing.
>
> And the Lord appeared unto them, and they rose up and blessed Adam, and called him Michael, the prince, the archangel.
>
> And the Lord administered comfort unto Adam, and said unto him: I have set thee to be at the head; a multitude of nations shall come of thee, and thou art a prince over them forever.
>
> And Adam stood up in the midst of the congregation; and, notwithstanding he was bowed down with age, being full of the Holy Ghost, predicted whatsoever should befall his posterity unto the latest generation.
>
> These things were all written in the book of Enoch, and are to be testified of in due time. (D&C 107:53-57.)

Joseph Smith taught that the blessing Adam gave his children was a "patriarchal blessing" and that Adam's hope was "to bring them into the presence of God."[7] That hope was realized as the Lord appeared to *them*, not just to Adam. What a marvelous scene—generations of Adam's righteous posterity gathered to honor and receive a blessing from their venerable father as he neared the completion of his mortal ministry, and having the Savior minister to them! And what a fitting tribute was given to Adam by the Lord, affirming that he is Michael, the prince, the archangel, and that he is to be the head or prince over his posterity forever.

In that grand setting Adam, by the power of the Holy Ghost, "predicted whatsoever should befall his posterity unto the latest generation." We do not have access currently to that prophecy, but we are assured that it is recorded in the book of Enoch and is "to be testified of in due time." Like Moroni, Adam saw down through the corridors of time to the winding up scenes of this earth's mortal existence and wrote, in effect, prophetic history (see Mormon 8:35). What a powerful testimony it will prove to be when that prophetic history is read, after the fact, by those who denied or doubted God's foreknowledge and his power to reveal the future to his prophets. And there will be plenty of evidence. All God's prophets have been shown these things and have left their records as testimonies. Elder Wilford Woodruff taught:

> Adam, our first great progenitor and father, after the fall, received this Gospel, and he received the holy Priesthood in all its power, and its keys and ordinances. He sealed these blessings upon his sons — Seth, Enos, Jared, Cainan, Mahalaleel, Enoch and Methusaleh. All these men received this high and holy Priesthood. They all professed to give revelation. They all had inspiration and left their record on the earth; and not one of them but what saw and prophesied about the great Zion of God in the latter-days. And when we say this of them, we say it of every Apostle and Prophet who ever lived upon the earth. Their revelations and prophecies all point to our day and that great kingdom of God which was spoken of by Daniel, that great Zion of God spoken of by Isaiah and Jeremiah, and that great gathering of the house of Israel spoken of by Ezekiel and Malachi and many of the ancient Patriarchs and Prophets.[8]

Three years after this momentous family gathering in Adam-ondi-Ahman,[9] Adam died. His mortal ministry came to an end, but his involvement with the world's history and earth's inhabitants did not. He still held the "keys of salvation under the counsel and direction of the Holy One" (D&C 78:16). Only one of the seven "days" of the earth's "temporal existence" (D&C 77:6) had passed. Adam's "keys of salvation" include, as Joseph Smith explained, the keys of all dispensations "to the end of the dispensations that are to be revealed."[10] There was still much to be done.

PRIESTHOOD AND KEYS REVEALED BY ADAM'S AUTHORITY

From Adam's death to the present there have been numerous universal apostasies necessitating the restoration of the gospel and the priesthood. The Prophet Joseph Smith explained that Adam has directed these restorations. "The Priesthood is an everlasting principle," he said, "and existed with God from eternity, and will to eternity, without beginning of days or end of years. The keys have to be brought from heaven whenever the Gospel is sent. When they are revealed from heaven, it is by Adam's authority."[11] In keeping with the order of heaven, there would be delegation or a chain of command through which Adam would accomplish this important work. The Prophet taught: "Christ is the Great High Priest; Adam next."[12] He also gave this explanation regarding Adam's position in authority: "The Priesthood was first given to Adam; he obtained the First Presidency, and held the keys of it from generation to generation. . . . Then to Noah, who is Gabriel: he stands next in authority to Adam in the Priesthood. . . . These men held keys first on earth, and then in heaven."[13] Hence, when John the Baptist brought the Aaronic Priesthood to Joseph Smith and Oliver Cowdery, declaring he acted under the direction of Peter, James, and John (Joseph Smith—History 1:72), we can assume Peter, James, and John also acted under someone's direction—namely, Adam or Noah or some other authorized individual. The same would be true of those who appeared on the Mount of Transfiguration (see Matthew 17:1–9), and it would be true of all who came in any dispensation.

Adam and Noah not only direct others in restoring the priesthood and its keys but they also have come themselves for varying purposes on occasion. Noah or Gabriel appeared to Zacharias, telling him of his future son, John (Luke 1:5–23). He also announced to Mary her singular privilege of becoming the mother of the Son of God (Luke 1:26–38). Both Michael and Gabriel were among those who came to Joseph Smith in this, the dispensation of the fulness of times. The Doctrine and Covenants recounts the latter-day appearances not only of Moses, Elias, and Elijah (see D&C 110) but also of Moroni; John the Baptist; Peter, James, and John; Raphael; and "divers angels, from Michael or Adam down to the present time, all declaring their dispensation, their rights, their keys, their honors, their majesty and glory, and the power of their priesthood; giving line upon line, precept upon precept; here a little, and there a little" (D&C 128:20–21). We know little of most of these visits except that they occurred and that they occurred under Adam's direction.

COORDINATING DIFFERENT SPHERES

It is interesting to contemplate the logistics of Adam's coordinating and directing the efforts of different beings from different spheres in these various restorations and visitations. Evidently Adam was in the post-earth spirit world from the time of his death until at least the time of Christ's resurrection. Since, at an earlier time, he had been given the keys to preside over the spirits of all men, he undoubtedly continued to preside over the spirits there. From his location in the post-earth spirit world, Adam must have continued to do all that he did "under the counsel and direction of the Holy One," which means he would have been in constant touch with the Savior. In addition, some of those who were sent to the earth to restore the priesthood and its keys under Adam's direction, before the first resurrection, were translated beings, such as Moses and Elijah. Joseph Smith, speaking of these translated beings, taught that "their place of habitation is that of the terrestrial order, and a place prepared for such characters He [God] held in reserve to be ministering angels unto many planets, and who as yet have not entered into so great a fullness as those who are resurrected from the dead."[14] Thus, for about three thousand years, Adam—from his abode in the post-earth spirit world—would have coordinated efforts of at least these three spheres of action. Then, after the resurrection was instituted in the meridian of time (and it seems only right that Adam would have been one of the first persons, if not the first one, resurrected after Christ), Adam's base of operation would be from wherever such righteous resurrected beings go to await the time when this earth will become celestialized and become their eternal home. Again we should remember that Adam's priesthood keys go with him—from the premortal world, through his mortal ministry, into the post-earth spirit world, and into the resurrection.

KEEPING THE DEVIL IN CHECK

The devil's obsession is to thwart the work of God, to "deceive and to blind men, and to lead them captive at his will" (Moses 4:4), to make all men "miserable like unto himself" (2 Nephi 2:27), to make "war with the saints of God, and [encompass] them round about" (D&C 76:29), to "seal [us] his" and have "all power over [us]" (Alma 34:35). In a vision Enoch saw that when Satan had temporarily succeeded in the days of Noah, "he looked up and laughed, and his angels rejoiced" (Moses 7:26). Satan looked up to mock God and rejoiced in his power. The devil does have power—within limits. As Joseph Smith taught:

> The spirits of good men cannot interfere with the wicked beyond their prescribed bounds, for Michael, the Archangel, dared not bring a railing accusation against the devil, but said, "The Lord rebuke thee, Satan."
> It would seem also, that wicked spirits have their bounds, limits, and laws by which they are governed or controlled, and know their future destiny; hence, those that were in the maniac said to our Savior, "Art thou come to torment us before the time," and when Satan presented himself before the Lord, among the sons of God, he said that he came "from going to and fro in the earth, and from wandering up and down in it;" and he is emphatically called the prince of the power of the air; and, it is very evident that they possess a power that none but those who have the Priesthood can control.[15]

The Prophet also gave this succinct explanation: "The devil has no power over us only as we permit him. The moment we revolt at anything which comes from God, the devil takes power."[16] It appears that, for the most part, we can avoid being overcome by the power of the devil by being submissive to God. There are times, however, when Satan attempts to overstep his bounds and must be held in check by someone with more power than he has. There are three occasions in the scriptural record when Adam was that someone.

A Dispute with the Devil Over the Body of Moses

Adam disputed with the devil over the body of Moses (Jude 1:9). Why? Evidently, the devil insisted that Moses die, that his body be turned over to him. Adam, however, overruled the devil and Moses was translated. Elder Joseph Fielding Smith has suggested that it was necessary for Moses and Elijah to be preserved from death "because they had a mission to perform, and it had to be performed before the crucifixion of the Son of God, and it could not be done in the spirit. They had to have tangible bodies."[17] Concerning this dispute between Adam and the devil, Elder Bruce R. McConkie has written: "It appears, then, that Satan—ever anxious to thwart the purposes of God—'disputed about the body of Moses,' meaning that he sought the mortal death of Israel's lawgiver so that he would not have a tangible body in which to come—along with Elijah, who also was taken up without tasting death—to confer the keys of the priesthood upon Peter, James, and John."[18]

As Moses was not the first to be translated from this earth, perhaps this same dispute—with the same principals—had occurred before.

Withstanding the Prince of the Kingdom of Persia

In Daniel, chapter 10, there is an account of a heavenly messenger sent to Daniel to help him understand his vision of the latter days. The messenger explained to Daniel that he had been detained because "the prince of the kingdom of Persia withstood [him] one and twenty days: but, lo, Michael, one of the chief princes, came to help [him]" (Daniel 10:13). It seems clear that the prince of the kingdom of Persia was Satan or one of his emissaries, stirring up a nation hostile to the Lord's people. Michael came to help.

Detecting the Devil When He Appeared as an Angel of Light

In reminding the Saints in 1842 of some of the marvelous events of the restoration of the gospel, Joseph Smith included an experience he had had with the devil and Michael on the banks of the Susquehanna River. The devil appeared as an angel of light. And Michael came to expose him. (See D&C 128:20.) How many other occasions have there been throughout the history of the earth when Lucifer and Michael have locked horns, as it were? It is reasonable to believe that there have been many.

ANOTHER COUNCIL AT ADAM-ONDI-AHMAN

Adam held an important meeting with his righteous posterity at Adam-ondi-Ahman three years before his death. Before the Lord's second coming, Adam will call another important meeting at that same sacred spot. Again it will be a gathering of the righteous, and again the Lord will appear. This time, however, instead of predicting "whatsoever should befall his posterity unto the latest generation," Adam will hear reports from his posterity. Of this future event, Joseph Smith taught:

> Daniel in his seventh chapter speaks of the Ancient of Days; he means the oldest man, our Father Adam, Michael, he will call his children together and hold a council with them to prepare them for the coming of the Son of Man. He (Adam) is the father of the human family, and presides over the spirits of all men, and all that have had the keys must stand before him in this grand council. This may take place before some of us leave this stage of action. The Son of Man stands before him, and there is given him glory and dominion. Adam delivers up his stewardship to Christ, that which was delivered to him as holding the keys of the universe, but retains his standing as head of the human family.[19]

Added insights are given by Joseph Fielding Smith:

> This gathering of the children of Adam, where the thousands, and the tens of thousands are assembled in the judgment, will be one of the greatest events this troubled earth has ever seen. At this conference, or council, all who have held keys of dispensations will render a report of their stewardship. Adam will do likewise, and then he will surrender to Christ all authority. Then Adam will be confirmed in his calling as the prince over his posterity and will be officially installed and crowned eternally in this presiding calling. Then Christ will be received as King of kings, and Lord of lords. We do not know how long a time this gathering will be in session, or how many sessions may be held at this grand council. It is sufficient to know that it is a gathering of the Priesthood of God from the beginning of this earth down to the present, in which reports will be made and all who have been given dispensations (talents) will declare their keys and ministry and make report of their stewardship according to the parable. Judgment will be rendered unto them for this is a gathering of the righteous, those who have held and who hold keys of authority in the Kingdom of God upon this earth. It is not to be the judgment of the wicked. When all things are prepared and every key and power set in order with a full and perfect report of each man's stewardship, then Christ will receive these reports and be installed as rightful

Ruler of this earth. At this grand council he will take his place by the united voice of the thousands who by right of Priesthood are there assembled. This will precede the great day of destruction of the wicked and will be the preparation for the Millennial Reign.[20]

Truly, that meeting at Adam-ondi-Ahman will be a high point for Adam. But the end is not yet. There is still a key role for him in the resurrection and final judgment and in the final battle with the devil and his angels.

ADAM'S ROLE IN THE RESURRECTION AND JUDGMENT

"Behold, verily I say unto you, before the earth shall pass away, Michael, mine archangel, shall sound his trump, and then shall all the dead awake, for their graves shall be opened, and they shall come forth —yea, even all" (D&C 29:26). It was the Savior who overcame death through his own death and resurrection, but evidently the keys of accomplishing the resurrection of all others are given to Adam and from him to others. President Spencer W. Kimball spoke of the keys of resurrection in the April 1977 general conference, quoting briefly from President Brigham Young. In the address from which he quoted, President Young said:

It is supposed by this people that we have all the ordinances in our possession for life and salvation, and exaltation, and that we are administering in these ordinances. This is not the case. We are in possession of all the ordinances that can be administered in the flesh; but there are other ordinances and administrations that must be administered beyond this world. I know you would ask what they are. I will mention one. We have not, neither can we receive here, the ordinance and the keys of the resurrection. They will be given to those who have passed off this stage of action and have received their bodies again, as many have already done and many more will. They will be ordained, by those who hold the keys of the resurrection, to go forth and resurrect the Saints, just as we receive the ordinance of baptism, then the keys of authority to baptize others for the remission of their sins. This is one of the ordinances we cannot receive here, and there are many more.[21]

How appropriate it is that Adam, who brought death into the world through the Fall, should be the one to call forth his posterity from the grave, to herald the resurrection with the sound of his trumpet. Inasmuch as all the dead do not arise at the same time, some even as far apart as one thousand years, that trumpet may have to sound again and again before all of Adam's children are brought forth (see D&C 88:94–102).

Resurrection and judgment are, in a sense, simultaneous events, as "your glory shall be that glory by which your bodies are quickened" (D&C 88:28). But, in addition, there will be an accounting, then commendation or otherwise, and an affirmation of our places in the varied kingdoms prepared to accommodate all mankind. As with the resurrection, undoubtedly the judgment will be a matter of keys and delegation. Elder Bruce R. McConkie has written: "The Ancient of Days, the oldest and most ancient of men, Adam our father, sits in judgment over the righteous of his race. Be it remembered that the Twelve Apostles of the Lamb, who were with the Lord in his ministry in Jerusalem, shall judge the whole house of Israel, meaning that portion of Israel who have kept the commandments, 'and none else.' (D&C 29:12.) There will be a great hierarchy of judges in that great day, of whom Adam, under Christ, will be the chief of all. Those judges will judge the righteous ones under their jurisdiction, but Christ himself, he alone, will judge the wicked."[22]

The Prophet Joseph Smith saw in vision a tender judgment scene, highlighting the role of Adam in presenting his righteous posterity to our Heavenly Father and to the Savior to receive their eternal reward. The vision is reported by Heber C. Kimball in his journal: "There Father Adam stood and opened the gate to them [the Twelve], and as they entered, he embraced them one by one and kissed them. He then led them to the throne of God, and then the Savior embraced each one of them and kissed them, and crowned each one of them in the presence of God. . . . The impression this vision left on Brother Joseph's mind was of so acute a nature, that he never could refrain from weeping while rehearsing it."[23]

During an 1861 address in the Salt Lake Tabernacle, President Kimball mentioned this same vision: "This brings to my mind the vision that Joseph Smith had, when he saw Adam open the gate of the Celestial City and admit the people one by one. He then saw

Father Adam conduct them to the throne one by one, when they were crowned Kings and Priests of God. I merely bring this up to impress upon your mind the principles of order, but it will nevertheless apply to every member of the Church."[24]

THE BATTLE OF THE GREAT GOD

Resurrection and judgment will go on during the thousand years from the time the Savior comes and the Millennium begins. "And Satan shall be bound, that old serpent, who is called the devil, and shall not be loosed for the space of a thousand years. And then he shall be loosed for a little season, that he may gather together his armies." (D&C 88:110–11.) Sadly, toward the end of the thousand years there will be those mortals on the earth who will "again begin to deny their God" (D&C 29:22). No doubt some of these will be part of the army Satan will gather at that time. The other part of his army will consist of all those spirits who have chosen to follow Lucifer. Satan will gather all who deny God, whose mentality and end are described in modern revelation: "That which breaketh a law, and abideth not by law, but seeketh to become a law unto itself, and willeth to abide in sin, and altogether abideth in sin, cannot be sanctified by law, neither by mercy, justice, nor judgment. Therefore, they must remain filthy still." (D&C 88:35.)

Satan and his "hosts of hell" will come up to battle against Michael and his armies, "even the hosts of heaven." This battle at the end of the Millennium is the final battle in the war that started in heaven. It is called the "battle of the great God" or the battle of Gog and Magog.[25] The outcome is sure. "The devil and his armies shall be cast away into their own place, that they shall not have power over the saints any more at all. For Michael shall fight their battles, and shall overcome him who seeketh the throne of him who sitteth upon the throne, even the Lamb. This is the glory of God, and the sanctified; and they shall not any more see death." (See D&C 88:112–16.)

When the battle of the great God is over and all are placed in their respective kingdoms, Adam will continue to preside over his posterity through all eternity.

NOTES

1. The day spoken of "was after the Lord's time, which was after the time of Kolob; for as yet the Gods had not appointed unto Adam his reckoning" (Abraham 5:13). The Lord instructed Abraham: "Kolob was after the manner of the Lord, according to its times and seasons in the revolutions thereof; that one revolution was a day unto the Lord, after his manner of reckoning, it being one thousand years according to the time appointed unto that whereon thou standest. This is the reckoning of the Lord's time, according to the reckoning of Kolob." (Abraham 3:4.) Adam's death fell within such a day.

2. Ezra Taft Benson, "What I Hope You Will Teach Your Children about the Temple," *Ensign* 15 (August 1985): 8.

3. Joseph Fielding Smith, *The Progress of Man* (Salt Lake City: Deseret News Press for the Genealogical Society of Utah, 1964), p. 39.

4. Speaking of his brother Alvin, the Prophet Joseph Smith said, "He was a very handsome man, surpassed by none but Adam and Seth" (*History of the Church*, 5:247; see also Genesis 5:3; D&C 107:43; 138:40).

5. *Teachings of the Prophet Joseph Smith*, comp. Joseph Fielding Smith (Salt Lake City: Deseret Book Co., 1976), p. 157.

6. Bruce R. McConkie, *A New Witness for the Articles of Faith* (Salt Lake City: Deseret Book Co., 1985), pp. 35–36.

7. *Teachings of the Prophet Joseph Smith*, pp. 158–59.

8. In *Journal of Discourses*, 16:264.

9. Adam-ondi-Ahman was named by the Lord and is located in Daviess County, Missouri (see D&C 116). Concerning the meaning of the term, Elder Orson Pratt explained: "Perhaps you may be anxious to know what 'Ondi-Ahman' means. It means the place where Adam dwelt. 'Ahman' signifies God. The whole term means Valley of God, where Adam dwelt. It is in the original language spoken by Adam, as revealed to the Prophet Joseph." (In *Journal of Discourses*, 18:343.) Adam-ondi-Ahman is a special place, not only for what has taken place there but also for what will yet take place there. It will be the site of another grand council, which will be called by Adam in preparation for the second coming of the Lord.

10. *Teachings of the Prophet Joseph Smith*, pp. 167–68.

11. Ibid., p. 157.

12. Ibid., p. 158.

13. Ibid., p. 157.

14. Ibid., p. 170.

15. Ibid., p. 208.

16. Ibid., p. 181.

17. Joseph Fielding Smith, *Doctrines of Salvation*, comp. Bruce R. McConkie, 3 vols. (Salt Lake City: Bookcraft, 1954–56), 2:110–11.

18. Bruce R. McConkie, *Doctrinal New Testament Commentary*, 3 vols. (Salt Lake City: Bookcraft, 1965–73), 3:423.

19. *Teachings of the Prophet Joseph Smith*, p. 157.

20. Joseph Fielding Smith, *The Progress of Man*, pp. 481–82. For additional commentary see Bruce R. McConkie, *The Millennial Messiah* (Salt Lake City: Deseret Book Co., 1982), pp. 578–88.

21. In *Journal of Discourses*, 15:137.

22. *The Millennial Messiah*, p. 584.

23. Quoted in Hyrum L. Andrus, *Joseph Smith, the Man and the Seer* (Salt Lake City: Deseret Book Co., 1960), p. 95. The reference cited is Heber C. Kimball's journal as quoted by Helen Mar Whitney, *Woman's Exponent* 9 (February 1, 1881): 130.

24. In *Journal of Discourses*, 9:41.

25. *Teachings of the Prophet Joseph Smith*, p. 280.

8

Stephen E. Robinson

The Book of Adam in Judaism and Early Christianity

The figure of Adam was powerful medicine in the literature of Judaism and of early Christianity, and the source of that power was the paradigmatic nature of Adam's role. He was *ha'adam*, the human being — the archetype, prototype, and pattern for all subsequent human beings. M. Eliade, among others, has shown from the evidence offered by many different cultures how powerful the figure of the original ancestor can be.[1]

In the mind of first-century Jews and Christians, what Adam was, we are; what Adam could become, we can become. Therefore, if one could alter the way Adam was perceived in the popular mind, one could change the contemporary view of the nature and function of man, of what it meant to be human. As E. Pagels notes: "Since everyone agreed that the story of Adam and Eve offered a basic paradigm for ordering human society, argument over the role of government most often took the form of conflicting interpretations of that story."[2] Pagels shows how the fifth-

Stephen E. Robinson is Associate Professor of Ancient Scripture and director of Pearl of Great Price research in the Religious Studies Center at Brigham Young University.

century church changed its understanding of the story of Adam
and Eve from an affirmation of free agency and the necessity of
voluntary choice to an affirmation of man's inability to govern
himself. Where Christians in earlier centuries had argued for
human free agency and the necessity of individual self-government
based on gospel principles,[3] Christians after Augustine rejected
both the doctrine of free agency and the possibility of individual
self-government. Consequently, they looked to the church or the
civil government to *control* humanity, to make right choices for
them, and to enforce those choices.[4] This is a prime example of
how, in religious societies or societies with a state religion, control
of the Adamic paradigm was also both theological and social control.

Such was the power of the Adamic paradigm that both sides of
a controversy would often appeal to it, just as both sides in a religious community today might still appeal to one and the same
Bible to support contradictory views. For example, the author of 4
Ezra, a determinist, blamed human failure on the sin of Adam,
who was created with a defect: "For the first Adam, burdened with
an evil heart, transgressed and was overcome, as were also all who
were descended from him. Thus the disease became permanent;
the law was in the people's heart along with the evil root, but what
was good departed, and the evil remained. . . . O Adam, what
have you done? For though it was you who sinned, the fall was
not yours alone, but ours also who are your descendants."[5] Thus,
in the pessimistic view of 4 Ezra, it was the "evil heart" with which
Adam was "burdened" by his creator that was the ultimate cause
of all human sin.

The author of 2 Baruch, however, insists that each of us is free
to make our own decisions, unburdened by the sin of Adam: "For,
although Adam sinned first and has brought death upon all who
were not in his own time, yet each of them who has been born
from him has prepared for himself the coming torment. And further, each of them has chosen for himself the coming glory. . . .
Adam is, therefore, not the cause, except only for himself, but
each of us has become our own Adam."[6]

Jesus himself used the Adamic paradigm to justify his break
with the traditions of the elders on the permissability of divorce.
Even though the law of Moses specifically permitted divorce, Jesus

argued: "Moses because of the hardness of your hearts suffered you to put away your wives: but *from the beginning* it was not so" (Matthew 19:8; italics added). In other words, man's original condition in Eden set a stronger precedent in the mind of Jesus than the subsequent legislation on Sinai. What happened in the case of our first parents is normative.

The normative power of the Adamic paradigm is manifest also in the pastoral Epistles: "But I suffer not a woman to teach, nor to usurp authority over the man, but to be in silence. For Adam was first formed, then Eve. And Adam was not deceived, but the woman being deceived was in the transgression." (1 Timothy 2:12–14.) Again the pattern set by the Adamic paradigm was called upon to justify the practice of the contemporary Church, just as in the modern Church the example of Adam and Eve are of paramount importance to the Latter-day Saint understanding of the relationship between husbands and wives and of the nature and purpose of life.

Modern secular society has difficulty in understanding how powerful the Adamic paradigm could be in other times and places, but that is because modern secular society no longer believes in Adam and Eve. The experience of the first parents has become irrelevant to modern society because modern society no longer believes there were first parents. We either have chosen other less compelling paradigms ("man is the featherless biped"—the purely scientific model) or have attempted to do away with paradigms altogether ("existence precedes essence"—the existential model).

Nevertheless, anciently the normative power of the Adamic paradigm was such that a considerable literature was spawned among both Jews and Christians in an attempt to redefine the nature of man by repainting the picture of the first man, Adam.

THE BOOK OF ADAM

According to Joseph Smith's translation of the Bible, Adam wrote a book of remembrance in which was kept a genealogy of the children of God and also the things which he wrote under the influence of the Spirit of God (see Moses 6:5, 46; see also 1:40–41). The Doctrine and Covenants records that Adam called his posterity together at Adam-ondi-Ahman to bless them and that he, "being full of the Holy Ghost, predicted whatsoever should befall his posterity unto the latest generation" (D&C 107:56). The information revealed to Adam was to be made available to Adam's posterity in the book of Enoch (D&C 107:57). This is also the view expressed in 2 Enoch, where Enoch is to preserve the writings of Adam and Seth as well as his own in the book which bears his name: "And give them the books of thy handwriting, children to children, kinsmen to kinsmen, race to race, as mediator, Enoch, of my general Michael, because thy handwriting and the handwriting of thy fathers Adam and Seth shall not be destroyed till the end of time."[7] Both Adam's prophecy of the future of the world and the book which he left to his posterity are well attested in the ancient literature.

Beginning with the rabbinic literature, we find several references to the Book of Adam in the Midrash Rabbah: "While Adam lay a shapeless mass before Him at whose decree the world came into existence, He showed him every generation and its Sages, every generation and its judges, scribes, interpreters, and leaders. Said He to him: 'Thine eyes did see unformed substance: the unformed substances [viz., thy potential descendants] which thine eyes did see have already been written in the book of Adam': viz., THIS IS THE BOOK OF THE GENERATIONS OF ADAM."[8] Notice the interesting claim that Adam, like Moses in the Pearl of Great Price, witnessed the primeval creation out of unformed substance (or "matter unorganized").

Also from the midrashim is the following: "God did not, however, tell Moses whom he should appoint, hence Moses inquired: 'To whom shall I speak?' God replied: 'I will show thee.' So what did the Holy One, blessed be He, do? He brought him the book of Adam and showed him all the generations that would arise from Creation to Resurrection, each generation and its kings, its leaders, and its prophets, saying unto him: 'I have appointed all these [for their destinies] from that time [Creation], and Bezalel, too, I have appointed from that time.' "[9] Again we have the clear belief that Adam had a knowledge of the entire history of the world from the Creation to the end and that the information was preserved in the Book of Adam. Moreover, Moses was allowed the same vision that had originally been given to Adam.

The Babylonian Talmud contains at least two references to the Book of Adam:

> But did not Resh Lakish [himself] say, What is the meaning of the verse *This is the book of the generations of Adam*? Did Adam have a book? What it implies is that the Holy One, blessed be he, showed to Adam every [coming] generation with its expositors, every generation with its sages, every generation with its leaders.[10]

> Samuel Yarhina'ah was Rabbi's physician. Now, Rabbi having contracted an eye disease, Samuel offered to bathe it with a lotion, but he said, "I cannot bear it." "Then I will apply an ointment to it," he said. "This too I cannot bear," he objected. So he placed a phial of chemicals under his pillow, and he was healed. Rabbi was most anxious to ordain him, but the opportunity was lacking. Let it not grieve thee, he said; I have seen the Book of Adam, in which is written, "Samuel Yarhina'ah [86a] shall be called 'Sage,' but not 'Rabbi,' and Rabbi's healing shall come through him."[11]

Note the common element in the rabbinic traditions that the Book of Adam recorded his predictions of future history down to the end of the world, or, in other words, "whatsoever should befall his posterity unto the latest generation" (D&C 107:56).

The so-called Book of Raziel should also be mentioned here, since it deals with many of the same themes as the Book of Adam. The book itself is a late medieval compilation of magical and mystical Jewish lore, some of which goes back to talmudic times (ca. A.D. 800). That part of the collection called the Sefer ha-Razim (Book of Secrets) relates that after the Fall, God sent the angel Raziel, whose name means "secrets of God," to Adam with a book which told him the future of the world down to its end. Raziel read passages from the book to Adam until the latter fell down in fear. But the heavenly messenger raised him up, saying, "Arise, Adam!" and gave him possession of the book which was then passed on to Adam's righteous posterity.[12] As we shall see below, the heavenly messenger(s) who raises Adam up and reveals the future or the knowledge necessary for redemption is a theme common to much of the Adam literature of antiquity.

In Christian sources, the Apostolic Constitutions mention a Book of Adam that was considered to be "pernicious and repugnant to the truth," even though it was written by "the ancient ones."[13] A Book of Adam is also mentioned as one of the apocryphal books of the Old Testament in the eighth century canon list of books called the "Sixty Books."[14] In the thirteenth century, Mechitar of Ayrivank compiled a canon list in which a Book of Adam known to him was listed among "the books which the Jews have in secret."[15] However, while mention of an ancient Book of Adam may be found in the sources, no actual text with this title has survived to modern times. Nevertheless, several other books attributed to or associated with Adam have come down to us.

Though the above are the specific witnesses to a Book of Adam, rabbinic literature in general has a few more things of interest to say about the first man. For example, the rabbis interpreted Genesis 1:27 ("So God created man in his own image, in the image of God created he him; male and female created he them") to mean that Adam and Eve were originally one perfect creation containing both male and female characteristics. When the female Eve was taken out of the male Adam, the two parts were less than perfect unless and until they could be joined together again.[16] The Zohar tells us that Eve was not Adam's first wife but that he had been married before to Lilith. Since Lilith was created out of the ground like Adam, she would not obey him but left him and became the evil spirit that causes crib death in babies. God corrected the mistake by creating Eve out of Adam's own flesh and bone so that she would be obedient to her source.[17] According to Aboda Zara 8a, Adam was the first man to offer sacrifice to God.

The early rabbis also accepted the pre-existence of souls, since they believed that all souls were created within the soul of Adam at creation though deposited in the heavens until their individual bodies were created.[18] The creation of Adam was seen as a microcosm for the creation of the world: Adam's hair was like the forests, his tears like the rivers, and so forth.[19] An expanded form of this idea appears in medieval times in the kabbalistic doctrine of Adam Kadmon (primordial man). According to this view, the created Adam, indeed creation itself, proceeds from and is patterned after a prior Adam, the divine Adam Kadmon, as Gershom Scholem explains: "In contrast to the First Man Adam, this spiritual man is called in the Zohar proper the *adam kadma'ah ila'ah* ('primordial supreme man'), and in *Tikkunei Zohar* he is called *Adam Kadmon* ('primordial man') or *Adam Kadmon le-khol ha-*

kedumim ('prototype of primordial man'). . . . This *Adam Kadmon* is the most sublime manifestation of the Deity that is to some extent accessible to human meditation."[20] Concerning this doctrine of Adam Kadmon, the same writer has observed: "The tendency to interpret human life and behavior as symbols of a deeper life, the conception of man as a *micro-cosmos* and of the living God as a *macro-anthropos*, has never been more clearly expressed and driven to its farthest consequences."[21]

The ancient Mandaeans, whose descendants still inhabit the area of the Shatt-al-Arab waterway between Iran and Iraq, also believed in the two Adams: "The earthly or bodily Adam and his sons, the Adamites, were, according to this mythology, only images of the heavenly Adam, called *Addam r(ab)ba* or Adakas (from *adam kasya* or 'hidden Adam'). The earthly Adam had a wife, called Eve (Hawwa), and there was also the heavenly Adam whose wife was called the 'cloud of light.' "[22]

Philo of Alexandria shared with the later kabbalists, Gnostics, and Mandaeans a belief that there were two Adams—the heavenly, spiritual man and the earthly, carnal man.[23] Philo interpreted the two accounts of the creation of man (Genesis 1:27 and 2:7) as describing two separate creations of two separate Adams: "Who is the 'moulded' man? And how does he differ from him who is (made) 'in accordance with the image (of God)?' The moulded man is the sense-perceptible man and a likeness of the intelligible type. But the man made in accordance with (God's) form is intelligible and incorporeal and a likeness of the archetype, so far as this is visible. And he is a copy of the original seal. And this is the Logos of God, the first principle, the archetypal idea, the pre-measurer of all things."[24]

Philo interpreted the story of Adam and Eve in completely allegorical terms along Platonic philosophical lines. As a thoroughly hellenized Jew, he interpreted the story as though it were a lesson in Platonic philosophy. For Philo, Adam symbolized *nous* (Greek for "mind"). He stood for all the higher, noble, and rational aspects of human personality. Eve, on the other hand, symbolized *aisthesis* (Greek for "sensation") and represented all the lower, physical, and emotional qualities of humans, including the appetites and passions.[25] Of course, Philo's view represents a hybrid of the language he inherited from scripture and the philosophical concepts he had adopted from the hellenistic world. While his philosophy mingled with scripture had great influence on later Christian theology, he does not represent a widespread religious view among Jews of the first century.

The cosmic or universal nature of Adam is revealed in another common tradition, namely that Adam's name represents the four points of the compass.[26] In Greek the four directions are *Anatole* (East), *Dusis* (West), *Arctos* (North), and *Mesembria* (South). Thus the name Adam could be understood as an acronym for the four directions. This was supported by the belief that the dirt used in Adam's creation was taken from the four corners of the earth. D. Cerbelaud believes that the symbolism involves Adam's body being understood as a temple and that it was therefore necessary for it to be cosmically oriented to the four points of the compass. She further suggests that since Adam's name is equivalent to the number forty-six in Jewish gematria, Jesus' statement about destroying and raising the temple (see John 2:19–22) should be interpreted symbolically as a statement concerning the replacement of the temple represented by the body of the first Adam with the temple represented by the body of Christ, the second Adam.[27]

Another topic which generated a surprising amount of commentary among the rabbis is the "garments of skins" given to Adam and Eve in the Garden of Eden. One interpretation has been that the garment of skins was the physical body itself. Another is that the first parents were dressed in the skin of the serpent of Leviathan, the great sea-monster. Since in Hebrew the word for "skin" is almost identical to the word for "light," some have suggested that the term should be read "garments of light." Others have insisted that the garments were made of wool or linen. In the Pseudepigrapha the celestial garments of Adam and Eve are often identified with the garments the righteous receive in the hereafter. Adam's garments of skins were generally perceived to have mystical qualities and were identified as high priestly garments which Adam passed down with the priesthood to his righteous posterity.[28]

The rabbis were divided on whether Adam was created mortal or immortal. It seems that there were three basic viewpoints. The first was that Adam was created immortal in the garden but was punished with death, which was hereditary in his posterity.

The second view was that Adam was created immortal but that his punishment was personal, not hereditary. That is, men die because of their own sins and not because of Adam's sin. Thus if a man were to live without sin, he would still be immortal. In fact, the rabbis pointed to Enoch and other translated individuals as examples of this kind of man. The third view was that Adam was created mortal and that his eventual death was inevitable; his sin, however, brought about violent, painful, and premature death. Had he not sinned, death would have been, after a long and happy life, a beautiful transition from this life to the next.[29] More recent theologians have pointed out that Adam cannot be considered to have been "immortal" at his creation, at least not in the strict sense, since he had the ability to die in the event of his sinning. In this sense, the state of the first Adam parallels the state of the second Adam, Christ. For in their respective gardens, Eden and Gethsemane, each had the ability to die if they so chose, but neither was under the necessity of dying.

THE APOCALYPSE (REVELATION) OF ADAM

While no book entitled the Apocalypse (Revelation) of Adam is mentioned in the surviving Jewish sources, Epiphanius of Salamis states that more than one such work was circulating among Gnostic Christians in the fourth century.[30] In 1945, a collection of Gnostic writings was found at Nag Hammadi in Upper Egypt which date to around the fourth century A.D. Among these there is indeed an Apocalypse (Revelation) of Adam (CG V, 5).[31]

In the Nag Hammadi Apocalypse, Adam, in the last year of his life, reveals to Seth the secrets of creation and the future history of the world, including the promise of a coming Savior. Bentley Layton maintains that the Apocalypse is based on some independent form of the Adam myth known to the Gnostics rather than on Genesis itself.[32] This is intriguing to Latter-day Saints especially, since our own understanding of Adam is also largely determined by an independent tradition. In the Apocalypse, Adam is approached after the Fall by three heavenly messengers who wake him from his slumber. Saying, "Arise, Adam!" they reveal to him his true origin and identity. Again we have the common theme of the raising of Adam by heavenly messengers. Usually these messengers reveal the future of the world, the esoteric knowledge needed for salvation, and / or the coming of a future Savior from the highest heavens in later times. In the Apocalypse of Adam the information and promise given to Adam by the heavenly messengers is transmitted to his posterity through Seth rather than by a general convocation of Adam's posterity.

George MacRae, among others, has argued that the theme of the promised Savior found in the Apocalypse of Adam must be pre-Christian, since he sees no evidence of Christianity in the document.[33] Other scholars resist the idea that there could have been any ancient "redeemer myth" before the appearance of Christianity in the first century. Yet among the Mandaeans, who are hostile in the extreme to the identification of Jesus as the Messiah, Adam is said to have been taught the mysteries of the cosmos and the rituals of salvation after the Fall by a heavenly messenger called Manda d'Hayye, which means "the knowledge of life."[34] For Mandaeans the promised Messiah was not Jesus but John the Baptist.

In the Apocalypse of Adam and some other Gnostic texts, the Fall is attributed not to the partaking of forbidden fruit but specifically to the separation of the male and female aspects within Adam.[35] This may be the reason why several Gnostic texts define salvation as an eternal reunion of the male and female principles within a single entity.[36]

Finally, the Nag Hammadi Apocalypse of Adam was not the only document which circulated in antiquity under that title. The Epistle of Barnabas and the Christian writers Irenaeus and Clement of Alexandria all share a common, identical passage which the Constantinople manuscript of Barnabas identifies as coming from an Apocalypse of Adam: "A sweet smelling fragrance to the Lord is a heart that glorifies the one who made it." Since this passage is not found in the Apocalypse of Adam from Nag Hammadi, it must be taken from a different Apocalypse of Adam which has not survived.

In Gnostic sources generally, though generalization is sometimes difficult, Adam is perceived as the first human—as in Judaism and Christianity—but his physical body is created by lesser beings, the archons, while his spirit comes from the realm of the Eternal Father. Since many of the Gnostic sources equate the creator, Jehovah, with Satan, true religion for Adam consists in learning to avoid the deception of the god of this world (Jehovah / Satan / Ialdabaoth) while receiving messengers from the Father in Heaven who teach him the *gnosis*, the esoteric knowledge needed for him to ascend past the archons set in his way and enter into salvation.[37]

The Gnostic Adam is created in the image of a heavenly Man. In fact, the heavenly Man, the divine model for the creation of earthly Adam, is sometimes called Geradamas or Pigeradamas, which means "the alien Adam," or the Adam from another place.[38] Thus there is in these sources, as in the Judaism and Mandaeism sources, an Adam senior, the perfect heavenly Adam, and an Adam junior, the first earthly prototype or copy.[39] According to H. Jackson, the Gnostics "coined the name Geradamas with the intent of distinguishing the heavenly Adam who, like them, was a stranger to this world, from the earthly, corporeal Adam created by and owing allegiance to the cosmic powers."[40] The idea found in 2 Enoch 32 may be related. F. Andersen comments on that passage: "This curious exegesis of Gen 3:19b," he notes, "seems to be unique. It implies that Adam, made in a heavenly Paradise from materials brought from the earth, is now sent back to his native element to live there."[41]

The Life of Adam and Eve (Apocalypse of Moses)

One of the most influential of the Adam books appears to have been a Jewish composition of the first century A.D. entitled the Life of Adam and Eve.[42] This is found in two roughly similar versions which unfortunately have quite different titles. The Latin version of the Life of Adam and Eve is known as the *Vita Adae et Evae*, but the Greek version is called the Apocalypse of Moses. The Latin version, but not the Greek, contains an account of Satan's being cast out of heaven, Adam and Eve's repentance, and the birth of Cain. The Greek version, but not the Latin, contains the story of the Fall as narrated by Eve and an account of the death and burial of Adam. The Life of Adam and Eve is a Jewish document written around A.D. 100, probably in a Hebrew original.

The familiar themes of Adam's prophecy of the future and specifically the coming of Christ are found in the *Vita* at 25–30 and 42.2, respectively. The convocation of his posterity (Adam-ondi-

Ahman) is described at 30.1–3. Also of interest in this document are the appearance of Satan as an angel of light to deceive Adam and Eve[43] and the importance of washing and anointing. When Adam and Eve are first expelled from the garden, they stand up to their necks in the Jordan and Tigris rivers, respectively, in an attempt to expiate their guilt.[44] But when Satan appears, disguised as an angel of light, Eve is deceived a second time and the attempt at penance fails. However, in the Slavonic version Eve is warned by Adam: "Take great care of thyself. Except thou seest me and all my tokens, depart not out of the water, nor trust in the words, which are said to thee, lest thou fall again into the snare."[45] Thus, properly equipped, Eve does not succumb to Satan the second time, according to the Slavonic version.

In his prophecy of the future, Adam describes the purification by water that will be available only when the Messiah comes (*Vita* 29.14), and when Adam is dying he sends Seth to fetch the oil of mercy from the tree of life in the garden, that Adam might be anointed and saved from pain and death. But Seth is turned away with the promise that Adam will receive the oil of mercy in the last days through Christ. After his death, Adam is carried off by angels and washed three times in the presence of God in the Acherusian Lake.

In this document there is an interesting variation on the theme of the heavenly messenger(s) who calls out "Adam, Arise!" Here it is Eve who cries out, "Adam, Adam, where are you? Arise! Come to me and I will show you a great secret." This image of Eve as motivator and revelator was picked up and expanded in Gnosticism, sometimes to the point where she actually becomes the heavenly messenger.[46] At other times Eve was identified, or at least associated, with the serpent as the bringer of wisdom on the one hand, or as the tool of Satan in the seduction of Adam on the other. Very early in Judaism the idea developed that Adam was saved by the wisdom of God. For example, we read in the Wisdom of Solomon 10:1–2: "Wisdom protected the first-formed father of the world, when he alone had been created; she delivered him from his transgression, and gave him strength to rule all things." In subsequent Jewish sources the wisdom of God is identified with the Torah, the law of Moses. But in Gnosticism, since the Greek word for wisdom is *sophia*, the wisdom of God became Sophia, the heavenly woman. From there it was a short step to associate the heavenly

Sophia with the earthly Eve, particularly since the wisdom (*sophia*) which saves Adam could so easily be identified with the knowledge (*gnosis*) Eve brought to Adam in the forbidden fruit.[47] The association of Eve and the serpent was supported by an unfortunate similarity in many of the Semitic languages between the name Eve and the word for "serpent" (*hawwah/hiwya* in Hebrew; *hayyat/hauyat* in Arabic; *hawah/hawyah* in Syriac).[48]

According to the Life of Adam and Eve, and those later works dependent upon it, the body of Abel could not be buried in the earth until after the body of Adam had been buried. Cain had tried to bury his slain brother but could not. Only after he who had been taken from the earth, Adam, had been buried would the earth receive the body of slain Abel.[49] After the burial of Adam, Eve instructs Seth to write down the life and teachings of Adam and Eve. The death of Eve is said to have occurred six days after that of Adam, whereupon "his rib" was returned to him.

JUBILEES

The Book of Jubilees has been called the Little Genesis, and it does relate the story of Adam and Eve. Written in the second century B.C., its purpose was to support the legislation of the law of Moses against the creeping hellenization of Judaism. Thus the stories of Adam and the patriarchs are retold from the perspective of a Torah-observing hasidic Jew, complete with an anachronistic concern for the details of the law of Moses. Little is added to the tradition concerning Adam, but the author does suggest a solution to the problem of "in the day that thou eatest thereof thou shalt surely die," pointing out that when Adam died he "lacked seventy years from one thousand years, for a thousand years are like one day in the testimony of heaven and therefore it was written concerning the tree of knowledge, 'In the day you eat from it you will die.' Therefore he did not complete the years of this day because he died in it [i.e. in the same thousand year period]."[50]

THE TESTAMENT OF ADAM

Adam was just as powerful a figure in early Christianity as he was in Judaism, and several Christian books belong to the Adam cycle. Sometime in the late third or early fourth century A.D. a

Christian author used older Jewish traditions about Adam to create the Testament of Adam. This document was very popular in the Christian church, and versions have been found in six different languages. The original language was Syriac.[51]

The Testament of Adam consists of a description of who and what praise God at which hour of the day and night, Adam's prophecy of the future of the world, and a description of the nine classes of angels and their different functions. Like the Life of Adam and Eve, the Testament of Adam adds many midrashic details about our first parents and their fall. For example, we are told that the forbidden fruit was the fig[52] and that Cain really killed Abel out of jealousy over their sister Lebuda.[53] Adam tells Seth that, before he fell, he used to hear the sounds of the angels praising God in their ranks at their appointed times and that he could hear the sound of mighty waves from the ocean above the heavens. We find an elaboration on this in 2 Enoch 31:2, which states that in Paradise the heavens were open and that Adam saw and heard everything that went on there. Of course, the standard theme of Adam's prophecy is the whole substance of the second section of the Testament of Adam, and once again the information is handed down through Seth in written form. The specific information of the prophecy centers on the Flood and the coming of Christ into the world.

It is theologically significant that in this document Adam is promised that he will eventually become a god through the merits of the promised Messiah. He says to his son, Seth: " 'He [God] spoke to me about this in Paradise after I picked some of the fruit in which death was hiding: "Adam, Adam do not fear. You wanted to be a god; I will make you a god, not right now, but after a space of many years. . . . And after three days, while I am in the tomb, I will raise up the body I received from you. And I will set you at the right hand of my divinity, and I will make you a god just like you wanted." ' "[54]

The Testament of Adam also divides history into a seven-thousand-year scheme — one thousand years from the Creation to the Flood, and six thousand years from the Flood to the end.

THE PENITENCE OF ADAM

A book called the Penitence of Adam is listed in the Gelasian Decree (sixth century A.D.) as apocryphal. At the end of the twelfth century A.D., Samuel of Ani noted a Penitence of Adam as one of the books Nestorian Christians had brought into Armenia from Syria, and in 1896 the Armenian Penitence of Adam was published by S. Josepheanz.[55] The Armenian Penitence is very similar to the Life of Adam and Eve. In the former as in the latter, Satan reveals that his animosity against Adam had its origin in the preexistence, when they were both in the presence of God.[56] Also here, as so often in the Adam literature, Adam is promised that he will be redeemed when Christ shall come into the world.

Other books of the Adam cycle found in the Armenian tradition are an Armenian version of the Life of Adam and Eve and six very short documents: History of the Creation and of the Transgression of Adam; History of the Expulsion of Adam from the Garden; History of Cain and Abel; the Promise of Seth; Adam's Words to Seth; and the Death of Adam.

THE CAVE OF TREASURES

Another early Christian composition dealing with Adam is the fourth-century work called the Cave of Treasures.[57] Widely distributed anciently, it has come down to us primarily as part of a later composite work called the Book of the Rolls.[58] The real focus of the Cave of Treasures is not Adam but Christ, and the document is a lengthy reinterpretation of Genesis from a narrowly Christian and, unfortunately, anti-Jewish point of view: the sacrament of bread and wine is read back into the Genesis account to replace the practice of sacrifice; Jesus wasn't really a Jew and wasn't really circumcized; and so forth. Beyond the Genesis material, the book is quite pedestrian, spending a great deal of time on chronology, genealogies, and the number of generations between biblical events.

A few points can be found in this book, however, that are worthy of note: Adam is said to have been created in Jerusalem; the fall of Adam and Eve, as well as the fall of Satan from heaven, was effected by removing from them their heavenly garments; Eden is understood as a mountain, with symbolic parallels to the later temple, the mountain of the Lord's house. Also, according to the Cave of Treasures, Christ was crucified over the exact spot upon which Adam had been buried, and he was crucified on the poles once used to carry the ark of the covenant. Like the Testament of Adam, this document also divides up the history of the world into seven one-thousand-year periods.

THE CONFLICT OF ADAM AND EVE WITH SATAN

A later Christian work entitled the Conflict of Adam and Eve with Satan is heavily dependent upon the Life of Adam and Eve, the Penitence of Adam, and the Cave of Treasures.[59] Originally found in an Ethiopic version, it is divided into three parts, of which only the first actually deals with Adam and Eve. In this is described the struggles Adam and Eve had with Satan *after* their expulsion from the Garden of Eden. The second part of the work is a history of the patriarchs from Adam to Melchizedek, and the third part gives a history of Israel from Moses to the birth of Christ.

THE HOMILY OF ADAM IN HADES TO LAZARUS

A late medieval composition in Old Slavonic entitled the Homily of Adam in Hades to Lazarus describes a message sent from Adam to the mortal Christ via the revivified Lazarus.[60] According to this work, when Jesus restored Lazarus to life, Lazarus brought the plea from Adam in Hades not to leave the patriarch and his righteous posterity any longer in their sufferings. The theology and the view of Hades reflected in this document are thoroughly "orthodox."

CONCLUSION

There was a rich tradition of Adam literature in ancient Judaism and early Christianity. The interest in Adam and the focus on his experiences both before and after the Fall were much more intense during those earlier periods of history than in the modern world generally, where the figure of the primal ancestor has lost its normative character. Perhaps as a result of that loss of interest, many of the ancient books attributed to or associated with Adam have not survived, among them the Book of Adam, the Book of the Generations of Adam, the Testament of the Protoplasts, the other Apocalyse(s) of Adam, and the Book of the Daughters of Adam.[61]

Among the Latter-day Saints, however, the figure of Adam largely retains its normative character. In this sense the Latter-day Saints are closer to the ancient world and to the early Church than are most of our contemporaries. Indeed, the Latter-day Saint temple endowment may be said in some sense to be our own "Book of Adam and Eve," and functions in the Latter-day Church in precisely the same way that extra-canonical Adam literature functioned in ancient Judaism and early Christianity.

It is also remarkable that Joseph Smith could reconstruct the main outlines of the ancient extra-canonical Adam literature without benefit of acquaintance with the Pseudepigrapha known to us in the twentieth century. Among the non-canonical themes found in the writings of Joseph Smith — themes confirmed to be ancient ones in light of the literature discovered only after his death — are the heavenly messengers, the raising of Adam, Adam's detection of Satan disguised as an angel of light (a false messenger), the promise to Adam of a coming Savior, the gathering of Adam's righteous posterity to receive his final blessing or testament, and Adam's prediction of future world history. In addition, the doctrine of the two Adams — the divine, heavenly Adam and the created, earthly Adam — found in many of the ancient traditions but mostly unknown to scholars until around the turn of the century, may have some application to certain cryptic remarks of Brigham Young on the subject of our primal ancestor.

NOTES

1. See "Archetypes and Repetition," in *The Myth of the Eternal Return or, Cosmos and History*, trans. W. R. Trask (Princeton University Press, 1974), pp. 3–48.

2. E. Pagels, *Adam, Eve, and the Serpent* (New York: Random House, 1988), p. 100.

3. Compare Joseph Smith's famous maxim: "I teach the people correct principles and they govern themselves" (as recalled by John Taylor, in *Journal of Discourses*, 10:57–58).

4. See Pagels's chapter on "The Politics of Paradise," in *Adam, Eve, and the Serpent*, pp. 98–126.

5. 4 Ezra 3:21–22; 7:118. See B. M. Metzger, trans., "The Fourth Book of Ezra," in James H. Charlesworth, ed., *The Old Testament Pseudepigrapha*, 2 vols. (Garden City: Doubleday, 1983–85), 1:529, 541.

6. 2 Baruch 54:15, 19. See A. F. J. Klijn, trans., "2 (Syriac Apocalypse of) BARUCH," in Charlesworth, ed., *The Old Testament Pseudepigrapha* 1:640.

7. 2 Enoch 33:9-11. See N. Forbes, trans., "2 Enoch, or the Book of the Secrets of Enoch," in R. H. Charles, ed., *The Apocrypha and Pseudepigrapha of the Old Testament*, 2 vols. (Oxford: Clarendon, 1913), 2:452.

8. Genesis Rabbah 24.2. See H. Freedman, *Midrash Rabbah: Genesis* (London: Soncino, 1939), p. 200.

9. Exodus Rabbah 40.2. See S. Lehrman, *Midrash Rabbah: Exodus* (London: Soncino, 1939), pp. 492-93.

10. Abodah Zarah 5a. See A. Cohen, *The Babylonian Talmud: Abodah Zarah* (London: Soncino, 1935), pp. 19-20. Similar passages can be found at Sanhedrin 38b, ARN 31:91, PR 23:115.

11. Baba Metzia 85b-86a. See H. Freedman, *The Babylonian Talmud: Baba Mezia* (London: Soncino, 1939), pp. 492-93.

12. Louis Ginzberg, *The Legends of the Jews*, 7 vols. (Philadelphia: Jewish Publication Society, 1937), 1:90-93; "Raziel, Book of," *Encyclopedia Judaica* (Jerusalem, New York: Macmillan, 1971), 13:159-60.

13. Apostolic Constitutions 6.16. See Roberts and Donaldson, *The Ante-Nicene Fathers*, 10 vols. (Grand Rapids: Eerdmans, 1975), 7:457.

14. See Hennecke-Schneemelcher-Wilson, *New Testament Apocrypha*, 2 vols. (Philadelphia: Westminster, 1963), 1:51-52.

15. See M. E. Stone, "Armenian Canon Lists III — the Lists of Mechitar of Ayrivank," *Harvard Theological Review* 69 (1976): 289-300.

16. See, for example, Genesis Rabbah 8.1, Erubin 18a. As noted below, this idea also recurs in an elaborated form in Gnosticism.

17. See Zohar 3.19 and 7.34. See also Ginzberg, *The Legends of the Jews* 1:64-66.

18. Ginzberg, *The Legends of the Jews* 1:55-59.

19. See Ginzberg, *The Legends of the Jews* 1:49-50.

20. G. Scholem, "Adam Kadmon," *Encyclopedia Judaica* 2:248-49.

21. G. Scholem, *Major Trends in Jewish Mysticism* (New York: Schocken, 1974), p. 269. However, as noted below, a similar doctrine was taught in Gnosticism.

22. K. Rudolph, *Mandaeism* (Leiden: E. J. Brill, 1978), p. 14.

23. Indeed, the Apostle Paul employs this same theme of the earthly and heavenly Adams in Romans 5 and 1 Corinthians 15.

24. Questions on Genesis 1.4. See also 1.8 and 2.56. The translation here is from R. Marcus, *Philo* (Cambridge: Harvard, 1971), suppl. vol. 1, p. 3.

25. Legum Allegoricum 2.2, 2.6, 3.161.

26. See 2 Enoch 30:13-15 and Sibylline Oracles 3:24-26. It is also known to Islam.

27. See D. Cerbelaud, "Le nom d'Adam et les points cardinaux," *Vigiliae Christianae* 38/3 (1984): 285–301.

28. See the notes in Ginzberg, *The Legends of the Jews* 5:103–4.

29. See the notes and discussion in Ginzberg, *The Legends of the Jews* 5:129–30. For "untimely death" in the Pseudepigrapha, see 2 Baruch 56:6.

30. Panarion 26.3. See F. Williams, *The Panarion of Epiphanius of Salamis* (Leiden: E. J. Brill, 1987), p. 88.

31. See J. M. Robinson, *The Nag Hammadi Library*, 2d ed. (San Francisco: Harper & Row, 1988), p. 277.

32. Bentley Layton, *The Gnostic Scriptures* (Garden City: Doubleday, 1987), p. 52. The point is also made by G. MacRae, "The Apocalypse of Adam," in Robinson, *The Nag Hammadi Library*, p. 277.

33. See, for example, his introduction to the Apocalypse of Adam in J. M. Robinson, *The Nag Hammadi Library* (San Francisco: Harper and Row, 1977), p. 256.

34. Rudolph, *Mandaeism*, pp. 14–15.

35. ApocAd (64:20–25). See also the Gospel of Philip 70:10.

36. As in the Gospel of Philip 68:23–26: "When Eve was still in Adam death did not exist. When she separated from him death came into being. If he again becomes complete and attains his former self, death will be no more." See also 70:10–20; 85:32–35; and Gospel of Thomas 51:21–25.

37. As, for example, in the Books of Jeu from the Bruce Codex. See C. Schmidt and V. MacDermot, *The Books of Jeu and the Untitled Text in the Bruce Codex* (Leiden: E. J. Brill, 1978).

38. See Howard M. Jackson, "Geradamas, the Celestial Stranger," *New Testament Studies* 27 (1981): 385–94.

39. See, for example, Melchizedek (IX, 1): 6–12, or the Apocryphon of John (II, 1): 8 and 15.

40. Jackson, "Geradamas," p. 391. See also note 39: "In the texts Pigeradamas is always the name of the celestial, incorporeal Adam, not the terrestrial Adam."

41. F. Andersen, "2 (Slavonic Apocalypse of) ENOCH," in Charlesworth, *The Old Testament Pseudepigrapha* 1:155. The idea that Adam was created in a heavenly garden and transported to earth is also found in the Quran (Sura 2:30, 36; 7:24).

42. See M. D. Johnson, "Life of Adam and Eve," in Charlesworth, *The Old Testament Pseudepigrapha* 2:249–95.

43. *Vita* 9.1–3, 12.1, ApMos 17.1. Here, as also in the Penitence of Adam, it is Adam (Michael) who detects Satan's deception and declares his true identity to Eve. Compare with D&C 128:20; 129:8.

44. According to Jewish tradition recorded in Yoma 87a, the *mikveh* (ritual bath) only purifies if the water reaches to the neck.

45. See L. S. A. Wells, "The Books of Adam and Eve," in Charles, *The Apocrypha and Pseudepigrapha of the Old Testament* 2:135.

46. See, for example, the Hypostasis of the Archons 89:11–13: "And the spirit-endowed woman came to him and spoke with him, saying, 'Arise, Adam.' " Also, On the Origin of the World 115:30–116:8.

47. See one of many possible examples in the Apocryphon of John 20–23.

48. See A. J. Williams, "The Relationship of Genesis 3.20 to the Serpent," *Zeitschrift für die alttestamentliche Wissenschaft* 89 (1977): 357–74 and S. Robinson, *The Testament of Adam* (Chico, California: Scholar's Press, 1982), p. 142.

49. This conflicts, however, with the rabbinic traditions (Midrash Rabbah on Deuteronomy 4:41, and elsewhere) that Adam buried Abel and with Josephus' statement that Cain had buried him.

50. Jubilees 4:30. See O. S. Wintermute, trans., "Jubilees," in Charlesworth, *The Old Testament Pseudepigrapha* 2:63–64.

51. See S. E. Robinson, trans., "Testament of Adam," in Charlesworth, *The Old Testament Pseudepigrapha* 1:989–95.

52. The fruit is variously described as wheat, the fig, dates, and grapes (Apocalypse of Abraham 23:6, 3 Baruch 4:8). The identification of the fruit with the apple comes from reading the Latin version of Genesis, where the last word of the serpent, "evil," is in Latin *malum*. *Malum* is also a Latin word for "apple."

53. This sister of Cain and Abel is also called Awan in Jubilees 4:1 and Noaba in Pseudo-Philo 1:1.

54. Testament of Adam 3:2, 4. See Robinson, "The Testament of Adam," p. 994. Compare with 2 Enoch 42:3, where Adam is (merely) promised Paradise.

55. An English translation by J. Issaverdens followed in 1901, *The Uncanonical Writings of the Old Testament* (Venice: Armenian Monastery of St. Lazarus). However, the definitive work on the Penitence and other Armenian Adam literature is M. Stone, *Armenian Apocrypha Relating to Patriarchs and Prophets* (Jerusalem: Israel Academy of Sciences, 1982). See also W. L. Lipscomb, "The Armenian Apocryphal Adam Literature" (Ph.D. diss., Columbia University).

56. This is also the tradition of the Quran (Sura 2:34, 20:115–17).

57. See E. A. W. Budge, *The Book of the Cave of Treasures* (London: Religious Tract Society, 1927).

58. M. D. Gibson, *Apocrypha Arabica* (Studia Sinaitica 8; London, 1901).

59. S. C. Malan, *The Book of Adam and Eve* (London: Williams and Norgate, 1882). See also E. C. Quinn, *The Quest of Seth for the Oil of Life* (Chicago: University of Chicago Press, 1962).

60. No author listed, "The Homily of Adam in Hades to Lazarus," *The Slavonic and East European Review* 10 (1931): 244–52.

61. See the discussion in Robinson, *The Testament of Adam*, pp. 15–16.

9

Roger R. Keller

Adam: As Understood by Four Men Who Shaped Western Christianity

The original purpose of this chapter was to examine Adam as he was understood in traditional Western Christianity from the Council of Nicaea in A.D. 325 until the Restoration that began in A.D. 1820. But how does one recount fifteen hundred years of theological thought about Adam in the Catholic and Protestant traditions? As the list of writers who could have been considered grew, it became apparent that a survey was simply impossible. There needed to be some way to convey to the reader what the majority of Christendom have believed without having to convey the thought of a dozen major thinkers.

In the end, the answer was relatively simple. In the time span in which we are interested there are four theologians, giants in their times, to whom every subsequent author was forced to refer. While such later authors may have tinkered with the machinery, they added few truly new insights to the work of these four. It therefore seems best to examine carefully the thought of these four

Roger R. Keller is Associate Professor of Church History and Doctrine at Brigham Young University.

shapers of Western Christianity —namely, Saint Augustine, Saint Thomas Aquinas, Martin Luther, and John Calvin—since in the end most of western theological thought about Adam, that thought which would be found among Catholics and Protestants, was molded by these four men.

Augustine provided the base from which all traditional western systematic theology began. He set the pattern for issues that were to be examined as well as the method by which they were to be considered.

Thomas Aquinas shaped Catholic theology for centuries. His *Summa Theologiae* was *the* theological study manual for virtually every Catholic priest until Vatican II in the 1960s. Even now, no Catholic theologian can be taken seriously who does not stand in dialogue with Aquinas.

Martin Luther is the bridge from Catholicism to Protestantism. He taught that people must return to the scriptures and let these records speak anew. His writings are enjoyable —far from sterile —and his humanity shows through virtually every line.

John Calvin was the systematic theologian *par excellence* of the Reformation. He put every doctrine in its proper place, and while Calvin's work does not have the warmth of Luther's, it does have a cohesiveness that Luther's writings lack.

Thus, Catholicism was and continues to be primarily influenced by Augustine and Aquinas—and even Luther and Calvin had to deal with these two. Similarly, Protestant theology can never travel far from Calvin and Luther, no matter what the denominational affiliation. Protestant writers may continue the thought of these two reformers, or they may violently reject their positions, but they can never escape their influence. For the above reasons, we will explore traditional Western Christianity's understanding of Adam through the eyes of these four men.

As we proceed we will discover that each author had certain issues and presuppositions in his environment which shaped the way in which he dealt with the subject of Adam. Augustine, for example, was influenced by Platonic and Neoplatonic philosophy and devoted extensive space to the issues of procreation and punishments for sin. Aquinas, on the other hand, used Aristotle as his foundational philosopher and was mostly concerned with explicating the concepts of the "image of God," the temptation, and the ensuing punishments. By contrast, Luther and Calvin were principally concerned with explicating the biblical story line by line and thus dealt with a much broader set of issues. Luther, therefore, commented broadly on the "image of God," the meaning of the trees in the garden, marriage, procreation, the temptation, our first parents' excuses, and the punishments meted out for sin. Calvin focused primarily on marriage and divine punishments.

In examining the views of these four men, it is hoped that readers will not simply look for the differences between our own Latter-day Saint theological tradition and the traditions of the authors considered here. Much more beneficial is to recognize the sacred truths that the Lord has preserved in the traditions which were the forerunners of the Restoration. The Father never leaves his children without guiding lights. The inspiration and guidance received by the men whose writings we will examine laid the groundwork which enabled the Restoration to occur by keeping ever before God's people the atonement of Jesus Christ, which answered the transgression of Adam and gave hope to the human family.

To see clearly what these four authors did with the scriptural narratives concerning Adam, we will examine each author's views individually. As noted above, they do not all treat every element of the Adam narrative. Thus, we will examine those issues which each author felt were important for his day and time.

Saint Augustine (a.d. 354–430)

Out of Nothing

For Augustine, God has always existed and there was never anything apart from him until he created it. All created entities were brought into being by God from nothing, and thus all creation is different from God. God is independent of his creation and does not require its existence in order to be complete in himself.[1] How many ages passed before man was created, Augustine does not know, but he implies that he questions the six-day creative framework.[2] He raises the question of whether the angels might have assisted in the Creation but says that here too he does not know and therefore ascribes all creative and originating activity to

God.[3] The Creation is good because God has placed all things in their appropriate rank and given each its own internal harmony.[4]

The Creation of Man

When he turns to the creation of man, Augustine's first concern is to state his understanding of "the image of God" in man. As with all the authors we will consider, Augustine does not conceive of the image in physical terms. Instead, God's image is to be found in a soul endowed with intelligence and reason. In this, man is like God and wholly unlike other created beings. Augustine leaves open the question of whether this soul was created before God "breathed" it into the body or whether it was created at the time of the "breathing."[5]

Augustine's principal concern is with the soul, and thus his comments on the body are limited. He does, however, make it clear that he does not believe that Adam was created with a spiritual body which degenerated into an animal body when he sinned.[6] The body was created from the dust of the earth[7] and enlivened by the soul, which made it a "soul-informed body." It could ultimately become a "Spirit-informed body" fit to live in the presence of God.[8] As long as the soul was in relation to God it was immortal, not by nature but by its relationship to its creator.[9] Hence, the soul which God created from nothing, and which therefore was not of his divine nature, was not subject to death in Adam and Eve's original perfection. In that perfection they had a perfect love of God, no desire to sin, and no desire for anything which they did not have.[10] They desired what God desired and lived in true gladness in the presence of God.[11] All this they did out of love and not out of fear of punishment.[12]

Eve

In preparation for his commentary on the major topic of procreation, Augustine turns to the relationship between Adam and Eve and discusses Eve's creation from Adam's rib, a creation which took place not carnally but by the invisible power of God.[13] Eve was not created as was Adam, that is, from the dust of the earth, but rather from the very material of Adam himself. This was done that there might be a unity in society, a harmonious bond of family affection between all of Adam's progeny.[14] By creating Eve out of Adam, God demonstrated how close the bond between husband and wife should be.[15] The wife is the indispensable helper of Adam, the one without whom there could be no generation of their kind.

Procreation

But could that generation take place in the garden before man fell? Augustine's answer is a resounding yes! Adam and Eve were not given a command they could not fulfill when they were told to multiply and replenish the earth. God created two sexes for the purpose of procreation.[16] Children were a part of the glory of marriage,[17] and Adam and Eve would have had children without the sorrow of labor pains or death.[18] If anyone were to say that generation could not occur before the Fall, they would be saying that sin was necessary to complete the full number of the saints whom God intended to bring into existence.

The procreative act would have taken place without lust. It would have been an act motivated by the will and by reason, those entities in which man bears the image of God.[19] Fertilization would have occurred differently than it does now, for the woman would have remained a virgin. "To be sure, the seed could be introduced in the same way through which the menses can be emitted."[20] Thus, procreation was a principal purpose for which man and woman were created.

The Temptation

Having established what life might have been like had Adam not fallen, Augustine turns to the question of what happened to human life as the result of the Fall. In dealing with the temptation of our first parents, he is most concerned to protect God from any suspicion that he somehow created imperfect and evil beings in Adam and Eve. They did not sin because there was evil in their nature. Instead, Satan's attack on them was designed to instill in them a dissatisfaction with what they had, thereby leading them to an act of sin.[21] The will to sin, however, was created in them by

Satan, not God. What made the will evil, and thus led to overt sin, was the will's defection from God.[22] Adam and Eve turned toward themselves in pride and away from God. They preferred themselves to God.[23] They listened with pleasure to the promise from Satan, "Ye shall be as god."[24]

Satan first attacked Eve because he did not believe that Adam could be easily persuaded directly. Thus he approached the weaker of the two, thinking it easier to corrupt Adam through Eve.[25] Eve was deceived by the enticements of Satan, but Adam was not. However, he could not bear the thought of being parted from his wife and therefore sinned, being deceived only about "the judgment which would be passed on his apology."[26] Even so, he too fell because he was secretly corrupted, having turned toward himself.[27]

The Sin

The awful element in the first sin, according to Augustine, was that there was no reason to do it. Every possible need of our first parents had been met, and the command to abstain from one tree out of the entire garden was miniscule.[28] "The iniquity of violating it was all the greater in proportion to the ease with which it might have been kept."[29] However, having eaten, Adam and Eve were then able to discern between the good they had lost and the evil into which they had fallen. They recognized that they were now naked of the grace which the Lord had given them, and this led to their shame at their bodily nakedness, a nakedness now motivated by lust.[30] When confronted by God with their disobedience, they did not go as far as Cain did in denying their actions; instead, they sought to blame others for them. They themselves were not really responsible.[31] The Lord, however, did not accept such rationalizing. He had told them what the result of disobedience would be, and that the Lord's word does not return empty to him.

The Punishments

As a result of sin, Augustine asserts, God abandoned man to man's own desires.[32] Adam and Eve's flesh, which had previously been obedient to their wills, began to torment them by its insubordination.[33] Also, the penalty of death was enacted. Originally, man could have moved from life to immortality without passing through death.[34] Having sinned, however, man dies both in soul and in body. Augustine does not view these two deaths as simultaneous. The soul died immediately due to its separation from God, and thus the Lord asks Adam where he is in order to cause Adam to consider his state without God. Bodily death occurred later ("earth thou art"), but the death threatened by God if Adam and Eve sinned was the death of the whole person, that is, body and soul. Though sequential, the full judgment of death is eventually meted out.[35] Infants are subject only to the first death, not to eternal damnation. "And if infants are delivered from this bondage of sin by the Redeemer's grace, they can suffer only this death which separates soul and body; but being redeemed from the obligation of sin, they do not pass to that second endless and penal death."[36]

None of this was accidental; God foresaw it all.[37] But he permitted man to fall knowing that man's seed, aided by divine grace, would one day conquer Satan, thereby bringing even greater glory on the whole of Adam's posterity.[38] Along with the potential glory, Adam also transmitted his curse to his posterity. Since like produces like, once Adam fell his offspring did likewise.[39] The basic harmony of a society produced from one individual is violated in the Fall, and thus the legacy of Adam is a legacy of violence. But even so, as Augustine views it, it is not a legacy without hope.

> For not even lions or dragons have ever waged with their kind such wars as men have waged with one another. But God foresaw also that by His grace a people would be called to adoption, and that they, being justified by the remission of their sins, would be united by the Holy Ghost to the holy angels in eternal peace, the last enemy, death, being destroyed; and He knew that this people would derive profit from the consideration that God had caused all men to be derived from one, for the sake of showing how highly He prizes unity in a multitude.[40]

Man's Hope

Thus, Augustine concludes, the real hope of mankind lies in Jesus Christ. He is the last Adam who wears the spiritual body to which we can look forward as we take his life upon us. We already wear the heavenly image through the grace and pardon of the Mediator, Jesus Christ, but this is only a foretaste of what is yet to come. We will receive bodies in the resurrection that surpass the glory of our first parents' bodies before they sinned. They had to use food to remain alive, even though they were perfect. However, in the resurrected state, having been created in the image of the second Adam, we will not need food but will live by the quickening Spirit of God, "for not the power, but the need, of eating and drinking is taken from these [resurrected] bodies. And so they will be spiritual, not because they shall cease to be bodies, but because they shall subsist by the quickening spirit."[41]

Thus, the cycle is complete. Man moves from created perfection, through the state of fallen man, finally to return to the presence of God as one perfected in Jesus Christ.

SAINT THOMAS AQUINAS (CA. A.D. 1225–1274)

The Image of God

Aquinas believed, as did Augustine, that the "image of God" in man relates to man's rationality or intelligence. For Aquinas, only intelligent creatures can properly be spoken of as bearing God's image, and angels bear the image more perfectly than men.[42] The image is found in both the male and the female, and it lies in the soul in so far as the soul stands in relation to God.[43] The only *true* image of God is found in the firstborn of the Father, Jesus Christ. Man's image is not quite so close to God's as is Christ's. Man is certainly *in* the image of God, since man bears a likeness to the original, but man is also *after* the image because the likeness is imperfect. Hence, one should never think that the image implies equality with God; rather, it reflects a distant approximation to the original. It is God who put the spiritual image in man, and thus man is subordinated to God.[44]

Aquinas also considers the way in which the image of God might relate to the body. He concludes, quoting Augustine, that due to the body's shape and vertical posture it is more suited to the contemplation of the heavens than other body forms. Thus, the body contains a trace of the image of God which is fundamentally lodged in the soul.[45]

Finally, Aquinas sees three tiers to the image.

> Thus God's image can be considered in man at three stages: the
> first stage is man's natural aptitude for understanding and loving
> God, an aptitude which consists in the very nature of the mind,
> which is common to all men. The next stage is where a man is ac-
> tually or dispositively knowing and loving God, but still imper-
> fectly; and here we have the image by conformity of grace. The
> third stage is where a man is actually knowing and loving God
> perfectly; and this is the image by likeness of glory. . . . The first
> stage of image then is found in all men, the second only in the
> just, and the third only in the blessed. . . .
> . . . God's image is found equally in both man and woman as
> regards that point in which the idea of "image" is principally real-
> ized, namely an intelligent nature. . . .
> . . . But as regards a secondary point, God's image is found in
> man in a way in which it is not found in woman; for man is the
> beginning and end of woman, just as God is the beginning and
> end of all creation.[46]

The Creation of Man

Having dealt with the question of the image of God in man,
Aquinas then turns to man himself. He notes that man is a special
creation of God and is thus the result of the activity of the whole
Godhead ("Let us . . .").[47] Despite this, however, man is not
wholly of the heavens. His soul is composed of spiritual substances, but his body is composed of the lower elements of creation, that is, of earth and water, or "slime." Thus, in his very person man is a microcosm of the created universe, combining in
himself both the spiritual and the earthy.[48]

Augustine left open the question as to whether the soul was
created before the body and was breathed into the body later, or
whether it was created at the time of God's "breathing." Aquinas,
on the other hand, answers this question by asserting that the
body and soul are inextricably bound to one another. It is the
soul's nature to be the form of the body, and consequently it could
not have been created apart from that which it was to actuate. It
must have been created *in* the body.[49] God's "breathing" does
mean to make a spirit or soul but only in conjunction with the
body.[50]

On the other side, the body was created to serve the rational soul, and it is of the earth because the soul, whose heavenly material is unimpressionable, needs the senses to gain knowledge of truth.[51] While agreeing with Augustine that angels may have helped somewhat in the creation of man by gathering the substances from which he was formed, Aquinas emphatically asserts that God alone formed both the body and soul of man. Only God could make a form from matter when there was no previous form to serve as a model.[52]

Man's Perfections

As created, man was perfect, according to Aquinas. Man had all knowledge of that which was naturally knowable. For example, he knew all there was to know about the animals as he named them. In intellectual or "academic" knowledge Adam would not have grown. He would have, however, increased in his experiential knowledge of the natural realm. Thus, nothing that should have been subject to him could have opposed him.[53] By contrast, he would have continued to grow in supernatural knowledge through the medium of revelation, even as the angels themselves increase in knowledge.[54] Adam's body was immortal, but not because of any natural characteristic in it. Instead, the body's immortality arose from God's having equipped the soul with a force capable of preserving the body from decay as long as the soul was submissive to God.[55] Further, man was perfectly virtuous, for the virtues are nothing more than a set of perfections produced when the reason or soul is subject to God and when the lower powers in man are subject to reason.[56]

Paradise

Aquinas next considers the Garden of Eden, or Paradise, as he calls it. Its location was in the noblest spot in the world. Since the east is on the right side of heaven, according to Aristotle, and the right side is nobler than the left, God suitably locates Eden to the east.[57] The reason that no geographers ever mention Eden is access to it is cut off by mountains and deserts, and its location is therefore unknown.[58] In the garden man was given the joyous work of caring for the garden. The work would have been good for man, since Paradise was created for man's good.[59] In the garden was the tree of life, which fortified the body, and although it could not give immortality, it could sustain man's life for an extended but finite length of time.[60]

Eve

Aquinas indicates that it was also in the garden that Adam was introduced to Eve, who had been taken from a rib in his side. God created Eve in this way, first, to emphasize the dignity of man. In his likeness to God, Adam is the one from whom the whole of his kind will arise, just as God is the One from whom the whole of the universe arose. Second, by creating Eve from Adam's rib God ensured that man would love the woman and stay with her, an important fact, since human couples stay together for life.[61] Third, it was appropriate that Eve be made from the rib, for it emphasized her essentially equal relationship with the man. She was neither his superior nor his slave, as she might have considered herself had she been created from either his head or his feet. Fourth, there is a typological reference in Eve's creation to the creation of the church which arose from the sacraments, the blood and water, which flowed from Christ's side.[62]

Eve was to serve as Adam's helper in the realm of procreation, for any other role could have been accomplished more efficiently by a man.[63] This last statement points to Aquinas' belief that woman was subject *by nature* to man, since the power of rational discernment was stronger in men than in women.[64] Thus, even in the garden, Adam is head of the woman.

Procreation

Since he proposes that Eve was created to be Adam's helper in procreation, Aquinas looks closely at what that would have meant in the garden. He holds, as did Augustine, that procreation was possible in the garden during the innocence of our first parents. He reasons that the very presence of the sexual organs indicates this reality, just as the presence of eyes and ears indicates that man could see and hear.[65] Moreover, to believe that man could not pro-

create in the state of innocence would have made sin urgently necessary.[66] Procreation was essential, and this is emphasized by the
double blessing given to Adam and Eve. The blessings stress that,
through Adam and Eve's procreative activity, the number of the
elect was to be filled, and the blessings also divert any suggestion
that there might be sin in the begetting of children.[67] In giving birth
to such offspring, there would have been no pain.[68] In addition,
intercourse would not have been motivated by lust, in which
reason did not temper desire. However, the absence of lust would
not have meant that the pleasurable sensation of intercourse
would have been lost. In reality it would have been heightened,
due to the purity of human nature and the pure sensitivities of the
body.[69]

The Temptation

Following a discussion of the condition of Adam and Eve in
their pristine state, Aquinas considers their fall and punishment.
Essentially, he agrees at most points with what Augustine held.
Adam and Eve's inner conceit preceded external sin, and thus the
first sin was pride.[70] They sought their own superiority, but this
was not the result of the flesh opposing the spirit. Instead, it was
because the spirit craved a nonmaterial good above its nature.[71]
Adam and Eve's itch "to know" caused an inordinate desire for
superiority.[72] Interestingly, Aquinas says that they did not sin in
wanting to be like God but in wanting to have knowledge like
God's, by which they could determine what was right and wrong
for themselves. They sought to achieve happiness by their own
powers. "The sin is not in simply wanting to be like God by
knowledge, but in wanting it inordinately, that is, above one's
measure."[73]

Whose sin was worse — Adam's or Eve's? If one considers the
question on an individual basis, Aquinas reasons, then Adam's
was worse, for he was the stronger of the two. If considered on a
generic level, then the sin was equal, for both sinned because of
pride. However, if one considers the sequence of sin, then Eve's
was worse. In addition, she sought the image of God directly
against God's will, while Adam sought it by his own power. Furthermore, Eve not only sinned herself but suggested sin to Adam,

thereby sinning against both God and man. Finally, as Augustine also suggested, Adam sinned in "friendly goodwill," agreeing to offend God rather than a friend.[74] However, Aquinas makes it clear that it was Satan who was the real agent of temptation. The woman was only his instrument in the process.[75]

The Punishments

In consequence of their sin, what were Adam and Eve's punishments? In answering this question, Aquinas says that the submission of the body to the soul was not something given to our first parents in their natures in the garden; rather, such submission was maintained by divine grace, and loss of the latter precipitated the loss of the former.[76] In addition, Adam and Eve lost paradise. They were cast out and forced to labor under a human nature without divine grace to assist it.[77] The woman was to have weariness during pregnancy and pain in childbirth. Further, she was to be subject to man's domination, submitting her will to his. Man was confronted with the barrenness of the soil and the drudgery of labor through which he would gain his food, as well as with the various hindrances to cultivation (e.g., weeds).[78] Both were confronted with disease and bodily defects due to the flesh's rebellion against reason.[79]

Death also entered the scene. In one sense it was natural, since the body was made of perishable materials, but in another sense it was truly penal. Adam and Eve lost the divine gift of grace which had preserved the body unblemished prior to their sin.[80] Yet God did not wholly desert them, for he made them clothing, partly to protect them, in their diminished state, from the elements and partly to cover the members of the body wherein the rebellion of the flesh against the spirit is most evident.[81]

Posterity

According to Aquinas, the sin of Adam and Eve and the attendant punishments affected not only them but also their entire posterity, even to the degree that an infant, needing to be cleansed of some infection, is in need of baptism.[82] The reason that we are participants in Adam's sin is we are all contaminated by the will of our first parent, a contamination which is passed through the male semen from generation to generation.[83] Paul says that through one *man* sin entered the world. A woman does not pass on original sin; only the man does.[84] Thus, Jesus is without original sin, for while he takes upon himself the material body derived from Adam, he does not receive the taint of original sin since his Father is God and his mother cannot pass it on. Christ is, therefore, able to be the second Adam who removes the sin of the first Adam[85] for those who cling to Christ as Lord.[86]

MARTIN LUTHER (A.D. 1483–1546)

The Sabbath

For Luther, the world was created in six days,[87] with man, the last creation, created uniquely for the knowledge and worship of God. The establishment of the Sabbath proves this, for had Adam not sinned, he would have instructed his family about the will and worship of God on that day. On the Sabbath, he would have glorified God, worshipped him, and offered sacrifice to him. He would have been busy with the word of God.[88]

"Let Us . . ."

The special nature of man, in Luther's view, caused God to take counsel within himself, and thus he said, "Let us make . . ." Man is the product of God's special plan and providence.[89] Like Aquinas, Luther understands the phrase, "Let us," to point to the plurality within the divine essense. Here is the mystery of the faith. We deal with one God, who is simultaneously Father, Son, and Holy Ghost. This phrase is a sure testimony to and proof of the doctrine of the Trinity.[90] While Luther contends, against Augustine, that the world was not made in a moment, he adds an interesting personal comment when he considers the creation of man. When God said, "Let us make . . . ," that included all whom God intended to create, although they did not come into view all at once. All things are present to God. There is no past, present, or future. God is outside the scope of time.[91] This suggests that in Luther's view, at least from the perspective of man, there might have been a period of time when we existed before our mortal lives.

The Image of God

Luther's approach to the image of God in man is also different from that seen in the writings of either Augustine or Aquinas. He is not concerned so much with how the image lodges in man but with how it affects man in his relationship with God. Thus he begins his discussion with the statement that since we are fallen men, we cannot really understand the image of God in our present state.[92] Only as we begin to experience redemption in Jesus Christ, and thus the beginnings of the restoration of the image of God in ourselves, can we begin to see dimly the essence of the image as it affected Adam.[93]

Having said this, however, Luther indicates that we can state some of the characteristics of both Adam and Eve[94] which reflected the divine image. They knew God and believed he was wholly good. They lived a completely godly life without any fear of death or danger. They were content with God's favor.[95] They possessed eternal life,[96] were completely engulfed by God's goodness and justice,[97] and had a complete understanding of heaven, earth, and the entire creation.[98] They were created to live with God finally in heaven, and in the meantime were to testify of him, to thank him, and to obey his word.[99] Such righteousness did not come from outside of the two. It was truly a part of their nature. For them to believe, love, and know God was as natural to them as sight was to the eye.[100] Finally, the image of God in Adam and Eve was an intimation that God would reveal himself in Jesus Christ, the real image of God.[101]

The Creation of Man

Adam, however, was not a man removed from the earth, Luther holds. He was a living being who was a compound of the brutes and the angels.[102] In his bodily form, he was nothing but a lump of earth before he was formed by the Lord into the most beautiful of creatures who had a share in immortality.[103] His body was similar to that of the animals.[104] He would have eaten, drunk, and procreated in the garden. There would have been conversion of food, "but not in such a disgusting manner as now."[105] There would have been no stench connected with excrement. Everything would have been beautiful and would have given no offense to any of the senses. Yet this would have still been *physical* life.[106]

In addition, Adam had a dependable knowledge of the stars and astronomy.[107] His eyesight would have exceeded that of the lynx or the eagle, and he would have had such strength that he would have treated the lions and bears like puppies.[108] He lived in peace with all the creatures, and his body was obedient to him, containing no evil inclinations or lust.[109] The tree of life would have preserved our first parents' perpetual youth, and they would have had bodies unimpaired by any hurt or disease until such time as they were translated from a physical to a spiritual, bodily life.[110]

But for all this, Adam was created in a middle state, halfway between the angels and the animals. He could have become immortal, for he was without sin, and thus he could have been translated to a deathless life. On the other hand, he could fall into God's curse, into sin, and into death, which is, from Luther's perspective, what happened. Here Luther adds a caution typical of him. He says that it is not our right or role to inquire too closely into why God willed to create man in such a middle state.[111]

Paradise

Following his discussion of man, Luther turns to the relationship between Adam and his place in the garden, particularly as that place related to the tree of the knowledge of good and evil and the tree of life. His treatment and understanding of the trees is unique. He sees the tree of the knowledge of good and evil as having been created to provide man with a way to express his reverence and worship to God by obeying the word and by not eating from the tree. The tree is Adam's altar. It is the place of obedience, of recognition of God's word and will, of giving thanks to God, and of calling on him to assist in resisting temptation. Thus, Luther says, "Let us learn that some external form of worship and a definite work of obedience were necessary for man, who was created to have all the other living creatures under his control, to know his Creator, and to thank Him."[112] Possibly the tree was really a grove of trees where Adam and his descendants could go each Sabbath, first to be refreshed from the tree of life and then to praise God and thank him for granting them dominion over creation.[113] In all this there was nothing laborious or difficult required of Adam.[114]

The presence of the tree of knowledge of good and evil further demonstrates that the church was established before the home, for Eve had not yet been created.[115] Luther suggests that after Eve's creation, on the first Sabbath in the garden, Adam preached to Eve, telling her that they should obey God's word to them, and perhaps even led her by the tree as they talked.[116] By nature the tree of knowledge was not deadly. Rather, it had a deadly nature toward man because God through his word had given it this property.[117] Similar to the tree of knowledge, the tree of life had no power of its own to give life, except as it was given such power by the potency of the word of God.[118] For Luther, the word is a powerful concept, representing God's creative, active power. What the word declares is either life-giving or death-dealing. In the end, the word in Luther's theology is Jesus Christ, the Word Incarnate.

Luther does not speculate about the location of the garden, for even though it was known (yet still inaccessible) to Adam's descendants for a time, the garden no longer exists. The Flood destroyed it along with everything else on the earth.[119] Thus, while Aquinas talks about the garden as being cut off from man today by mountains and deserts, Luther simply denies its present existence. In its original state, Paradise was God's garden or temple for Adam.[120] It had finer, better, and more delightful foods than the rest of the earth, which, though also beautiful, supplied food for the animals.[121] Thus, Paradise was a place uniquely designed for man and his well-being. For Adam, Paradise was not only a place but also a state—a state of peace and freedom from fear—as well as the place in which God could give all the good gifts associated with a lack of sin.[122] But life in the garden did not preclude work, for life is not designed for the purpose of leisure. The "idle" life of monks and nuns, as Luther had experienced it, was to be condemned. Adam would have farmed a small plot of aromatic herbs, an act which would have been as enjoyable and fulfilling as play is to us.[123]

Eve

Following the Genesis sequence, Luther turns to a discussion of
Eve and her role in the plan of God. He notes that Eve was full of
the knowledge of God in her own nature and was suited to live the
same kind of life that Adam lived in the garden. She was not inferior to Adam in her qualities of mind or body. She was created to
be useful for procreation.[124] Luther notes that, in the Hebrew,
Adam is *ish* (man) and Eve is *ishah* (woman), a she-man, a heroic
woman, who performs manly deeds.[125] Having said this, however,
Luther also holds that while the woman was similar to the man in
justice, wisdom, and happiness, she was still not equal to man in
glory and prestige. The male is like the sun, the woman like the
moon, and the animals like the stars. She is not excluded from the
glory of human nature, but she is inferior to the male.[126] What
then is the woman's role? She is the companion of man, a thought
which Luther sees as extremely important in the face of the practice of celibacy in the Roman church.

Eve was created in a way no less wonderful than was Adam,
for they were both created through the word of God.[127] Adam was
created from the dust of the earth, and Eve was created from a rib
of Adam's which still had flesh on it, for Adam says that she is
"*flesh of my flesh* and bone of my bone."[128] This knowledge was
not natural but was given to him by the Holy Ghost. It was a spiritual knowledge.[129] Thus, with the creation of Eve, the home was
established, for God brought to the lonely Adam his wife, a being
whom he needed that there might be increase in the human family.[130]

Marriage

It is interesting to see how Luther revised the perceptions of
marriage in his day and time. He makes the following very personal comments:

> What has come into the minds of the tools of Satan and the
> enemies of Christ? They have denied that there is any chastity in
> marriage, and they have declared that those most suited for the
> ministry of a congregation are celibates, because Scripture says

(Lev. 11:44): "You shall be pure." Are spouses impure? Is God the author and establisher of impurity when He Himself brings Eve to Adam? . . .

When I was a boy, the wicked and impure practice of celibacy had made marriage so disreputable that I believed I could not even think about the life of married people without sinning. . . . Thus many who had been husbands became either monks or priests after their wives had died. Therefore it was a work necessary and useful for the church when men saw to it that through the Word of God marriage again came to be respected and that it received the praises it deserved.[131]

Luther gives a new theological meaning to marriage as he discusses the marriage of Adam and Eve. He notes that God *brought* Eve to Adam. The first marriage was without the "epileptic and apoplectic lust of present-day marriage." It was a chaste and delightful affair, and even in their "coming-together" there would have been honor and sacredness. Since Adam didn't snatch at Eve but waited until the Lord brought her to him, marriage is not something to be looked down upon. What God has joined together no man should separate or denigrate. Where there is a lawful joining together of a man and a woman, there one finds a divine ordinance and institution.[132] Thus, in marriage, husband and wife possess all things together. There is no difference between the man and the woman, except for their sexual difference. The wife is mistress of the home, just as the man is the master of it.[133] Together they take care of the home, create children, and care for them.[134] Wives actually build up their husbands.[135] By contrast, divorce is an indication of the awful depravity which affects man, for it is totally counter to God's intention for marriage.[136] In Luther the Church finds an advocate for the sacredness of the marriage covenants. He elevates the married state to the position of honor and respect that it deserves.

The married state was also the appropriate state in which to conceive children. As already noted, there would have been no lust involved in the procreative act. As often as Adam and Eve wanted children, they would have come together without passion, admiring God and obeying him with complete restraint, "just as we now come together to hear the Word and to worship him."[137] In this sense, it seems that the sexual union would almost have been a sacrament. Birth would have occurred without pain, and the children would have had original righteousness. They would have immediately known God.[138]

Dominion

Luther also asserts that, in addition to their relationship with one another, Adam and Eve also were given the relationship of dominion over the rest of creation. Just as God ruled Adam and Eve, so they were given rulership over all that lived in the air, under the water, or upon the face of the earth.[139] In man's dominion one sees part of the divine image, for naked man, without weapons or clothes, ruled over all.[140] The animals would readily have given Adam any service he desired.[141] Given this, Adam would not have eaten meat, but the more healthy diet of grains and fruits. To Latter-day Saints, the following comment by Luther will have a ring of familiarity:

> Moreover, Adam would not have eaten the various kinds of meat, as the less delightful food, in preference to the delightful fruits of the earth, where as for us nothing is more delicious than meat. From the use of these fruits there would not have resulted that leprous obesity, but physical beauty and health and a sound state of the humors.
>
> But now people do not content themselves with meats, with vegetables, or with grain; and rather often, because of unsuitable food, we face dangers of health.[142]

Even in our fallen state, God has permitted man to retain a portion of the dominion he gave to Adam and Eve. In this one sees God's concern and blessing, for were Satan to have had dominion over the earth, he would have taken the animals and used them to annihilate humankind.[143]

The Temptation

Having dealt with man as he might have been had Adam not sinned, Luther turns his attention to what man has become due to sin. The temptation, directed first at Eve who was the weaker of the two,[144] was an attack on God's word. When Moses records that "the serpent says . . . ," he is noting that God's word was attacked by another word, the word of Satan. Satan's chief objective was to raise doubts in the mind of Eve about the truthfulness of the word of God. In essence he imitated God and preached to her,[145] inquiring whether God really meant what he said or whether Eve had perceived correctly the command of God, for Satan knew that the source of all sin was unbelief in or abandonment of the one true word.[146]

Eve, being led by the Holy Ghost, at first resisted admirably,[147] but then she began to doubt as Satan asked whether it is really logical that God would give them all the bounty he had and then exclude one tree from his gifts.[148] Eve began to waver, as seen in her changing the wording of God's threat. God had said that if Adam and Eve ate of the tree they would die. Eve, however, as is reflected in the Hebrew text of the Bible, said that God told them that they should not eat of the tree "lest *perchance* we shall die." Satan planted in Eve's mind the idea that God would not really kill them for eating the fruit of this one tree, and thus Satan poisoned Eve, creating in her another word which denies God's word.[149] Where the word is lost, contempt for God can enter in, and thus Eve could overtly sin against God's command by eating the fruit.[150] Hence the critical sin was not the eating of the fruit; rather, it was the spiritual change which made the overt act possible.

Why did God permit Satan to tempt our first parents? Luther states that we cannot question God, for he does not have to account for his actions. In the end, the only satisfactory response is that it pleased the Lord to tempt Adam and Eve and thereby to test their powers of obedience.[151]

The Sin

Adam and Eve probably sinned, Luther surmises, on the seventh day, the Sabbath. Wherever the word of God is, there is Satan in opposition to it, and thus he is often most active on the Sabbath, trying to destroy God's word. It grieves Satan that through the word we can become citizens of heaven.[152] Yet, for Adam and Eve, it was not enough to have a knowledge of God; in addition, they wanted a knowledge of evil. They wanted insight beyond what was given to them. Thus, comments Luther, the farther man withdraws from the word, "the more learned and wise he appears to himself."[153] With this disposition for unwarranted knowledge, Adam and Eve sinned overtly through all their senses by eating the fruit. Eve ate the fruit with pleasure and offered it to Adam, being unaware of her sin, for it is sin's nature not to be felt for some time.[154] In the end, Luther believed, what Adam and Eve willed was to become like their creator, to become equal to God.[155]

Aprons

Having sinned, Adam and Eve made coverings to hide their nakedness as though it were shameful. But, asks Luther, what parts of the body are more noble and honorable than those devoted to procreation?[156] Man's basic glory was that he needed no hair, feathers, or scales with which to cover himself as did the animals, for he was created with such beauty that he could walk about with a hairless and naked skin.[157] The disgrace greater than nakedness was that the will was now impaired, the intellect depraved, and the reason corrupted and utterly changed.[158] Proof of Adam's fall was that he then feared the wind (God's voice) which preceded the coming of the Lord. Man feared the very One who created him and was more comfortable in the presence of Satan.[159]

Excuses

Adam demonstrated his newly acquired fear when he was called to accountability, according to Luther. God, or perhaps an angel in God's place, asked Adam where he was, not because He did not know, but rather to show Adam that there was nowhere he could hide from God.[160] Confronted with God, both Adam and Eve tried to excuse themselves and thereby fell into the depths of blasphemy. Adam tried to excuse his act by pointing out that the woman enticed him, the very woman that *God* had made for him. Thus, Adam rationalized, it was God's fault that he sinned, for he certainly would not have done so if God had not made the woman. Likewise, the woman tried to excuse her act by pointing out that the serpent, which was God's creation and not hers, had tempted her. In their attempt to blame God for their actions, they took the last steps in disavowal of the word. They insulted God and charged him with being the originator of sin.[161]

The Punishments

Luther indicates that, in response to Adam and Eve's sin and their subsequent attempt to excuse themselves, the Lord leveled the punishments against them which he had promised. Everything became corrupted. The sun was less bright, the water less clear, the trees less fruitful, and the earth less fertile.[162] The earth was cursed, and the very presence of weeds and vermin became daily sermons, reminding us of our fallen state.[163] Although the power of procreation remains, it is tainted with a lust only slightly less than that of the beasts.[164] While the woman's role is still that of companion and mistress of the home, she also necessarily becomes the antidote for this lust. Few marry, notes Luther, solely out of duty.[165] Along with procreation come disease and the loss of fetuses.[166] The woman's life is threatened in childbirth.[167] Similarly, the man must endure trouble as he provides for his family and as he seeks to rule, direct, and teach them.[168]

Adam and Eve were banished from the tree of life, for the word of God was still attached to it, and had they eaten of it, they would have been returned to their former existence.[169] Finally, the serpent was cursed by God, and the creature which had once been most beautiful was changed into its present disgusting form.[170] In addition, death entered the picture. Had Adam and Eve remained in their state of innocence, death would have been delightful, it being the process by which they would have been translated into the spiritual life. After the Fall, however, it became a dreadful experience.[171] Even so, due to the long-suffering of God, death was postponed. This gracious interlude provided to our first parents was, however, used by Satan to lead our parents into smugness, Luther believed.[172]

Man's Hope

Yet, Luther concludes, the Lord did not leave Adam and Eve without hope. The garments he provided them were a mixed blessing. They protected, yet served to remind them of their wretched state. The skins of slain animals were to remind them of their mortality and of their now living in certain death.[173] The real hope, however, came in the cursing of the serpent: the Lord explained that the serpent may bruise the heel of the seed of the woman, but the woman's seed will crush the serpent's head. Luther argues that, by not being more definite, God mocked Satan, thereby causing him to fear the seed of all women.[174]

> Thus the first little expression, "I shall put enmity between you and the woman," seems to denote all women in general. God wanted to make all women suspect to Satan; on the other hand, He wanted to leave the godly with a very certain hope, so that they might expect this salvation from all who gave birth, until the real one came. In the same way this "her Seed" is spoken most individually, if I may use this expression, concerning the Seed which was born only to Mary of the tribe of Judah, who was espoused to Joseph.[175]

In Luther's mind Adam and Eve understood this. A future Redeemer would release them from death and sin and give them peace. In this hope they were truly righteous.[176] This is further underlined by Adam's assertion that Eve was "the mother of all living." She was the mother of the seed who would redeem all that had been lost. Adam's name for her is a prophecy of future grace. It is a comfort for daily life against all the temptations of Satan.[177] Thus, the first Adam knew of the coming of the last Adam.

JOHN CALVIN (A.D. 1509–1564)

Man's Purpose

Calvin begins by examining why man was created. The basic answer is that man is created to give obedience to God, to adore God, and to meditate on a better life, which is with God. God provided man with all things necessary for life that he might devote himself wholly to the task of contemplation and enjoyment of God.[178] By causing man to pass through mortality, God led him to meditate on the heavenly glory. From the blessings God provides, man might also learn of the divine parental benevolence toward man.[179] The giving of the Sabbath day only magnifies this purpose, for it is the day when man can wholly occupy himself with the contemplation of God. Such contemplation is in reality the proper business of man's entire life, but should man be remiss in his daily remembrance of his purpose in life, the Sabbath provides a day to remedy that. The Sabbath withdraws man from the distractions of the world and enables him to dedicate himself entirely to God.[180]

Man's Creation

Calvin's view is that, as God approached his most excellent creative act, he took counsel with himself. In other instances, he merely commanded the existence of something, but here he gave special significance to the creation with the phrase, "Let us . . ."[181] Calvin notes that Christians correctly see in this statement an argument for a plurality of persons within the Godhead.[182] To further emphasize man's uniqueness, Adam was not created all at once, but rather he was gradually formed, created in stages. First, his dead body was created from the dust of the earth, lest anyone might be tempted to become prideful at man's uniqueness. Knowledge of our earthy origin should lead us to humility before God. Next, the body was quickened by the soul which gives it motion. Finally, God engraved on the soul his image, and to that image he tied Adam's immortality. However, Adam was still of the earth. Thus, it is no accident that Paul distinguishes between Adam as a "living soul" and the "quickening spirit" that the second Adam, Christ, will grant (1 Corinthians 15:45). Adam was not perfected. That is a benefit conferred by Christ which leads to a celestial life.[183]

Paradise

In considering Paradise, or the Garden of Eden, Calvin notes that Moses was writing to his own people and therefore concludes that Paradise must have been located to the east of Judea.[184] It must have been on earth, therefore, otherwise the location designator would be meaningless. Further, had man not sinned the whole earth would have been much like Paradise.[185]

Calvin then turns to life in the garden and focuses on the two trees. He understands the tree of life to be a symbol of the life Adam received from God. It could not give life, in contrast to Luther's understanding of it, but rather it reminded Adam from whence all life came. At times God uses symbols to stretch out his hand to us that we might better ascend to him. As often as man tasted the fruit of the tree of life, he would be reminded that he lived not by his own power but by God's gift. It is also a type of Christ through which Adam comes to understand that he is to depend wholly upon the Son of God.[186]

By contrast, the tree of knowledge of good and evil was forbidden to man as the first lesson in obedience. Calvin asserts, "The only rule of living well and rationally, [is] that men should exercise themselves in obeying God."[187] Thus, the tree of knowledge was prohibited so that man might not seek more than was allotted to him. He was not to trust his own understanding nor to constitute himself a judge of what was best for him.[188] He was to turn to his God. This prohibition was, of course, far from a hardship on man. After all, he had all the other trees and fruits in the garden, and God denied only one to him. God then stated the punishment for violation of the command, thereby affirming the authority of the law. Ultimately, man would be judged as wicked because he failed in his duty to obey when there was no reason to violate the command.[189]

In addition to his duty to obey God, man's role in Paradise was to care for the garden. Adam and his descendants were created to work, not to live an idle and indolent life.[190] Coupled with this is the dominion God gave to Adam (and his posterity) over the world. The animals were singled out particularly because they have independent wills.[191] By bringing the animals to Adam, God demonstrated that he had endowed the animals with a disposition to obey, and thus they would voluntarily offer themselves to man for service.[192]

Eve

Calvin's concern with Eve focuses primarily on the role she played in marriage and the pattern that this then establishes for marriage in general. He begins by reflecting on Eve's origin out of Adam, and, like our three previous writers, sees in this creative act God's intention to emphasize the unity and bond between the two. In Eve, Adam saw himself, and, having been incomplete before her creation, the first man found himself completed. Had the two been created as separate individuals, there would have been the potential for contempt, envy, or contention between them. Coming from a common source, however, there should have been a mutual bonding.[193] Calvin further asserts that God let Adam know through his word or through revelation how Eve came into being and how the two of them were related.[194] The taking of Eve from Adam's side also bears a resemblance to the relationship between the church and the Son of God, who permitted himself to become weak that others of his body (the Church) might have strength.[195]

Marriage

Having established the fundamental relationship between Adam and Eve, Calvin goes on to explain his views on marriage. Since woman is taken out of man, it is clear that the man is incomplete without the woman, who is created to be his companion.[196] They are to cultivate "mutual society," for man is created to be a social animal. Thus, woman is to be man's companion and associate, assisting him to live well.[197] Far from being merely conjugal partners, the two are inseparably associated for life, and thus marriage extends to all aspects of life.

Further, marriage is an honorable estate because God created it. Calvin, like Luther, notes that Adam did not take Eve to himself but rather received her from God, who is the author and patron of marriage.[198] No one can pronounce unclean that which God has himself constituted. Thus, it is within the bonds of marriage that divine, or legitimate, procreation is to take place. Adam and Eve and their descendants were to replenish the earth, but not through promiscuous intercourse. Marriage is the prerequisite to the production of holy offspring.[199]

Calvin also notes that God said that Adam and Eve were to be "one flesh." He understands this to mean that two persons only are involved in marriage, and thus polygamy stands at variance with the divine decree. Similarly, divorce is a blot on the laws of nature. The husband ought to prefer the wife to his father and, by implication, to anything else.[200]

The Temptation

Calvin now turns to the temptation. He begins by noting the irony of the whole situation. Adam and Eve, knowing full well that the animals and all creation were placed under them, succumbed to the enticements of the serpent, who was in reality one of their slaves. Instead of punishing the apostate serpent, who was in revolt against God's commands, Adam and Eve submitted themselves to him.[201] What greater mark of depravity could there be?

After noting the irony, Calvin embarks on an explanation of the temptation that is very similar to that of Luther. He points out that Satan tempted Eve covertly by questioning whether God had actually intended that they should not eat of *every* tree in the garden. Calvin notes that it is very dangerous to believe that God is to be obeyed only when his commands coincide with reason. We should be content with the naked command of God, knowing full well that if it comes from God it must be right and just.[202] Eve did not do this, and she began to waver by indicating doubt, as Luther indicated, that God really meant that they would die. She said that "perhaps" they would die. Basically, Eve, in Calvin's view, desired to know more than God allowed.[203]

Calvin, too, asks why God should permit the temptation of Adam and Eve, but his answer is a little more definite than that of Luther. Calvin argues that, having made man free in everything, God chose to put Adam's obedience to the test. In the end, Adam was not pleased with the command not to eat of the tree of knowledge, and thereby he fell into sin. His perverseness in rejecting the command was shown in light of the mildness of the command itself. There was no fundamental reason to break it, for Adam lacked nothing.[204] The ultimate answer, however, is that God willed the Fall by giving his permission for it to occur. He had determined within himself what man's future condition should be. To ask why this was is to ask a question to which we do not have the answer, for it lies in the mystery of God.[205]

Aprons

Following their sin, according to Calvin, Adam and Eve began to be aware that they had disobeyed, but they were not conscious of the depth of their sin. Consequently, they were only ashamed of their nakedness and did not humble themselves as they should, nor did they fear the judgments of God. Thus, they simply made aprons as barriers between themselves and God.[206] The moment they heard God's voice, however, they realized that the leaves were of no value.[207] Then, when asked why he was hiding, Adam indicated that he feared the Lord's voice and that he was ashamed of his nakedness. This, of course, only shows the degree to which Adam had fallen, for never before had he feared the Lord's voice nor had he been ashamed of his nakedness. He did not recognize that sin was the root of his shame, nor did he yet feel his punishment to the degree that he was willing to confess his fault.[208] Instead, he blamed both Eve and God, who gave him Eve, for his failure. Eve similarly did not take responsibility for her behavior but blamed it on the serpent.[209] Thus, Adam and Eve stood in pride before God, not yet aware of the degree to which their acts would affect them and their posterity.

The Punishments

God, however, in Calvin's view, does not deny his word and executes punishment on man. First, God cursed the serpent because the serpent had been created for the benefit of man. God returned it to its previous station and rank in the created order.[210] Man himself became devoid of all good, blinded in his understanding, perverse in his heart, and cursed under a decree of eternal death.[211] Man must labor, a labor that will not be sweet.[212] Adam and Eve were also excommunicated from the church, for the tree of life was the sacrament which had been given to them.[213] In addition, Eve was cursed with all the problems and pains of pregnancy and became subject to her husband in servitude.[214] Further, marriage was disrupted,[215] and now Satan attacks marriage in two ways. First, he encourages the practice of celibacy, and, second, he insinuates that married couples may indulge themselves in whatever behavior pleases them.[216] Thus, Adam and Eve's condition became hopeless unless God provided hope.

The natural order, according to Calvin, is also influenced by the sin of our first parents. The nature of the world degenerates, leading God as avenger to create caterpillars, fleas, and other insects.[217] Frost, thunder, unseasonable rains, drought, hail, and diseases are also products of the Fall.[218] Thus, everywhere that man looks in the natural world he sees that God has withdrawn his favor and has cursed him.[219] Through all of these "disasters" the Lord partially invites us to repentance, partially instructs us in humility, and partially makes us more cautious of further violating the Lord's word.[220]

Death is, of course, the ultimate punishment. But for Calvin, death is much more than merely the death of the body and the alienation of the spirit from God. It includes all the miseries of life. Adam was cast down so that he and his posterity might learn what it is to live in death, to live in a life without God.[221] Yet, God does not wholly desert them. He does provide Adam and Eve with garments for protection, and Calvin here follows essentially the same reasoning as Luther. The garments are made of skins because they would be degrading, and in them man would behold his own vileness. He thus would be reminded constantly of his sin.[222]

Man's Hope

In considering the hope that God held out to our first parents, Calvin is much more concerned than any of the other authors to stay with the literal meaning of the text and not to see in it types and figures of Christ. Thus, he does not see the promise that the serpent will bruise the heel of the woman's seed and that the woman's seed will crush the serpent's head as being a prophecy of Christ. Rather, Calvin holds that, on one level, it is a statement which reflects the reality that there will always be enmity between humans and snakes.[223] But on another, the promise is a recognition that the snake is simply the tool of Satan, and therefore Calvin states that it has been ingrained into man's nature to flee from Satan.[224] The seed of the woman, that is, the human family collectively, will ultimately be victorious over Satan, and the power to be victorious is given to faithful men.[225] When Adam heard this promise, he immediately gave Eve a name that is derived from the Hebrew word for "life."[226]

In addition to this hope, God also softened the exile of Adam by providing him with a home on earth and by providing him with a livelihood, albeit one for which he must work. Thus, Adam saw that he was not wholly cut off from the Lord and that the Lord still cared for him. Also, even though God had cut Adam off from the tree of life, God provided a substitute symbol in the form of sacrifice.[227]

Posterity

From Calvin's perspective, all Adam's posterity shares in his sin because the whole of humankind was encompassed in the man Adam.[228] The trials that were heaped on Adam were to lead him to repentance so that he might seek in Christ a remedy to his situation.[229] Fundamentally, Adam received a promise of salvation which he could activate through his faith in the word of God, which had its roots in Jesus Christ.[230] Prior to his sin, Adam had received life through his direct communication with God, but from the moment of his fall he was forced to seek life through the death of Christ.[231] Thus, we, the posterity of the first man, may recover in Christ what was lost in Adam.[232]

CONCLUSION

We have reviewed the way four of the greatest theologians of traditional Western Christianity viewed Adam. Among them we find much agreement. It is also noteworthy that they do not agree with one another completely. Even so, we cannot help but perceive and appreciate their struggle to understand the biblical text and their desire to explicate it in such a way that it might make a difference in the lives of Christian peoples.

For those of us who are Latter-day Saints, we can discover in the writings of these four men many truths that are common with our own thought and beliefs. Yet at the same time we can see where these authors either have gone in a different direction than we do or have come close to our understanding and then stopped, and this because they did not have the additional information which we possess as a result of the Restoration. Having read the works of Saint Augustine, Saint Thomas Aquinas, Martin Luther, and John Calvin, one finds it hard to escape the impression that God led them as far as he could in their historical settings, according to the best light they possessed. Moreover, one sees these men, in their writings, pointing beyond themselves to something more complete and something more full. The Latter-day Saint knows what that "something" is. It is the fulness of the gospel of Jesus Christ, revealed to us in the latter days, a "something" which men like our four authors, through their faithfulness to the truths they then had, prepared the world to hear when the appointed time for the Restoration came.

NOTES

1. Saint Augustine, *The City of God*, trans. Marcus Dods (New York: Random House, 1950), 382, 400; Books 12.2 and 12.17.

2. Ibid., 398, Book 12.16. See also Luther's comment that Augustine believed all creation to have occurred in a moment of time, in *Luther's Works*, ed. Jaroslav Pelikan, vol. 1, *Lectures on Genesis, Chapters 1–5* (St. Louis: Concordia Publishing House, 1958), 121.

3. Augustine, *City*, 408; Book 12.25.

4. Ibid., 384; Book 12.5.

5. Ibid., 407; Book 12.23.

6. Ibid., 435; Book 13.23.

7. Ibid., 437; Book 13.24.

8. Ibid., 432–33; Book 13.23.

9. Ibid., 412; Book 13.2.

10. Ibid., 456; Book 14.10.

11. Ibid., 474; Book 14.26.

12. Ibid., 456; Book 14.10.

13. Ibid., 407; Book 12.23.

14. Ibid., 405–6; Book 12.21.

15. Ibid., 410; Book 12.27.

16. Ibid., 469; Book 14.22.

17. Ibid., 468–69; Book 14.21.

18. Ibid., 457; Book 14.10.

19. Ibid., 470; Book 14.23.

20. Ibid., 475; Book 14.26.

21. Ibid., 387; Book 12.7.

22. Ibid., 388; Book 12.9.

23. Ibid., 385; Book 12.6.

24. Ibid., 461; Book 14.13.

25. Ibid., 458–59; Book 14.11.

26. Ibid., 459; Book 14.11.

27. Ibid., 460; Book 14.13.

28. Ibid., 463; Book 14.15.

29. Ibid., 460; Book 14.12.

30. Ibid., 466; Book 14.17.

31. Ibid., 462; Book 14.14.

32. Ibid., 462; Book 14.15.

33. Ibid., 463; Book 14.15.

34. Ibid., 412; Book 13.1.

35. Ibid., 423; Book 13.15.

36. Ibid., 414; Book 13.3.

37. Ibid., 457; Book 14.11.

38. Ibid., 476; Book 14.27.

39. Ibid., 413–14; Book 13.3.

40. Ibid., 406–7; Book 12.22.

41. Ibid., 432; Book 13.22.

42. St. Thomas Aquinas, *Summa Theologiae*, eds. Thomas Gilby and T. C. O'Brien, 59 vols. (New York and London: Blackfriars in conjunction with McGraw-Hill Book Company and Eyre & Spottiswoode, 1964–76), 13:57 (Ia. 93, 3).

43. Ibid., 13:71 (Ia. 93, 6); 13:79 (Ia. 93, 8).

44. Ibid., 13:51 (Ia. 93, 1).

45. Ibid., 13:71 (Ia. 93, 6).

46. Ibid., 13:61 (Ia. 93, 4).

47. Ibid., 13:33 (Ia. 91, 4).

48. Ibid., 13:19 (Ia. 91, 1).

49. Ibid., 13:13–15 (Ia. 90, 4).

50. Ibid., 13:5 (Ia. 90, 1).

51. Ibid., 13:19 (Ia. 91, 1).

52. Ibid., 13:23 (Ia. 91, 2).

53. Ibid., 13:123 (Ia. 96, 1).

54. Ibid., 13:99 (Ia. 94, 3).

55. Ibid., 13:139 (Ia. 97, 1).

56. Ibid., 13:115 (Ia. 95, 3).

57. Ibid., 13:185 (Ia. 102, 1).

58. Ibid., 13:187 (Ia. 102, 1).

59. Ibid., 13:193 (Ia. 102, 3).

60. Ibid., 13:147–49 (Ia. 97, 4).

61. Ibid., 13:39–41 (Ia. 92, 2).

62. Ibid., 13:43 (Ia. 92, 3).

63. Ibid., 13:155 (Ia. 98, 2).

64. Ibid., 13:39 (Ia. 92, 1).

65. Ibid., 13:157 (Ia. 98, 2).

66. Ibid., 13:153 (Ia. 98, 1).

67. Ibid., 10:137 (Ia. 72).

68. Ibid., 44:177 (2a2ae. 164, 2).

69. Ibid., 13:157–59 (Ia. 98, 2).

70. Ibid., 26:67 (Ia2ae. 84, 2).

71. Ibid., 44:151 (2a2ae. 163, 1).

72. Ibid., 44:153 (2a2ae. 163, 1).

73. Ibid., 44:157 (2a2ae. 163, 2).

74. Ibid., 44:161 (2a2ae. 163, 4).

75. Ibid., 44:187 (2a2ae. 165, 2).

76. Ibid., 13:109 (Ia. 95, 1).

77. Ibid., 44:175–77 (2a2ae. 164, 2).

78. Ibid., 44:177 (2a2ae. 164, 2).

79. Ibid., 44:167 (2a2ae. 164, 1).

80. Ibid., 44:169 (2a2ae. 164, 1).

81. Ibid., 44:179 (2a2ae. 164, 2).

82. Ibid., 26:7 (Ia2ae. 81, 1).

83. Ibid., 26:11 (Ia2ae. 81, 1).

84. Ibid., 26:25 (Ia2ae. 81, 5).

85. Ibid., 52:5 (3a. 31, 1).

86. Ibid., 48:23 (3a. 1, 4).

87. *Luther's Works* 1:121. This, as Luther points out, is in opposition to both Augustine and Hilary, who believed all things were created in a moment.

88. Ibid., 79, 80.

89. Ibid., 56.

90. Ibid., 57, 224.

91. Ibid., 76.

92. Ibid., 61, 62.

93. Ibid., 65.

94. Ibid., 69.

95. Ibid., 62–63.

96. Ibid., 65.

97. Ibid., 67.

98. Ibid., 68.

99. Ibid., 131.

100. Ibid., 165.

101. Ibid., 87.

102. Ibid., 112.

103. Ibid., 84.

104. Ibid., 57.

105. Ibid., 92.

106. Ibid., 110.

107. Ibid., 66.

108. Ibid., 62.

109. Ibid., 113.

110. Ibid., 92.

111. Ibid., 111.

112. Ibid., 95.

113. Ibid., 105.

114. Ibid., 106.

115. Ibid., 103.

116. Ibid., 144.

117. Ibid., 95.

118. Ibid., 96.

119. Ibid., 90.

120. Ibid., 101.

121. Ibid., 92.

122. Ibid., 89.

123. Ibid., 102, 103.

124. Ibid., 67, 115.

125. Ibid., 137.

126. Ibid., 69.

127. Ibid., 123, 128.

128. Ibid., 129.

129. Ibid., 136.

130. Ibid., 115.

131. Ibid., 135.

132. Ibid., 134.

133. Ibid., 137.

134. Ibid., 133.

135. Ibid., 134.

136. Ibid., 138.

137. Ibid., 168.

138. Ibid., 104, 116–17.

139. Ibid., 64.

140. Ibid., 66.

141. Ibid., 77.

142. Ibid., 72.

143. Ibid., 133.

144. Ibid., 151.

145. Ibid., 146–47.

146. Ibid., 149.

147. Ibid., 150.

148. Ibid., 153.

149. Ibid., 155.

150. Ibid., 158.

151. Ibid., 144, 145.

152. Ibid., 70, 82.

153. Ibid., 160.

154. Ibid., 163.

155. Ibid., 223.

156. Ibid., 167.

157. Ibid., 140.

158. Ibid., 166.

159. Ibid., 170–71.

160. Ibid., 173.

161. Ibid., 178–79.

162. Ibid., 64.

163. Ibid., 204, 209.

164. Ibid., 71.

165. Ibid., 116.

166. Ibid., 133.

167. Ibid., 198.

168. Ibid., 203.

169. Ibid., 227.

170. Ibid., 186–87.

171. Ibid., 110.

172. Ibid., 159.

173. Ibid., 221.

174. Ibid., 194.

175. Ibid., 195–96.

176. Ibid., 197, 199.

177. Ibid., 220.

178. John Calvin, *A Commentary on Genesis*, ed. and trans. John King, two volumes in one (Edinburgh: The Banner of Truth Trust, 1964), I:64, 65. All the material used for this paper is in the first volume of this work. Hereafter, only the page number will be given.

179. Ibid., 115.

180. Ibid., 105–6.

181. Ibid., 91.

182. Ibid., 92–93.

183. Ibid., 111–13.

184. Ibid., 113.

185. Ibid., 114.

186. Ibid., 116–17.

187. Ibid., 126.

188. Ibid., 118.

189. Ibid., 126–27.

190. Ibid., 125.

191. Ibid., 96.

192. Ibid., 132.

193. Ibid., 132, 133.

194. Ibid., 134.

195. Ibid., 133.

196. Ibid., 97.
197. Ibid., 128, 129.
198. Ibid., 131, 134.
199. Ibid., 97, 98.
200. Ibid., 136.
201. Ibid., 141.
202. Ibid., 147.
203. Ibid., 149, 151.
204. Ibid., 154.
205. Ibid., 144.
206. Ibid., 157, 159.
207. Ibid., 159.
208. Ibid., 162.
209. Ibid., 164–65.
210. Ibid., 166, 167.
211. Ibid., 65.
212. Ibid., 175.
213. Ibid., 184.
214. Ibid., 171, 172.
215. Ibid., 129.
216. Ibid., 134.
217. Ibid., 104.
218. Ibid., 177.
219. Ibid., 173.
220. Ibid., 179.
221. Ibid., 127.
222. Ibid., 181–82.
223. Ibid., 167.
224. Ibid., 169.
225. Ibid., 170, 171.
226. Ibid., 181.
227. Ibid., 184–85.
228. Ibid., 152.
229. Ibid., 179.
230. Ibid., 65.
231. Ibid., 184.
232. Ibid., 157.

10

Robert L. Millet

Adam: A Latter-day Saint Perspective

About twenty years ago I read a book by a noted psycho-analyst which discussed at length the episode in Eden. In the opening chapter the writer detailed the Genesis story and particularly focused upon the serpent's temptation of Adam and Eve. "Yea, hath God said," the serpent asked, "Ye shall not eat of every tree of the garden? And the woman said unto the serpent, We may eat of the fruit of the trees of the garden: but of the fruit of the tree which is in the midst of the garden, God hath said, Ye shall not eat of it, neither shall ye touch it, lest ye die. And the serpent said unto the woman, Ye shall not surely die: for God doth know that in the day ye eat thereof, then your eyes shall be opened, and ye shall be as gods, knowing good and evil." (Genesis 3:1–5.) The learned writer then spent the remainder of the book discussing Adam and Eve's decision to partake of the forbidden fruit as the beginning stages and symbolic representation of mankind's consuming passion for power and dominion. Imagine —he said, in effect —man

Robert L. Millet is Associate Professor and Chairman of the Department of Ancient Scripture at Brigham Young University.

seeking to know and be as God is. Why, the very idea is blasphemous and unthinkable!

Some years later I was driving across the country, listening to the car radio as I traveled. I especially enjoy listening to religious channels and networks to better understand the perspective of our Protestant and Catholic friends. On one channel the host of a rather popular program was taking calls from the listening audience, soliciting religious questions. One caller asked, "Reverend, why did Adam and Eve take the fruit of the tree of the knowledge of good and evil?" The minister's answer was simple. "I don't know," he said. "That's the dumbest thing anyone could have done! Why, if Adam and Eve had not been so selfish, so power-hungry, we might all have been in paradise today!" The answer at the time caused me to chuckle. I have since thought again and again about his answer and looked more soberly and sympathetically upon a Christian world which desperately needs what we as Latter-day Saints have to offer.

Much of what we do have to offer has come to us through the instrumentality of the Prophet Joseph Smith. In the Book of Mormon we read: "And the king [King Limhi] said that a seer is greater than a prophet. And Ammon said that a seer is a revelator and a prophet also; and a gift which is greater can no man have, except he should possess the power of God, which no man can; yet a man may have great power given him from God. But *a seer can know of things which are past*, and also of things which are to come, and by them shall all things be revealed, or, rather, shall secret things be made manifest, and hidden things shall come to light." (Mosiah 8:15–17; italics added.) To some degree it might be said that Joseph Smith the Seer, having been led and instructed of the Lord, revealed as much concerning the past ages and dispensations as he did concerning our present age and the future. Consider what we now know, thanks to the Prophet's ministry, of Enoch and Noah and Melchizedek; of Abraham and Joseph and Moses—precious truths and sacred insights from modern revelation concerning some of the greatest of the ancient noble and great.

And what of Adam? Through the modern seer, Joseph Smith, we learn that Adam was earth's first Christian. To Adam the gospel was first preached. To him and his posterity came the doctrine and proclamation, the commandment that we should do all that we do in the name of the Son, and that we should repent and call upon God in the name of the Son forevermore (Moses 5:8). Adam —his very name means man or mankind. Adam —his very title implies the first man of all men, which are many (Moses 1:34). Indeed, in the words of President Brigham Young, "The name that was given to Adam was more ancient than he was."[1] Through the work of the Restoration, the knowledge of antiquity and the understanding of God's dealings with earth's first prophets and Apostles —special witnesses of him and his message —have been made known.

Because God has spoken anew in our day about Adam and Eve, we know things about ourselves —about our nature and true relationship to Deity —that we would not know otherwise. For example, through Joseph Smith's inspired translation of the early chapters of Genesis —some of which constitutes "Selections from the Book of Moses" in our Pearl of Great Price —we know the following:

1. Adam and Eve were vital parts of God's purpose and plan —the plan of salvation —which plan has been in existence since the days that they first walked the earth. The Saints today, and all who will listen, become privy to a foundational truth concerning Christ's eternal gospel —the knowledge that Christian prophets have taught Christian doctrine and administered Christian ordinances since the days of Eden.

2. Adam and Eve's doings in Eden are not to be understood in a spiritual vacuum. And Lucifer's actions in the garden must be seen as a part of his malevolent mischief begun in the premortal councils. The War in Heaven simply continues on earth. (See Moses 4.)

3. The fall of Adam and Eve was an essential part of God's plan. Thus the Fall is viewed by Latter-day Saints with an optimism that is uncharacteristic of traditional Christianity. Simply stated, Adam and Eve came into the Garden of Eden to fall. In fact, their partaking of the fruit was as much a part of the foreordained plan as the atonement of Christ. "Because that Adam fell," Enoch explained, "we are" (Moses 6:48; compare 2 Nephi 2:25).

4. God forgave Adam and Eve their transgression in the Garden of Eden. Though children are "conceived in sin" —though conception becomes the vehicle through which the effects of the

Fall are transmitted to man — they are free from any original sin or guilt. Little children are whole from the foundation of the world. These blessings come as unconditional benefits of the atonement of Jesus Christ. (Moses 6:53–55.)

5. Through the redemptive labors of Christ and their own repentance, Adam and Eve were forgiven of their sins, born again, changed from a carnal and fallen state to a state of righteousness; they were justified, sanctified, and made ready for an entrance into the eternal presence (Moses 6:57–60). We can receive these blessings as well. Through the ordinances of salvation, Adam, Eve, and their posterity are "quickened in the inner man," are born of the Spirit, and thus become the sons and daughters of Christ (Moses 6:64–68). Then, through receiving the blessings of the new and everlasting covenant of marriage, these Saints may ultimately qualify to become sons and daughters of God the Father and receive, as joint-heirs with Christ, all that the Father has.[2]

In summary, much of what we know of the Creation, the Fall, and the Atonement — the three pillars of eternity — we know in large measure because of what God has revealed, principally in the latter days, regarding our first parents.

Adam stands in a vital priesthood role in relation to his posterity. He also stands as an example, a pattern for all mankind to follow. Knowing as we do that the plan of salvation was taught and understood in earth's earliest ages; that "the Gospel began to be preached, from the beginning, being declared by holy angels sent forth from the presence of God, and by his own voice, and by the gift of the Holy Ghost" (Moses 5:58); and knowing that apostasy, a counterfeit gospel, and false orders of priesthood were also in effect from the beginning (see Moses 5:16–55; Abraham 1:21–27), we should not be surprised that elements of truth concerning Adam and Eve, truth mixed with error, or semblances of the ordinances or rituals should be evident in the literature of antiquity or among peoples and cultures all over the globe.[3]

Sadly, it seems that most in society live in ignorance in regard to the role of Adam. A large segment of the world's population dismisses him as myth and metaphor. Others, like my minister friend, spurn his actions in Eden and condemn him as rebellious. Still others, also misinformed and misled, worship him as a god. To misunderstand Adam is to misunderstand our own identity, as well as our relationship to the Lord and his plan. The gospel light has shone forth, and people need not wander in darkness as to who they are, whose they are, and what they may become. Searching the revelations and attuning ourselves to the living oracles in our own day will prepare us for a time when further light and knowledge concerning the Adamic dispensation will be given (D&C 107:57), a time when the faithful will know "things which have passed, and hidden things which no man knew, things of the earth, by which it was made, and the purpose and the end thereof—things most precious" (D&C 101:33–34). A knowledge of the origin and destiny of man—this is the legacy of the Latter-day Saints.

NOTES

1. From an address delivered by Brigham Young on 28 December 1845.

2. See Ezra Taft Benson, "What I Hope You Will Teach Your Children about the Temple," *Ensign* 15 (August 1985): 8–9.

3. See Spencer J. Palmer, "Mormon Views of Religious Resemblances," *Brigham Young University Studies* 16 (Summer 1976): 660–81; Milton R. Hunter, *The Gospel Through the Ages* (Salt Lake City: Bookcraft, 1945); Hugh Nibley, *The World and the Prophets* (Salt Lake City and Provo: Deseret Book Co., and Foundation for Ancient Research and Mormon Studies, 1987), pp. 232–39.

Subject Index

— A —

Aaron (son of Mosiah), 42, 43, 72
Aaronic Priesthood, 120
Abel, 143, 144
Abinadi, 43
Aboda Zara, 136
Abraham, 83, 190
  creation account of, 16, 17, 20, 47
  foreordination of, 14, 94
  vision of premortality, 4, 9, 14
Acherusian Lake, 142
Accountability, 105
  age of, 51, 105
  for own sins, 58
Adam, 16, 17, 127
  "Ancient of Days," 1, 124, 126
  appearance to Christ, 84
  baptism of, 108, 114
  birth of, 26
  body changed after the Fall, 18, 28
  book of remembrance, 66, 77, 79,
    115–16, 117, 133–34
  burial of, 145
  children baptized, 105
  Church organized by, 107–8
  confrontations with Satan, 113–14,
    121–23, 147

  council at Adam-ondi-Ahman, 108, 114,
    117–19, 123–25, 134, 141–42, 147
  death of, 50, 114, 119, 143
  "deep sleep" of, 97
  dominion of, 170
  faith of, 102–3
  foreordination of, 13, 14, 87, 96–97
  garments of, 30, 98, 104, 138, 163,
    173–74, 180
  gospel revealed to, vii, 2, 65–85, 114–15,
    117, 119, 190–91
  government of, 116–17
  in premortal life, 1–10, 13–14
  in spirit world, 121
  judge, 126
  keys of dispensations held by, 2, 79, 91,
    107, 113, 119–21, 124
  keys of presidency given to, 2–3, 90,
    107, 116–17, 120
  keys of priesthood given to, 29
  keys of resurrection held by, 125–26
  keys of salvation held by, 9–10, 87, 109
  keys restored under direction of, vii,
    113, 119–21
  language of, 115–16
  marriage to Eve, 29, 96–99, 100, 169–70
  mortal ministry of, 113–19
  name of, 138, 191

on Eve, 26, 97–98
on the Fall, 61
paradigm of, 131–33
patriarchal blessings given by, 105, 117–19
priesthood held by, *vii*, 9, 98–99, 114–15, 116
priesthood role of, 192
prophecies of, 61, 76, 106, 118–19, 134, 141, 144, 147
prototype of all mortal men, 67, 131
raising of, 135, 139–40, 147
repentance of, 77–79
resurrection of, 109, 121
rib of, 25, 95, 96–97, 99, 154–55, 161, 168, 177
role in the Creation, 9–10, 13, 87, 107
role in resurrection and judgment, 125
sacrifices offered by, 20, 73–77, 117, 136
second to Christ, 87, 107
stewardship delivered to Christ, 124
transgression forgiven, 58, 77–78, 108
visited by God, 100
worship of, *viii*, 192
See also Fall; Michael
Adam Kadmon, 136–37
Adamic dispensation, 193
Adamic paradigm, 131–33
Adam-ondi-Ahman, 20, 27–28
council at, 108, 117–19, 123–25, 134, 141–42, 147
future gathering at, 114, 123–25
Adam's Words to Seth, 145
Age of accountability, 51, 105
Agency, 5–6, 8, 67, 89, 101, 132
Aisthesis, 137
Allegory, of Eden, 29–31
Alma the Younger, 43, 102
on baptism, 108
on the Fall, 32–33
on justice of God, 6
on plan of redemption, 70–71
on spiritual death, 50
America, 20, 82
Ammon (son of Mosiah), 43
on seers, 190
Amulek, 43
on the Atonement, 81
on resurrection, 17
"Ancient of Days," 1, 124, 126
Andersen, F., 141
Angel, 172
appearance to Adam, 30, 66, 74, 77
appearance to Christ, 84
Angel of light, appearance of Satan as, 114, 123, 142, 147

Angels, 144, 153, 158, 160, 165, 166
ministering, 121
of Michael, 4, 6–7
of Satan, 4, 7, 10, 72, 113–14, 122, 125
under direction of Adam, *vii*, 2, 120
Animal sacrifices. *See* Sacrifices
Animals, 28, 41, 44, 46, 48, 53–54, 166, 176
Anointing, 104, 142
Antionah, 43
Apocalypse (Revelation) of Adam, 139–41, 146
Apocalypse of Moses, 141
Apocryphal literature, 98, 132–47
Apostasy, 56, 119, 192
Apostles, 83, 126, 191
Apostolic Constitutions, 135
Aprons, 172, 179
Aquinas, Thomas, 152, 158–64, 165, 167, 182
Summa Theologiae, 152
Arabic language, 143
Aristotle, 152, 160
Ark of the Covenant, 145
Armenia, 145
Astronomy, 166
Atonement, *viii*, 6–7, 23, 27, 30–31, 39, 41, 45, 49, 50–52, 55–56, 58–59, 65–68, 72–85, 90, 100, 108, 109, 114, 117, 153, 191–92
See also Redemption
Augustine, 56, 132, 152–61, 164, 165, 182

— B —

Babylonian Talmud, 135
Baptism, 78, 125
infant, 56–58
of Adam, 108, 114
of Adam's children, 105
of fire and the Holy Ghost, 114
Barnabas, Epistle of, 140
Baruch, 132
Battle of Gog and Magog, 127
"Battle of the great God," 114, 127
"Behold the Great Redeemer Die" (hymn), 82
Benjamin (Nephite prophet-king), 43, 72
on the Atonement, 58
Benson, Ezra Taft, on the fall of Adam, 41
on the order of the Son of God, 114–15
Bible, 25, 35, 39, 57, 62, 66, 116, 132
Joseph Smith Translation, 22, 43, 45, 57, 66, 76, 79, 116, 133, 191
Birth, 46, 48, 51, 79, 162, 170
of spirits, 11–12, 22–23

Blasphemy, 172, 190
Blood, brought by the Fall, *vii*, 18, 23,
    45–46, 63, 83–85
    of Christ, 45, 75, 80–85, 93
Blood atonement, 84–85
Bodies, 158, 159–60, 163, 165–66, 175
    mortal, 3, 16, 21, 46–47, 63, 65, 71, 73,
    95
    of Adam and Eve before the Fall, 28,
    45–46
    resurrected, 45, 47
    spirit, 46–47
Bones, 48, 97–98
Book of Adam, 133–39, 146
Book of Enoch, 118, 134
Book of Jubilees, 143
Book of Mormon, 20, 26, 41, 43, 56, 58,
    59, 60, 77, 83, 116, 190
Book of Moses, 26, 42, 43, 44, 47, 57, 66,
    67, 73, 76, 77, 79, 191
Book of Raziel, 135
Book of remembrance, of Adam, 66, 77,
    79, 115–16, 117, 133–34
Book of the Daughters of Adam, 146
Book of the Generations of Adam, 134–35,
    146
Book of the Rolls, 145
Brass plates, 43, 45, 66, 67, 76
Broken heart and contrite spirit, 80
Brother of Jared, on the Fall, 52

— C —

Cain, 141, 143, 144, 156
Cainan (son of Enos), 22, 115, 117–19
Calvin, John, 152–53, 174–81, 182
Catholicism, 57, 151–52, 168, 190
Cave of Treasures, 145–46
Celestial City, 126–27
Celibacy, 168, 179
Cerbelaud, D., 138
Childbearing, 89, 106
Childbirth, 163, 173
Children, 169
    free from original sin, 34, 55–59, 192
    not born in Eden, 45, 76–77, 96, 102
    of Adam and Eve, 105
    of Eve, 103, 109–10
    See also Original sin
Christianity, 32, 55–59, 77, 151–82
    early, 131–47
Church, 177
    established before the home, 167
    organized by Adam, 107–8
Clement of Alexandria, 140
Commandments, 39, 74

Conflict, of Adam and Eve with Satan,
    146
Corianton, 6
Council of Nicaea, 151
Councils of God, 85
Councils of heaven, 87, 88, 191
    See also Grand Council in Heaven
Covenant, 114
    between members of Godhead, 12–13,
    68
Covenants, 27, 104
    made by Eve, 89, 109
    marriage, 96–99, 169
    premortal, 89
    temple, 29, 30, 79
Cowdery, Oliver, Aaronic Priesthood
    restored to, 120
Creation, 2, 4, 11–23, 37–39, 41, 43, 48,
    59–60, 63, 67–70, 116, 192
    days of, 20–21
    fall of, 53–54
    involvement of Adam in, *vii–viii*, 9–10,
    87, 93–96, 107
    involvement of Eve in, 88, 93–96, 109
    Judaic and early Christian understand-
    ing of, 134, 136–42, 145
    natural, 11
    paradisiacal, 16–20, 47
    spirit, 4, 11–12, 19, 47, 49, 95
    spiritual, 11, 17, 19, 23, 44, 47, 49
    Western Christian understanding of,
    153–55, 159–61, 164–68, 174–77
Curse, on the earth, 53–54, 173

— D —

Daniel, 119, 123
    on "Ancient of Days," 1, 124
Death, *vii*, 27, 56–57, 60, 99, 108, 125,
    154, 173
    nonexistent before the Fall, 20, 23,
    44–45, 96
    of Christ, 82–84, 145, 181
    of plants and animals, 53–54
    spiritual, 5, 33–34, 39, 48–52, 55–56,
    84, 101, 114, 157, 163, 180
    temporal, 11, 17, 26, 31–33, 39, 46, 47,
    48–53, 55–56, 63, 65, 84, 101, 114,
    139, 157, 163, 180
Death of Adam, 145
Delegation, 93, 120, 126
Determinism, 132
Devil. *See* Lucifer; Satan
Diogenes of Sinope, 38
Discernment, 156

Dispensation of the fulness of times, 2, 52, 107, 120
Dispensations, 124, 190
  keys held by Adam, 2, 79, 91, 107, 113, 119–20
Divine investiture of authority, 22
Divorce, 132–33, 169, 178
Doctrine and Covenants, 26, 44, 56, 83, 116, 120, 133

— E —

Earth, 41
  created near Kolob, 15
  creation of, 23, 67, 93–95
  curse on, 53–54, 173
  death of, 53–54
  paradisiacal creation of, 16–20, 47
  paradisiacal state of, 31
  redemption of, *viii*
  renewal of, 16
Eden, 3, 11, 18, 25–35, 43, 53, 67, 72, 73, 78, 81, 84, 88, 96, 114, 133, 138, 139, 145, 146, 160–61, 175, 189, 191
  conditions of life in, 44–46
  location of, 20, 160, 167, 175
  nature before the Fall, 17
  temple to Adam and Eve, 30, 145, 167
Egypt, 139
Egyptian drawings, 29
Egyptian papyri, 12
Eliade, M., 131
Elias, 120
Elijah, 120, 121
  translation of, 122–23
Elohim, 13
  Creation under direction of, *vii*
  See also God; Heavenly Father
Endowment, 79, 147
  See also Temple ceremony
Enoch, 13, 22, 26, 66, 77, 79, 83, 115, 117–19, 122, 190, 191
  book of, 118, 134, 141
  on the Fall, 45
  on gospel taught to Adam, 57
  translation of, 139
Enos, 22, 115, 117–19
Epiphanius of Salamis, 139
Epistle of Barnabas, 140
Epistles, pastoral, 133
Eternal families, 88
Eternal life, 1, 8, 19, 31, 32, 33, 35, 39, 71, 85, 95, 105, 109, 110, 113, 165
  represented by tree of life, 100
Eternal marriage, 30, 96–99
  See also Marriage
Eternal principles, 8

Ethiopia, 146
Eve, *vii*, 16, 17, 67, 73, 79, 87–110, 115, 137, 142–43, 154–56, 167, 170–71
  Adam's name taken by, 98
  birth of, 26
  changed after the Fall, 28
  children trained by, 106
  creation from rib of Adam, 25–27, 95, 96–97, 99, 154–55, 161, 168, 177
  death of, 143
  faith of, 102–3
  foreordination of, 14
  full partner with Adam, 97
  garments of, 30, 98, 104, 138, 173–74, 180
  involvement in the Creation, 88, 93–95, 109
  marriage to Adam, 96–99
  mother of all living, 31
  on having children, 45
  on joy through the Fall, 18–19, 32, 35, 61, 76, 109
  premortal role of, 88–93
  pride of, 162
  revelation received by, 107
  See also Fall
Evolution, theory of, 54, 63
Exaltation, 16, 61, 79, 81, 89, 99, 101, 104, 125
Excommunication, of Adam and Eve, 179
Existentialism, 133
Ezekiel, 27, 119
Ezra, 132

— F —

Faith, 6–7, 35, 41, 73, 74, 81, 93
  of Adam, 181
  of Adam and Eve, 30, 99, 102, 104, 105
  of Eve, 89, 109
  worlds framed through, 94
Fall, *viii*, 27, 37–64, 87, 88, 99–103, 116, 141, 145
  a blessing, 61–63
  blood brought by, *vii*, 18, 23, 45–46, 63, 83–85
  children brought by, 45, 76–77, 96, 102
  children shielded from, 55–59, 191–92
  Christ not totally subject to, 55, 80
  death brought by, *vii*, 18, 32, 114, 125
  effects of, 43, 48–54, 76, 96, 100
  essential to God's plan, 191–92
  foreordained, 67–69, 90
  natural creation through, 11, 19, 20
  nature of Eden before, 17
  of whole creation, 53–54
  reality of, 27, 37, 43

redemption through, 65–66, 68–69, 72, 109
statements about, 41–43
time system before, 16
traditional Christian views on, 156, 162–63, 170–73, 178–80
Families, government of Adam administered through, 116
Family, championed by Eve, 92
Fatherhood, of Adam, 104, 105–6
Fathers, 116
Fear, 7, 172, 179
Fig, 144
First Presidency, keys obtained by Adam, 2–3, 116–17, 120
on Adam, 3
on creation of man, 95
Firstlings, 73–74
Flaming sword, 43
Flesh, 47–48
Flood, 144, 167
Foreordination, 14, 67, 71, 84, 191
of Adam, 14, 87, 96
of Eve, 14, 87, 97
Forgiveness, 6
of Adam's transgression, 58, 78, 191–92
Free agency, 5–6, 8, 67, 89, 101, 132
Fruit, forbidden, vii, 28, 30, 31, 32, 44, 61, 63, 67, 73, 102

— G —

Gabriel, 2, 120
Garden of Eden. See Eden
Garments, heavenly, 145
of light, 98, 138
of salvation, 30
of skins, 30, 104, 138, 163, 173–74, 180
Gelasian Decree, 144
Genealogy, 133
Genesis, 42, 47, 58, 145
Joseph Smith's translation of, 43, 191
Geradamas, 141
Gethsemane, 27, 83, 139
Gift of the Holy Ghost, 57, 78
See also Holy Ghost
Gnosticism, 137, 139–41, 142
God, 38, 40–42, 60, 67, 164
appearance at Adam-ondi-Ahman, 118
becoming like, 69–70
foreknowledge of, 119, 157
government of, 116–17
image of, 95, 152, 158–59, 165, 175
justice of, 6–7
love of, 31, 100
man's relationship to, 79
presence in Eden, 46, 100

rebellion against, 4
spirit children of, 41, 71
See also Elohim; Gods; Heavenly Father; Jehovah; Jesus Christ
Godhead, 159, 175
covenant between members of, 12–13, 68
Godhood, 5, 69–70
Gods, 8, 14, 16, 21, 69, 87, 94
Gog and Magog, battle of, 127
Gospel, 31, 59, 73, 90
always the same, 67, 88
revealed to Adam, vii, 25, 65–85, 114–15, 77–79, 117, 119, 190–91
taught in premortal life, 71
Grace, 157, 159, 163
Grand Council in Heaven, 5, 10, 71, 93–94
role of Eve in, 90–91
See also Councils in heaven
Greed, 41
Greek language, 82, 137, 141, 142–43
Greek philosophy, 38, 137

— H —

Ha'adam, 131
Happiness, 8, 50, 162
Hatred, 41
Health, 170
Heaven, 38
councils of, 87, 88
government of, 117
Grand Council in, 5, 10, 71, 90–91, 93–94
Heavenly Father, 9, 39, 88, 93, 153
father of spirits, 3, 12, 15–16, 21, 69
man created by, 21–22
See also Elohim; God
Heavenly messengers, 147
See also Angel; Angels
Heavenly mother, 12, 15–16, 88, 91
Heavenly parents, 3–4, 12, 88–89, 98
Hebrew language, 82, 97, 98, 101, 102, 104, 106, 138, 143, 168, 181
History, 3, 42
History of Cain and Abel, 145
History of the Creation and of the Transgression of Adam, 145
History of the Expulsion of Adam from the Garden, 145
Holy Ghost, 59, 76, 77, 106, 114, 117, 118, 134, 157, 168, 171
gift of, 57, 78
Home, 93, 95, 167, 168
Homily of Adam in Hades to Lazarus, 146

Hope, 33, 65–66, 70, 153, 157–58, 173–74,
    180–81
Humanism, 58–59
Humility, 8, 175
Hymns, 81–82

— I —

"Immaculate conception," 57
Immortality, 1, 39, 84, 85, 95, 96, 100,
    113, 157
Improvement Era (magazine), 95
Infant baptism, 56, 163–64
Infants, 157
    See also Children
Inspiration, 153
Intellect, 172
Intelligence, 16, 61, 88, 154, 158, 159
Intelligences, 11
Irenaeus, 140
Isaiah, 119

— J —

Jackson, H., 141
Jackson County, Missouri, 20
Jacob (son of Lehi), 18, 43
    on the Atonement, 72
    on being clothed with purity, 98
    on effects of the Fall, 48, 50, 51–52
Jared (son of Mahalaleel), 115, 117–19
Jehovah, vii, 9, 13, 19, 23, 70, 92, 107,
    140–41
Jehovah-Christ, 21
Jeremiah, 119
Jerusalem, 145
Jesus Christ, vii, 2, 3, 62, 122, 140, 141,
    144, 145, 146, 147, 157–58, 161, 164,
    165, 174
    Adam second to, 87, 107
    Adamic paradigm used by, 132–33
    atonement of, viii, 6–7, 23, 27, 30–31,
        41, 45, 50–52, 55–56, 58–59, 65–68,
        72–85, 90, 100, 108, 109, 114, 117,
        153, 191–92
    baptism in name of, 57
    blood of, 45, 75, 80–85, 93
    Creator, 9, 13, 14, 22
    crucifixion of, 145
    death overcome by, 125
    foreordination of, 4–8, 13–14, 67–68,
        71, 90
    Mediator, 108
    mortal ministry, 113
    not totally subject to the Fall, 55, 80
    of Eve's seed, 106
    on nature of resurrected beings, 48

Only Begotten in the flesh, 95–96
    perfect example, 69–70
    priesthood power of, 93
    resurrection of, 121
    "second Adam," vii, 139, 164, 175
    second coming of, 114, 123–25, 127
    serpent's head crushed by, 103–4
    sons and daughters of, 192
    taking name of, 30
    testimony of, 27, 108
    testimony to Nephites, 13
    types of, 180
    visit to spirit world, 113
    Word Incarnate, 167
    worlds created by, 9
Jewish legends, 98
John, on becoming like God, 70
    on creation by the Son, 13
    on Satan, 4
    on tree of life, 30
    on the War in Heaven, 5, 7–8, 93
John the Baptist, 120, 140
    Aaronic Priesthood restored by, 120
Jordan River, 142
Joseph of Egypt, 190
Josepheanz, S., 145
Joy, 18–19, 32, 33, 34, 61, 76, 77, 107–8,
    109
Jubilees, Book of, 143
Judaism, figure of Adam in, 131–47
Judgment, 3, 39, 50, 52, 104, 124, 126
    involvement of Adam in, vii, 114
Justice, 81
    of God, 6–7
Justification, 192

— K —

Kabbalism, 136–37
Keys, 98
    of the dispensation of the fullness of
        times, 2, 107
    of dispensations, 2, 79, 91, 113, 119–21,
        124
    of First Presidency, 2–3, 116–17, 120
    of presidency, 90, 107
    of resurrection, 125–26
    of salvation, 9–10, 87, 90, 109
    priesthood, 29, 123
    restored under direction of Adam, vii,
        113, 119–21
Kimball, Heber C., on role of Adam in the
    Creation, 9
    on vision of Joseph Smith, 126–27
Kimball, Spencer W., on keys of the resur-
    rection, 125

Knowledge, 115, 162
Kolob, 15–16

— L —

Lamech, 115, 117
Latin, 141
Law of Moses, 132–33, 142, 143
Law of sacrifice, 29–30
  See also Sacrifices
Laws, eternal, 8
  immutable, 40
  of creation, 94
Laying on of hands, 29
Layton, Bentley, 139
Lazarus, 146
Lebuda, 144
Lectures on Faith, 7, 69–70
Lehi (father of Nephi), 43, 72
  on agency, 101
  on children of Adam and Eve, 31
  on conditions before the Fall, 44, 45, 46
  on the Fall, 18, 76, 103
  on the Fall and the Atonement, 60
  on fruit of the tree of life, 31
  on opposition, 100
Life, purpose of, 77, 133
Life of Adam and Eve, 141–46
Lilith, 136
Limhi, 190
Love, 95
  of God, 31, 100, 154
Lucifer, 43, 191
  armies of, vii, 127
  rebellion of, 14, 71–72, 73, 91–93
  See also Satan
Luke, 22, 48, 84
Lund, Anthon H., 3, 95
Lust, 155, 156, 162, 166, 169, 173
Luther, Martin, 152–53, 164–74, 176, 178,
  182

— M —

McConkie, Bruce R., on appearance of
    angel to Christ, 84
  on blood, 45
  on the Creation, 9, 13–14, 19–20
  on creation of man, 21–22, 95–96
  on days of the Creation, 20–21
  on dispute over the body of Moses, 123
  on Eve, 87, 91, 97, 107
  on the Fall, 102
  on fallen earth, 54
  on forbidden fruit, 102
  on the Judgment, 126
  on partaking of the fruit, 28

  on patriarchal theocracy, 116–17
  on the priesthood, 93
  on rebellion of Satan, 71
  on role of women in the Creation,
    94–95
McConkie, Joseph Fielding, on the tree
    of life, 100
MacRae, George, 140
Mahalaleel, 115, 117–19
Malachi, 119
Man, divine origin of, 3, 37
  origin and destiny of, 193
Manda d'Hayye, 140
Mandaeans, 137, 140, 141
Marriage, 133, 153, 168–70, 176–78,
    179
  covenants of, 169
  eternal, 30, 96–99
  new and everlasting covenant of, 192
  of Adam and Eve, 29, 62, 96–99, 100,
    169–70
Mary (mother of Jesus), 27, 57, 98, 120,
    174
  foreordination of, 14, 94
Meat, 170
Mechitar of Ayrivank, 136
Melchizedek, 146, 190
Melchizedek Priesthood, 115
Mercy, 6–7, 81
Meridian Twelve, 83
Metaphors, 26, 29
Methuselah, 115, 117–19
Michael, 17, 118, 120, 124, 125, 134
  armies of heaven led by, vii, 4–8, 107,
    127
  confrontations with Satan, 121–23
  foreordination of, 87, 90–91
  involvement in the Creation, vii–viii, 9,
    14, 21, 23, 87, 93–94, 107
  keys given to, 1–2, 87, 90–91, 93, 107
  See also Adam
Midrash, 144
Midrash Rabbah, 134
Millennium, 16, 31, 114, 125, 127
Millet, Robert L., on tree of life, 100
Ministering angels, 121
Misery, 32
Monks, 167
Mormon, on baptism of children, 59
  on sorrow of the Nephites, 80
Moroni (son of Mormon), 43, 59, 118, 120
  on the Fall, 41
Mortal probation, 31–32, 33, 39, 96, 99
Mortality, 3, 40, 42, 46, 69, 114
  blood the badge of, 84
  brought by the Fall, 11, 28, 48, 54, 60,
    63, 67, 69, 90–91, 96

flesh, 47–48
    purpose of, 14
    symbolized by tree of knowledge of
        good and evil, 99–100
    See also Death
Moses, 5, 20, 29, 83, 120, 121, 134, 146,
    170–71, 175, 190
    book of, 26, 42, 43, 44, 47, 57, 66, 67,
        73, 76, 77, 79, 191
    creation account of, 17, 19
    law of, 132–33, 142, 143
    translation of, 122–23
Motherhood, of Eve, 103–4
Mount of Transfiguration, 120
Mountains, 27, 145

— N —

Nakedness, 98, 156, 172, 179
Neoplatonic philosophy, 152
Nephi (son of Lehi), 31
    on the tree of life, 100
Nephite prophets, 43
Nephites, 13, 66, 80
Nestorian Christians, 145
New and everlasting covenant of marriage,
    192
New Testament, 57, 58
Noah (Old Testament prophet), 2, 13, 83,
    115, 117, 120, 122, 190
Nouss, 137
Nuns, 167

— O —

Obedience, 8, 19, 29, 71, 74, 77, 104, 114,
    166, 171, 174, 178
Olaha Shinehah, 105
Old Testament, 57
    apocryphal books of, 136
Opposition, 6, 61, 100–101
Ordinance, of naming and blessing, 105
    of resurrection, 125
    See also Baptism
Ordinances, 2, 39, 67, 89, 114, 191, 192
    beyond this world, 125
    received in Eden, 98–99
    temple, 79
Ordinations, 117
Organic evolution, 54, 63
Original sin, 34, 55–59, 163–64, 191–92

— P —

Pagels, E., on paradigm of story of Adam
    and Eve, 131–32
Pain, 5–6

Paradigm, of story of Adam and Eve,
    131–33
Paradise, 160–61, 163, 166–67, 175–76,
    190
    See also Eden
Paradisiacal creation, 16–20
Paradisiacal glory, 31, 53
Paradisiacal state, 34, 94
Patriarchal blessings, given by Adam, 105,
    117–19
Patriarchal order of the priesthood, 114,
    117
Patriarchal theocracy, 116–17
Patriarchs, ancient, 22, 66, 67, 71, 116,
    143, 146
Paul, 164
    on Adam and Christ, 52
    on the Atonement, 82
    on faith, 74, 94
    on the Fall, 55–56
    on godly sorrow, 80
    on men and women, 97
    on resurrected bodies, 17
    on second Adam, 175
    on the Son, 13
    on women, 133
Peace, 16, 174
Pearl of Great Price, 56, 66, 79, 116, 134,
    191
Peculiar people, 82
Penitence of Adam (apocryphal work),
    144–45, 146
Perfection, 41, 42, 69, 160
Peripoiēsis, 82
Perspective, 41
Peter, on the Atonement, 82
    on Church members being a "peculiar
        people," 82
Peter, James, and John, 120, 123
Philo of Alexandria, 137
    on two separate Adams, 137–38
Physical death. *See* Death, temporal
Pigeradamas, 141
Plan of salvation, *vii*, 3, 4–5, 7, 33,
    39–40, 57, 63, 67–71, 75, 83, 84, 89,
    102, 191, 192
Planets, 41, 121
Plants, 28, 53–54
Platonic philosophy, 137, 152
Polygamy, 177–78
Posterity, of Adam and Eve, 99, 100, 181
Pratt, Orson, 96
    on Adam-ondi-Ahman, 128 n.9
    on antiquity of plan of salvation, 68–69
    on fall of the earth, 53
    on immortality after the Creation, 17–18
Pratt, Parley P., on fall of the earth, 53–54

Prayer, of Eve, 106
Premortal bodies, 45
Premortal Church, 89
Premortality, 11–20, 40, 46, 68, 71, 73, 84, 136, 145, 165
  role of Adam in, *vii*, 1–10, 87–93, 121
  role of Eve in, 87–93
Pride, 156, 162, 179
Priesthood, 124–25
  given to Adam, *vii*, 2–3, 9, 29, 93, 98–99, 105, 114–15, 116, 119, 138
  keys of, 29, 123
  restoration of, 113, 119–20
  See also Adam, individual keys; Keys
Prince of the kingdom of Persia, 123
Principles, eternal, 8, 69
  fixed, 40
Probation, mortal, 31–32, 33, 39, 96, 99
Procreation, 31, 54, 63, 152, 153, 154–55, 161–62, 166, 172, 177
  not possible before the Fall, 18, 20, 23, 45–46, 100
Promise of Seth, 145
Prophecies, of Adam, 61, 76, 106, 118–19, 134, 141, 144, 147
Prophets, *viii*, 42, 71, 92, 119, 191
  latter-day, 38
  living, 71, 193
Protestantism, 151–52, 190
Pseudepigrapha, 138, 147
Psychoanalysts, 189
Punishments, 156–57, 163, 173, 176, 179–80
Purification, 70

— R —

Radio programs, 190
Raphael, 120
Rationality, 158
Raziel, Book of, 135
Reason, 154, 160, 172
Rebellion, 41
  of Lucifer, 4, 14, 71–72, 73, 91–93
Records, 74
Redemption, *vii*, 37, 39, 41, 45, 68–69, 72, 76, 77, 81, 108
  See also Atonement
Reformation, 152
Repentance, 31–32, 33, 45, 57, 78, 79–80, 81, 108, 115, 141, 180, 191
Restoration, 26, 88, 103, 119–20, 123, 151, 153, 182, 191
Resurrected beings, 48
Resurrected bodies, 17, 45, 47, 158
Resurrection, 3, 16, 20, 33, 39, 47, 48, 65, 68, 109, 114, 134, 158

involvement of Adam in, *vii*, 121, 125–27
  keys of, 125–26
  ordinance of, 125
Revelation, 38–40, 119, 160
  modern, 17, 26, 190, 192, 193
  received by Adam, 66, 117
  received under direction of Adam, *vii*
Rib, of Adam, 25, 95, 96–97, 99, 154–55, 161, 168, 177
Righteousness, 32, 34, 104, 165
Rituals, 192

— S —

Sabbath, 164, 167, 171, 175
Sacraments, 145, 161
Sacrifice, by mothers, 106
  law of, 29–30
Sacrifices, 66, 73–77, 83, 145, 164, 181
  offered by Adam, 20, 73–77, 117, 136
  symbolic of the Atonement, 74–75
Salt Lake Tabernacle, 126
Salvation, 2, 30, 33, 40, 60, 69–70, 73, 81, 106, 107, 110
  for the dead, 60
Samuel of Ani, 145
Samuel the Lamanite, 43
  on effects of the Fall, 52
Sanctification, 192
Sarah (wife of Abraham), foreordination of, 14, 94
Satan, 92, 104, 105, 140–41, 145, 146, 157, 168, 180
  Adam and Eve tempted by, 29, 52, 73, 101, 155–56, 163, 170–74, 178
  angels of, 4, 7, 10, 72, 113–14, 122, 125
  appearance as angel of light, 114, 123, 142, 147
  army of, 127
  binding of, 127
  confrontations of Adam with, 113–14, 121–23
  War in Heaven fought against, 4–8, 10, 113–14
  See also Lucifer
Scholem, Gershom, 136
Scriptures, *viii*, 1, 7, 9, 37–38, 39, 42–43, 46–48, 65, 71, 72, 88, 152
"Second Adam," *vii*, 139, 164, 175
Second Coming, 114, 123–25, 127
Secular society, 133
Seers, *viii*
  See also Prophets
Segullâ, 82
Selfishness, 41
Semitic languages, 143

Serpent, 28–29, 53–54, 101, 142–43, 172, 173, 174, 178, 179, 189
Seth, 22, 87, 105, 115, 117–19, 134, 139, 142–44
Sexual sin, 62
   See also Procreation
Sickness, 41
Sin, 55, 60, 61, 101, 104, 105, 108, 152, 153, 156, 162, 170, 171–72
   not possible in Eden, 46
   original, 34, 55–59, 163–64, 192
Slavonic language, 142, 146
Smith, Joseph, 7, 13, 59, 79, 88, 96, 106, 116, 147, 190
   Aaronic Priesthood restored to, 120
   appearance of Satan as angel of light, 123
   Bible translation, 22, 43, 45, 57, 66, 76, 79, 116, 133, 191
   on Adam, 1–2, 79, 90, 107, 120
   on celestial glory of the earth, 15
   on contention in heaven, 5, 71
   on council at Adam-ondi-Ahman, 118, 124
   on covenant made by members of God-head, 12–13, 68
   on Eve, 103
   on faith, 102–3
   on the Fall, 60
   on fixed principles, 40
   on foreordination, 90
   on Grand Council in Heaven, 93, 94
   on happiness, 8
   on keys brought by authority of Adam, 119–20
   on location of Eden, 20
   on marriage, 98
   on Michael, 90
   on paradisiacal glory of the earth, 16
   on power of Satan, 122
   on priesthood position of Adam, 2–3, 9, 116
   on resurrected bodies, 45
   on revelation, 38
   on the things of God, 22
   on translated beings, 121
   on visits of God to Adam and Eve, 100
   vision of the Judgment, 126–27
Smith, Joseph F., 3, 95
   on love of mothers, 106
Smith, Joseph Fielding, on blood, 18, 45
   on council at Adam-ondi-Ahman, 124–25
   on the Fall, 62–63
   on fallen earth, 54
   on language of Adam, 115

   on role of Adam in the Creation, 13
   on spirit creation, 12
   on spiritual creation, 17
   on translation of Moses and Elijah, 122–23
Snakes, 25
   See also Serpent
Snow, Lorenzo, on offspring of Heavenly Father, 12
Sophia, 142–43
Sorrow, 5, 53, 104
Souls, 46–47, 70, 136, 154, 158, 159, 163
   definition of, 46–47
Spirit bodies, 46–47, 88
Spirit children, 3, 41
Spirit creation, 4, 11–12, 19, 47, 49, 95
Spirit world, 15, 17, 113, 121
Spirits, 47, 65, 73, 113
   birth of, 11–12, 22–23, 88
   female, 88
Spiritual bodies, 47, 154
Spiritual creation, 11, 17, 19, 23, 44, 47, 49
Spiritual death. *See* Death, spiritual
Spiritual rebirth, 30, 51, 79, 192
Standard works, 37
   See also Scriptures
Stars, 41
Suffering, 6–7
   of Christ, 7
Summa Theologiae (multi-volume work), 152
Susquehanna River, 123
Symbolism, of mountains, 27
   of name of Adam, 138
Symbols, 176
Syria, 145
Syriac language, 143, 144

— T —

Taylor, John, on divine origins, 15–16
Temple, Adam's body, 138
Temple ceremony, 26, 29
Temple endowment, 79, 147
Temple ordinances, 79
Temples, 27–28, 29, 30, 145
Temporal death. *See* Death, temporal
Temptation, of Adam and Eve, 43, 53, 101–3, 152, 155–56, 162–63, 166, 170–71, 178, 189
Temptations, 114
Tenth article of faith, 53
Terrestrial glory, of the earth in Millennium, 16
Terrestrial order, 121

Testament of Adam, 143–44, 145–46
Testament of the Protoplasts, 146
Testimony, 8, 27, 73, 93, 95
Tigris River, 142
Time, reckoning of, 16
Torah, 142
Transgression, 82
  of Adam and Eve, 43, 108
  See also Sin
Translated beings, 51, 121, 139
Tree of the knowledge of good and evil,
  vii, 16, 25, 28, 43, 50, 99–102, 104,
  114, 143, 153, 156, 166–67, 176, 178,
  190
Tree of life, 25, 31, 33, 43, 99–102, 105,
  108, 153, 161, 166–67, 173, 176, 179,
  181
  type of Christ, 176
Tribulation, suffered in name of Christ,
  108
Trinity, 164
Trust, 89, 102, 110, 192
Tyrus, 27

— U —

Unity, of Adam and Eve, 98, 177

— V —

Vatican II, 152
Veil, 53, 105

Virginity, 155
Visions, 4, 9, 126–27

— W —

War, 41
War in Heaven, *vii*, 4–8, 10, 14, 71–72,
  87, 88, 91–93, 113–14, 191
  role of women in, 14, 94–95
Washing and anointing, 142
Whitney, Orson F., on the Fall, 60
Winder, John R., 3, 95
Wisdom, 35, 61, 99, 101, 104, 115
Wisdom of Solomon, 142
Women, 26–27, 161, 173, 174
  in the War in Heaven, 14, 94–95
Woodruff, Wilford, on location of Eden,
  20
  on prophecies, 119
Word Incarnate, 167
Work, 167, 176, 179, 181
Worlds, creation of, 13, 16, 69, 94
Worship, of Adam, *viii*, 192
  of God, 110

— Y —

Young, Brigham, 96, 147
  on the Fall, 61–62
  on fallen earth, 54
  on glory of the earth, 15
  on location of Eden, 20
  on name of Adam, 191
  on ordinances beyond this world, 125

Scripture Index

OLD TESTAMENT

Genesis

1	47, 49
1:26, 27, 28	2
1:27	136, 137
2	47
2:5	12
2:7	46, 137
2:17	50, 51
3	42, 49
3:1–5	189
3:6	111
3:15	103
3:19	141
3:20	150
5:3	128
5:5	114
6:23 (JST)	22
9:2–6	45

Exodus

13:2	74
18:20	92
19:5	82
34:19	74

Leviticus

11:44	169
17:10–15	45
17:11–14	84

Deuteronomy

4:41	150

Ecclesiastes

3:20	26

Isaiah

14:13–14	91
40:6	47
45:12	22

Jeremiah

17:5	47

Ezekiel

28:13–14	27

Daniel

10	123
10:13	123

NEW TESTAMENT

Matthew		15:45	*vii*, 175
17:1–9	120	15:50	45, 84
19:5–6	27		
19:8	133	2 Corinthians	
26:39	83	7:9–11	80

Mark		Galatians	
14:36	83	5:19	48

Luke		Ephesians	
1:5–23	120	1:3–4	89
1:26–38	120	3:9	13
3:38	22	4:16	40
3:45 (JST)	22		
22:41–44 (JST)	84	1 Timothy	
22:44	83	2:12–14	133
24:39	48	2:15 (JST)	106

John		Hebrews	
1:1–3 (JST)	13	1:2	9, 13
1:3	9	2:14	103
2:19–22	138	5:9	90
3:16	72	11:3	94
5:26	55	11:6	74
8:44	92		
10:17–18	55	1 Peter	
10:34–35	15	1:18–19	82
15:1–6	73	1:19–20	67
21:21–23	51	2:9	82

Acts		2 Peter	
4:12	75	2:1	82
17:24–26	31		
17:26	91	1 John	
		2:16	48

Romans		Jude	
5	148	1:9	10, 92, 122
5:12, 15, 19	56		

1 Corinthians		Revelation	
6:19–20	82	2:7	31
11:3, 8–9	96	12:1–17 (JST)	72
11:12	97	12:7–9	4
15	148	12:9	92
15:22	52, 55, 84	12:10	4, 92
15:23	109	12:10–11	93
15:42, 44	17	12:11	5, 6, 8, 10, 92
15:42–49	47	13:8	67, 90

BOOK OF MORMON

1 Nephi		8:10–12	31
2:20	20	8:11–12	34
5:10–11	43, 66	10:6	72

11:4–21	31	4:2	9
11:4–23	100	4:8	75
11:14	98	8:15–17	190
11:18	14	26:23	22
19:12	82		
22:23	48	Alma	
		5:62	108
2 Nephi		11:45	17, 47, 55
2:8	72	12:20–21	43
2:11–12	6	12:22–37	79
2:15	100	12:25, 26, 30, 32, 33	39
2:15–26	79	12:25–27	90
2:16	101	12:32	50
2:17	76	13:3	89
2:17–20	43	17:16	39
2:18	101	18:39	39
2:20	31	21:9	72
2:21	32	22:12–14	42
2:22	28, 32, 44, 53, 100	22:13–14	39
		24:14	39
2:22–23	18, 100	29:2	39
2:22–25	103	32:21	93, 102
2:23	32, 45, 46	32:42	34
2:23, 25	76, 77	34:9	39
2:24	60	34:9–12, 14–16	81
2:24–25	32	34:10	6
2:25	34, 191	34:16	39
2:27	121	34:31	39
4:34	47	34:35	5, 122
9	114	39:17–19	71
9:4, 6	48	39:18	39
9:6	18, 39	41:1–3	6
9:6–9	66	41:2	39
9:7–9	50, 72	41:10	80
9:10, 19	51	42	114
9:13	39	42:1	6
9:14	98	42:2	102
10:19	20	42:2–4	33
11:5	39	42:5	33, 39
25:23	60	42:6	33
28:31	47	42:7–8	33
31:20–21	75	42:8	39, 40
		42:9–10	34
Jacob		42:11, 13	39
6:8	39	42:12	60
		42:13, 22, 25	6
Jarom		42:15	6
1:2	39	42:15, 31	39
		42:23	55
Mosiah			
2:25	26	Helaman	
3:7	7, 83	14:15–18	52
3:11	58	14:16	52
3:11–16	83	14:17	55
3:11–17	72		
3:16	58	3 Nephi	
3:17	75	8:12	82

9:15	13	3:2	52
28:6–8, 17, 36–40	51	3:14	68
		3:14–17	88
Mormon		3:15–16	22
2:13	80		
8:35	119	Moroni	
9:12	41	8:7–9, 12, 19–20	59
Ether			
2:9–10	20		

DOCTRINE AND COVENANTS

1:8	8	88:94–102	126
10:20–21	113	88:110–11	127
18:23–24	75	88:110–15	114
19:16–18	7	88:112–16	127
19:16–20	83	93:25	92
20:17	13	93:29	88
20:17–20	42	93:33–34	33
20:17–29	79	93:38	58
22:1	114	101:33–34	193
27:2	80	107:40–41	117
29:12	126	107:42–50	105
29:17	80	107:43	128
29:20–32	20	107:53–56	108
29:22	127	107:53–57	118
29:26	125	107:54	1, 10
29:34–35	44, 60	107:56	134, 135
29:36	4	107:57	134, 193
29:37	72	110	120
29:39	6	116	128
29:40	101	117:8	105
29:40–42	52	121:41	105
29:40–43	114	128:20	123, 149
29:40–44	79	128:20–21	120
45:4	83	128:21	10
66:2	114	129:6–8	47
76:24	9, 13	129:8	149
76:26	8	130:20–21	68, 83
76:28	92	131:7–8	47, 88
76:29	113, 122	132:5	68
76:69	7, 83	132:5, 11	83
77:2	88	132:11	68
77:6	119	132:19–20	15
78:16	1, 119	132:63	89
84:16	105	133:57	114
88:15	46	138:12–13	108
88:25–26	53	138:18–19	109
88:26–28	47	138:38–39	108
88:27	17	138:39	87
88:28	126	138:40	128
88:35	8, 127	138:51	109

PEARL OF GREAT PRICE

Moses		5:6–8	74
1:28–35	94	5:7	30
1:32–33	13	5:8	30, 106, 191
1:34	191	5:9	76
1:39	39	5:10	61, 106
1:40–41	66, 133	5:10–12	35, 76
2	21, 49	5:11	19, 32, 45, 63,
2:22, 28	18		100, 109
2:26	95	5:11–12	61, 77, 106
2:27	22, 95	5:12–13	115
2:31	95	5:13	108
3	49	5:16	106
3:4–5	19	5:16–55	192
3:5	4, 12, 19, 49	5:57	68
3:7	9, 48, 95	5:58	107, 192
3:7, 9, 19	46	5:59	115
3:9	18, 28, 44, 53, 96	6	65
3:15	96	6:1	115
3:16–17	28, 114	6:4	27
3:17	99, 100	6:4–9	116
3:18	97	6:5, 46	133
3:21	97	6:9	98
3:21–25	95	6:10	105
3:22–24	97	6:12	50
3:23	26	6:22	22, 95
3:23–24	98	6:23	106
3:24	27	6:48	45, 77, 191
3:25	98	6:49–59	26
4	49	6:51–52	77
4:1	5, 92	6:51–54	58
4:1–4	72	6:51–62	66
4:2	90	6:51–68	105
4:3	5, 101	6:52	75, 78
4:4	121	6:53	78, 108
4:6	101	6:53–54	78
4:9	99	6:53–55	192
4:10–11	101	6:55	6
4:12	101, 102	6:57–60	192
4:17	51	6:58–61	79
4:21	103, 106	6:59	18
4:22	104	6:59–60	80
4:25	26	6:62	39, 79
4:26	104	6:64–68	114, 192
4:27	30	7:1	105
4:28	104	7:26	122
4:29	104	7:47	67
4:31	31		
5	49, 65	Abraham	
5:1–8	30	1:21–27	192
5:1–12	65, 66, 105	3:4	31, 50
5:3	115	3:22	9, 11, 21, 93
5:4	27, 46	3:22–23	4
5:4–5	73	3:22–24	14, 94

3:22–28	14	5:7	46
3:23	93	5:12–13	16
3:24	9, 14, 95	5:13	31, 50
3:24–25	100		
4	21, 49	Joseph Smith — History	
4:1	14, 94	1:72	120
4:21	39		
5	49		
5:3	94	Articles of Faith	
5:3–5	94	1:10	6